CW00409898

ADVANCE PRAISE FOR
THE MISSING BUDDHAS

"A fascinating detective story that traces the origins, ownership and sale of a unique set of lost Buddhist treasures - an exciting read."
— Rose Kerr, Art Historian and Former Keeper of the Far Eastern Department at the Victoria and Albert Museum, London

"The author has unlocked the mysteries surrounding a unique set of life-size glazed pottery luohan sculptures, each with an outstanding individual and human portrayal. With strong evidence, he eschews the former dealers' stories and hearsays and instead provides reliable new verdicts for their provenance and patronage. Written in plain language the book is not only for scholars but also for all lovers of Chinese art."
— Peter Y. K. Lam, Honorary Fellow, Institute of Chinese Studies. The Chinese University of Hong Kong

"The Missing Buddhas' reads like a great murder mystery. For anyone interested in Chinese antiquities and art, the study and journey of these porcelain figures is a must read. The feel for the people involved in the search, the intrigue and acquisition of these treasures is fascinating. Tony's research is meticulous and extensive, covering a very wide range of source material. It is an extraordinary story. All I can say is "well done Mr. Miller!"
— Tad Beczak, Chairman of Old Peak Investments Limited, Former Publisher and Deputy Chairman of the SCMP Group

"A fascinating account of historical/cultural detective work which will leave the rest of us deeply impressed by a blend of meticulous scholarship and a sense of wonder at the powerful beauty of these 900 years old Buddhist statues. Where were they made? Why did they disappear? And how did they start to appear on the Peking antiquities market in the early part of the last century? Tony Miller tackles all the historical puzzles. But even more fascinating is the untangling of the skulduggery that was a major feature of the Peking art market. This book should have every museum, including the specialist Musée Guimet, where the last statue now is, re-examining their records and their attributions of the origins and provenance of these statues."
— David Wilson, Baron Wilson of Tillyorn, former Governor of Hong Kong

THE MISSING BUDDHAS

The mystery of the Chinese statues
that stunned the Western art world

Tony Miller

The Missing Buddhas

By Tony Miller

ISBN-13: 978-988-8552-92-4

HISTORY / Asia / China

EB146

Published by Earnshaw Books Ltd. (Hong Kong)

DEDICATION

To the one who makes me complete…

學貴乎雅

禮成於貞

Contents

Note on Title and Transliteration

AN INNATE PEDANTRY prompts the author to state up front that this is categorically **not** a book about missing Buddhas — the statues whose story is told here are actually disciples of the Lord Buddha, not images of Buddha himself. So, why not use the Chinese word for these disciples? Well, for one, the term "Luohan" might not be familiar to many and a title such as "The Missing Luohans" would therefore not have resonated. More particularly, the mystery of these statues is bound up with the story of the German dealer who claimed to have found where they were hidden, and reported seeing engraved on a nearby stone stele the words:

"All these Buddhas came from afar."

This enigmatic remark has puzzled many people over the years because, whether they came from near or far, the statues were all Luohans. The German dealer must have known the difference, but he seems to have sacrificed accuracy for familiarity in order not to confuse his audience. I have followed his example. Actually, this book should really have been called "The Legend of the Yixian Luohans," but that would have required an even lengthier explanation.

Several systems for transliterating Chinese names and place names were employed before the Chinese Government's adoption of *Pinyin*. This can cause confusion. Where quoting from older sources, the author has chosen to leave these as originally rendered, relying on context to make matters clear, but annotating where the thread would otherwise be lost. There are, however, two terms that require early clarification:

- *Arhat* is the Indian word, derived from Sanskrit, for the disciples of the Lord Buddha chosen by him to protect the Law. The Chinese translation for this name in modern *pinyin* is Luohan (羅漢), but it frequently still appears in its older form of Lohan; and
- Yixian (易縣) is a county to the southwest of Beijing where the terracotta Luohans were allegedly found. At the beginning of the 20th century, it was called I-chou (易州), which was sometimes rendered as Ichou. Today the Luohans are generally referred to as the "Yixian Luohans", but the older names are used in earlier writings on them and sometimes reappear even today.

FOREWORD

"The Lohan represents art which is intelligible in all lands and in all ages."

R.L. Hobson[1]

I DO NOT think that I am alone in the sense of shock I experienced on first encountering the Luohan in the British Museum. It was not a shock of horror, rather one of wonder. Here was a man, a monk, who had been dead for a millennium or more, who was yet reaching out, not reaching out to me but to something beyond me. He was not speaking, but everything about his poise and expression spoke to me of that beyond as something infinitely far off and yet attainable. One did not have to know anything about Oriental religions, or Asian sculptural conventions to grasp that this was one of those rare examples of great art that communicates across time and space and cultures.

It would be several years before I caught up with the monk's brethren in the Metropolitan Museum, in New York. I had not gone in search of them; I had not known they were there, but as soon as I saw them I recognized them. Quite when I began puzzling about them is lost to me; the unconscious mind works in curious ways. However, at some point in my researches into other matters something triggered the thought *"I wonder how many of them there are?"* and I dug a few books off the shelves of our library and quickly found that what I had experienced on first encounter at the British Museum was no less profound than that of its former curator:

"It is no conventional deity which sits before us. The features

---

1   Hobson, Robert L., *Chinese Pottery Statue of a Lohan*, London, 1925, p.7.

are so human as to suggest an actual portrait, but for the supernatural enlargement of the ears in Buddhist fashion. The contracted brows bespeak deep concentration; the eyes, dreamy yet wide awake, look through and past us into the infinite; the nostrils are dilated in deep breathing; the lips compressed in firm yet compassionate lines. It is the embodiment of the Buddhist idea of abstraction and aloofness; yet it lives in every line, the personification of mental energy in repose."[2]

Exhausting references in our own books, I went online to ask again "*How many?*" At which point things became more confused and my attention was distracted by more immediate tasks. Whether I recognized it or not at the time, however, I was already hooked. The monks had grown in number, even if there seemed to be disagreement about exactly how many there were; the lyrical praises heaped on them by curators and scholars confirmed my amateur judgement as to their quality; and yet they were nagging at me, and asking me a host of different questions.

Then I came across the name of Friedrich Perzynski and translated excerpts from his extraordinary tale, and suddenly the antennae tuned by a lifetime of listening to special pleading began to twitch, the bureaucrat's instinct honed by experience to suspend belief came to the fore and a voice inside me said "*Hold on a minute! No, this cannot be!*" The voice had hardly stilled when a little more surfing on the web produced some excerpts from a newly-published book, and I headed for New Asia Library at the Chinese University of Hong Kong. I ploughed through the volume at speed and came up bewildered and angry that anybody could have the temerity to suggest that the statues dated only from the Ming dynasty rather than earlier.

---

2   Hobson, Op. Cit. 1915, p. 36.

As usual when confused about such matters, I consulted my mentor, Professor Peter Lam, the former Director of the Art Museum at CUHK, the Chinese University of Hong Kong, who was as amused to find that I had strayed so far from my normal areas of interest, as I was to find him equally incensed by the same book. So, I began to take the subject more seriously.

The journey since has been fascinating and the people I have met along the way, a motley crew of scholars and engineers, soldiers and adventurers, antiquarians and archaeologists, dealers, collectors and curators have become familiar friends, even when they have been rogues and villains. I hope that I have done none of them any injustice here, either in the inevitably brief pen-portraits I have sketched, or the quotations attributed to them. I have preferred to allow all the actors to speak for themselves for the immediacy such dialogue brings to the story.

Likewise, I hope that I cause no offense to the museums that are now home to these remarkable works of art. No disrespect is intended. In many places, I have used the familiar short forms of their famous names for convenience and ease of reading. In each case, I have endeavored to use the proper name in full the first time it is mentioned and in all attributions for illustrations. I trust also that my debunking of a myth and re-telling of an extraordinary story will cause their curators and sponsors to feel neither embarrassment nor difficulty. Rather I hope that they and other readers will be entertained and even amused.

PROLOGUE

IT IS NOT often that the international art market is taken completely by surprise, but in June 1913, it was stunned. Two life-size sculptures of Oriental monks were exhibited for sale at the Musée Cernuschi in Paris and were immediately snapped up by the Penn Museum in Philadelphia and the Museum of Fine Arts in Boston. Then, five months later, two more appeared in Berlin; or at least one-and-a-half. The whole one went to another North American museum, while the head-and-shoulders torso of the fourth was bought by a German collector. It was not just that Western cognoscenti of Chinese art had never seen terracotta statues of this scale, glazed in the three-color palette that today we take for granted as emblematic of China's Tang dynasty (618-907), but that these monks were unnervingly life-like. They looked not so much at you as straight through you to some other-worldly beyond.

Word of this wholly new aesthetic traveled fast and the cry went up from the curators of museums that had missed out in these first sales: "*I want one too!*" Already, it was clear to them that the monks were Arhats — Luohans, 羅漢 in Chinese — the disciples chosen by the Lord Buddha himself to protect the Law, and they knew that there should therefore be at least 16 of them, if not 18 in a full set. So, curators dialed their dealers and, sure enough, over the next few years, the First World War notwithstanding, several other Luohan statues from the same set surfaced in Britain, Canada, Japan and the United States. Where had they come from?

As part of his promotional material for the Berlin sale, the German dealer Friedrich Perzynski published a dramatic account of how he had tracked the Luohans down to inaccessible caves above the town of Yixian (易縣) south-southwest of Beijing. They had, he suggested, been hidden there in ages past by pious monks anxious to save them from pillage or destruction by nomadic invaders. He offered little by way of historical evidence, but what his essay lacked in academic precision was amply outweighed by atmospheric detail of the death of an empire. Western powers had spent the preceding one hundred years strong-arming China into ceding Treaty Ports, granting trading privileges and awarding lucrative railway franchises. Popular discontent at these intrusions had exploded at the turn of the century in the ugly form of the Boxer Rebellion, and Allied Forces had had to force their way into Beijing to relieve a fifty-five day siege of the foreign legations. In the ensuing chaos, imperial treasures were looted, whetting Western appetites for more and, while an uneasy peace was restored, the prospect of easy pickings lured archaeologists and antiquarians, dealers and collectors from all corners of the globe. Only the year before the first Luohans appeared in Paris, in 1912, Puyi (溥儀) the last emperor of the Qing dynasty, had abdicated, ushering in a period of prolonged instability for China and a Golden Age for Western museums.

The first sales were barely concluded before polite fisticuffs began amongst curators and art historians as to the correct dating of the statues. Had they been sculpted during the Tang dynasty (618-907), or was it the later Ming (1368-1644)? Most took Perzynski's promotional text at face value, so few questions were asked about from whence they had originally come. Alone at the British Museum, Robert Hobson lamented with typical understatement that their "provenance has been kept discreetly concealed". Nobody else seemed to think that odd and, as a result, the various theories that today surround their origins owe so much to Perzynski's account of their "discovery" that more than one generation of curators and scholars would appear to have either deliberately shut their eyes, or had difficulty separating hard fact from romantic fiction. That is a pity. The Luohans are extraordinary works of art and, frankly, they deserve better. Hence this humble attempt to clear away the cobwebs of myth and mystery that have been allowed to festoon the Luohans and to shine a little light on their true history.

Let us start with a quick a look at the broader historical backcloth against which events unfolded, and the cultural context from which these religious icons emerged.

1

MONKS, MERCHANTS AND MILESTONES

"Buddha was a man of the barbarians who did not speak the language of China and wore clothes of a different fashion."

Han Yu (韓愈; 768-824 CE)

ONE OF THE Luohan statues that journeyed to the West in 1913 sported a beard and had distinctively South Asian features. This provides a gentle reminder of Buddhism's foreign origins, for that religion is not native to China. It was born of the teachings of Siddhartha Gautama, the Lord Buddha (c. 5th to 4th Century BCE), who attained enlightenment under a Bodhi tree somewhere in the foothills of the Himalayas in north-eastern India.

Buddhism was already five hundred years old when, sometime in the second century of the Christian era, it made its way from India into China through Afghanistan and the high passes of the Karakorum that funnelled North-South trade to and from the great Central Asian crossroads at Dunhuang (敦煌) on the south-eastern edge of the Tarim Basin. By that time, the Han dynasty (漢, 260 BCE–221 CE) had held power for three centuries, ruling over a flourishing country that covered some six million square kilometres, a land mass larger than all twenty-seven nations of today's European Union combined.

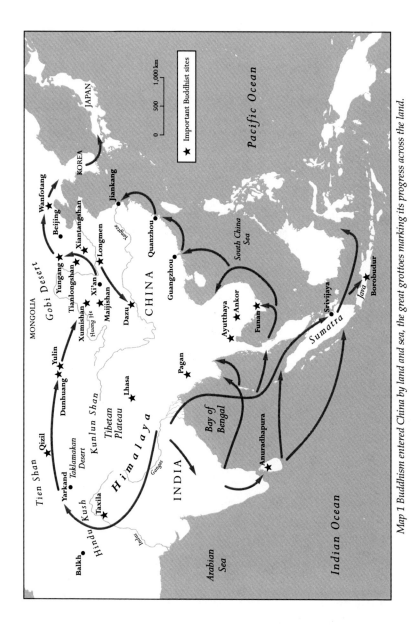

Map 1 Buddhism entered China by land and sea, the great grottoes marking its progress across the land.

*Fig.1 Longmen Grottoes, Luoyang, Henan province, date from the late 5ᵗʰ Century.
Author's photograph.*

Buddhism proved popular. The murals and sculptures that decorate China's numerous caves and grottoes bear mute but eloquent testimony to the patronage of both courts and commoners. They also provide convenient milestones for its progress across the land (**Map 1**). In the West, the Qizil Caves (克孜爾千佛洞), Dunhuang (敦煌) and the Yulin caves (榆林窟) all have art dating from the 4ᵗʰ Century. By the 5ᵗʰ the new belief had run the length of the Gansu corridor, eastwards via the Bingling grottoes (甘肅) to Maijishan (麥積山) and to Xumishan (鬚彌山) in Ningxia (寧夏), before following the Yellow River (黃河) northwards up-stream to Yungang (雲崗), then capital of the Northern Wei dynasty in Shanxi Province, and east again to Korea and Japan. The monks followed the money and, by the 6ᵗʰ Century, the busy chisels of Buddhist sculptors had chipped a path southward through Hebei to the "Resounding Halls" grotto at Xiangtangshan (響堂山) and on to Gongxian (鞏縣) and

THE MISSING BUDDHAS

Fig.2 The Terracotta Warriors, Xi'an, Shaanxi province. Author's photograph

the Longmen Grottoes (龍門石窟) near the Northern Wei's new capital at Luoyang (洛阳) in Henan. **(Fig.1)** Buddhism also entered China via its ports. Like trade and water, it worked its way around obstacles and, together with its art, it excited the interest and attracted the sponsorship of rulers across the whole Asian region.

Unification of China's earlier Warring States had been achieved in the latter half of the previous millennium by the First Emperor of the Qin, Qin Shihuangdi (秦始皇帝 r. 221-210 BCE). The accidental discovery of his entombed Terracotta Army outside Xi'an (西安) in Shaanxi Province, which hit the world's headlines in 1974, merely confirmed the grandiose ambitions of this extraordinary genius. **(Fig.2)** China is famous for its record-keeping, and the official *Records of the Grand Historians* written by Sima Qian (司馬遷; c. 145-86 BCE) a century after the First Emperor's demise detailed his relentless pursuit of standardization: a single currency, Chinese script, weights and measures, and even axle widths to fit the ruts in the network of

4

three-carriageway roads he had built, which covered the entire country, and were longer even than those built by Rome.

His administrative system was the template that other dynasties were in large part to follow for the next two millenia. From then on, a united, centrally governed China was the norm, interrupted only relatively briefly by periods of internal strife or external invasion. Compare and contrast Europe where, over the same period, fragmentation along linguistic lines has been the norm, despite occasional attempts to impose unity by the soldiers of Rome, of Charlemagne's Frankish Kingdom, of France and of Germany, and, more recently, by the bureaucrats of Brussels.

China's borders are Nature's gift: the Himalayan range to the south; deserts and more rugged mountain chains to the west and much of the north, enclosing three great river systems that rise in those surrounding heights to flow all the way to its long eastern seaboard. So, China has been clear about its borders, relatively secure within them and wary of adventuring without, but it has always been curious about what lies beyond. As a result, those borders have more often than not remained open to commerce and ideas. China was by no means isolated or introverted.

Thus, Buddhism was not the only foreign religion to enter China. Zoroastrian beliefs padded in with camel trains from Persia. So also did Judaism, and Manichaean and Nestorian Christianity. All left souvenirs along the way for later archaeologists to discover. In due course, with the development of Indian Ocean trade, they were followed by Moslems. Indeed, ports on the eastern seaboard hosted numerous foreign communities, all of whom brought their own beliefs with them and were routinely granted freedom of worship. The Jewish bankers of Kaifeng had their own synagogue; the Moslem merchants of Guangzhou (廣州) and Quanzhou (泉州) their own mosques.

The First Emperor's mania for standardization did not extend to religious beliefs. There was no state religion. If there was a common denominator amongst ordinary men and women it would have been a mix of superstition and animist beliefs little different in substance from those of their counterparts in pre-Christian Europe. Like the latter, these were intertwined with popular mythology and a pantheon of often mischievous immortals. Over time their beliefs became infused with a clearer philosophical focus on the ideal of living in harmony with Nature, which lies at the core of Taoism, as elaborated by the philosopher Laozi (老子) in the 6th Century BCE. For the aristocracy and the intellectual elite, the challenge, as elsewhere in the world, was how to moderate the excesses of powerful military leaders and, ultimately, to channel the energies of autocratic emperors. In this they were greatly assisted by the example and teachings of another philosopher, known in the West as Confucius (孔子; 551-479 BCE). A contemporary of Laozi, his was a code of conduct founded on a rigid social order, rather than a system of beliefs, but in its insistence on ritual it has sometimes been mistaken for such.

In the absence of any state, or state-sponsored religion, Buddhism could be said to have been knocking on an open door, but so were all other foreign religions. How then to explain its success? Several things worked in its favour, among them the fact that neither monotheistic tradition nor Messianic myth barred the way. While the promise of paradise has obvious attractions, the threat of eternal damnation does not. If that was the competition, then a cycle of re-birth and the possibility, open to all, of an end to suffering through self-improvement would have held greater appeal for commoners and courtiers alike. Most of all it would have appealed to those who wanted to live for ever.

The First Emperor's massive mausoleum, with its regimental

Fig.3 The Great Wall at Badaling. Author's photograph

guard of terracotta warriors, is emblematic of the traditional concern of China's emperors for the afterlife. Whether before or after the arrival of Buddhism, almost the first obligation for an emperor, or empress on "assuming the Mantle of Heaven" was to begin preparations for the construction of his, or her tomb. As with Egypt's Pharaohs, these were invariably large and elaborate subterranean constructions involving the employment of thousands of labourers. Those of the Ming (明) dynasty form a cluster in valleys to the East of Beijing; those of the Qing (清) a similar group to the West. Regrettably, the tradition that tombs should be finely furnished with goods and chattels for the hereafter was responsible for the early emergence of a tomb robbing profession and a ready market for the treasures they recovered.

The labour and resources expended by Qin Shihuangdi on his tomb were as nothing to those he devoted to defence of the empire. Tension between nomadic herders and settled farmers was not

7

unique to the Middle Kingdom[1], but from time immemorial it has had to guard against incursions from the North and West. Various stretches of defensive ramparts had been built before, but it was Qin Shihuangdi who linked them all together in a "Great Wall" designed to protect civilization from the barbarians beyond. **(Fig.3)** Thereafter successive dynasties traded silk and tea for horses and employed a combination of exchanges of tribute and diplomatic marriages to manage relations. They preferred to placate rather than to contest, in keeping with the maxim of China's earliest known military strategist, Sun Tzu (*Sunzi*, 孫子; c. 500 BCE), who advised the Duke of Zhou (周公; r. c. 500 BCE): "The supreme act of war is to subdue the enemy without fighting."[2]

In general terms, it is true to say that China has had more success securing its land borders to the South and West, and its seaboard to the East. The Northeast has always been more vulnerable. Here a little history may help both to illustrate the point, and to clear some of the confusion that arises from the swirling fortunes of the major dynasties and the shifting location of their capital cities.

As we saw, the First Emperor's last resting place is just East of Xi'an; his capital was just to its West, at Xianyang (咸阳). The Han Dynasty (漢; 206 BCE- 221 CE), which succeeded him shortly after Hannibal took his elephants for a short walk in the Maritime Alps, followed his example, as did the Tang (唐; 618-907). A period of chaos and internal strife followed the latter's collapse, during which originally nomadic tribes such as the Khitan and Jurchen took the opportunity to occupy large swathes of the northeast of the country. The difference between these tribes and the sporadic

---

1   The first scholar to draw attention to this phenomenon in the development of settled societies was the great 14th Century Arab historian Ibn Khaldun in his *Muqaddimah,* or *Introduction to History,* Tunis, c. 1377.

2   Sun Tzu, *The Art of War.*

raiders of the West were that they wanted to settle. They were attracted by all that Chinese culture had to offer. The Northern Song dynasty (北宋; 960-1126) resisted their advance from its capital at Kaifeng, but ultimately had to fall back on present-day Hangzhou. From here, the "Southern Song" (南宋; 1126-1279) ruled what was left until all were swept aside by the Mongols. Like other nomads before them, the Mongols quickly became Sinicized, building a new capital at Khanbaliq (today's Beijing) and ruling China for more than a century as the Yuan Dynasty (元; 1260-1368).

A peasant uprising toppled the Yuan and brought in the Ming Dynasty (明; 1368-1644), which initially took Nanjing as its capital, but eventually transferred back to Beijing. The Manchu invaders who dethroned them three centuries later, about the time when Royalists and Roundheads were busy battling it out in the English Civil War, kept the capital there and ruled as the Qing Dynasty (清) through to the beginning of the 20th Century. The rise and fall of China's dynasties sketched out above is sometimes portrayed as cyclical, as though regular fragmentation is ultimately inevitable. That is misleading. If there is a rhythm to such events, it is at best irregular. What is more remarkable and more telling is the routine return to stasis, a relative peace and stability not seen elsewhere in the world, that demonstrates the country's essential integrity.

Given the length of its borders and the number of potentially unfriendly neighbours, it is hardly surprising that China's earliest rulers should have been curious about the lands that lay beyond. In 139 BCE, for example, the Han Emperor despatched perhaps China's most famous ambassador from Xi'an to explore Central Asia and find out more about a loose and unruly coalition of nomadic tribes known as the Xiongnu, who had become a thorn in China's side. Zhang Qian (張騫; d. 113 B.C.)

succeeded in following the trade routes all the way through the passes separating the Pamirs from the Hindu Kush to the great fortress city of Balkh, in the north of today's Afghanistan just inside its border with Uzbekistan. His luck eventually ran out, however, and he was captured and detained for some seventeen years before he managed to escape and return home. Details of his exploits and the intelligence he gathered were faithfully recorded in Sima Qian's *Records of the Grand Historians*.

It took a little time, but in 90 CE, one of the Han Dynasty's greatest soldiers, General Ban Chao (班超; 32-102), subdued the Xiongnu in the West and secured the Tarim Basin. Designated Protector General of the region he set up his garrison on the river island fortress of Gaochang (高昌) just outside present-day Turpan (吐鲁番). From there he despatched an envoy named Gan Ying (甘英), to Rome, apparently looking for a way to cut out the Parthian and Soghdian middlemen in the silk trade. Gan Ying made it as far as the Characene port of Charax Spasinu at the head of the Persian Gulf, but was discouraged by suspicious locals from trying to go any further. His timing was bad. Had he arrived 18 years later, he would have been able to greet the Roman Emperor Trajan personally. The latter had somehow survived the great earthquake, which destroyed Antioch the Golden on the last night of the Brumalia Festival in 115 CE, and marched his army the length of the Fertile Crescent virtually unopposed. In the process, he expanded the Roman Empire to its greatest extent. Standing on the docks, gazing at all the sailing ships in that busy trading post, the aging wannabe Alexander mused wistfully, *"Were I still young, I should certainly have crossed over to India."*[3]

The arrival of Buddhism, heightened rather than reduced

---

3   Cassius Dio, *Roman History.*Book LXVIII, 29.

China's curiosity about that very different southern neighbour and, between 399 and 412, the Chinese Buddhist monk Faxian (法顯; 337-c. 442) journeyed on foot to India via Khotan and Yarkand in Central Asia, passing close to Kabul before heading south through Kashmir. During his time in India, he visited innumerable monasteries and sacred sites, collecting Buddhist texts as he went so that he could translate them on his return. Eventually, footsore and weary, he resolved to go home by boat and boarded a foreign trading vessel heading for Guangzhou. His description of the first part of that journey in his *Record of Buddhist Kingdoms,* provides the first detailed account of a sea voyage from India to China.

Two hundred years later, the precocious monk Xuanzang (玄奘; 602-64) followed Faxian's footsteps and wandered around India's monasteries and holy places from 629 to 645. He returned by land and, like Faxian, came back laden with Buddhist texts that he would spend the rest of his life translating. His exploits were later to become the basis of the popular Ming novel *Journey to the West.* More important for our purposes, however, it was Xuanzang who, in 654, translated the *Record on the Duration of the Law, spoken by the Great Arhat, Nandimitra,* a text known in Chinese as the *Fazhuji* (法住記).

According to Nandimitra, the Lord Buddha entrusted the Law to the care of his sixteen most faithful disciples. Called Luohans in Chinese, he chose them from among those of his adherents who had followed the Eightfold Path and attained the Four Stages of Enlightenment. Nadimitra lists the sixteen Luohans by name. That and the fact that they all had different personalities emphasized their humanity and ultimately made them popular characters. As with the spread of other religions, those responsible for preaching the word abroad would sometimes make reference to, or come to an accommodation with prevailing popular beliefs.

Fig.4 Guanxiu's caricatures of the luohans, as in this rubbing of an engraved copy, became iconic portraits.

Such syncretism is amply illustrated in the casual jumbling of Buddhist and Taoist sculptures at Dazu Grottoes (大足石刻) near Chongqing (重慶). In much the same fashion, the Luohans soon took on some of the supernatural attributes as well as the quirky human characteristics of China's Taoist Immortals. This enhanced their popularity and, in due course, a cult came into being; the cult of the luohan. The cult is normally associated with one or other of the two meditative schools of Buddhism, the Tiantai (天台) and the Chan (禪) ("Zen" in Japanese). These taught that Nirvana could be attained through the quietening of the active mind and looking inwards. Along the way, two additional names were added to the original tally of sixteen, and a set of eighteen statues is known to have been cast in bronze as early as 959 for a sanctuary in Guangxi province.[4]

Such temple statues, along with the grotto carvings played an important part in Buddhism's success. As in Europe, in a pre-digital age when literacy was largely the preserve of the elite, sculptural and pictorial guides were essential aids for spreading the word. Hence the importance of securing imperial patronage and protection. Without it the grottoes would have stayed bare and the temples un-built, for artists do not live

---

4   Levi, Sylvain, and Chavannes, Edouard, "Les Seize Arhats protecteurs de la loi", *Journal Asiatique*, XIe serie, Tome VIII, pp. 269-70, 275, 276 and 287.

by inspiration alone. One who was particularly inspired, however, the Buddhist monk, poet and painter Guanxiu (貫休, 832-912) conceived portraits of the Luohans that have become iconic. While living in Lanxi (蘭溪), Zhejiang Province, he had a dream in which they appeared and asked him to paint their likenesses. Most had come originally from the Indian sub-continent and Afghanistan and these origins are recalled in the Indo-European features found in many paintings and sculptures, including some in the caves at Dunhuang. However, Guanxiu took this alien aspect a stage further, painting their portraits in caricature, with exaggeratedly trailing bushy eyebrows, large eyes and noses and drooping jowls. In addition, a deliberate eccentricity of dress and vagabond appearance imparted a sense of their having renounced the world, its wealth and all earthly desires. **(Fig.4)**

On completion Guanxiu, donated the paintings to the Shengyin Temple in Qiantang (錢塘), or Hangzhou (杭州) as it is better known today. Their fame spread, their popularity increased and they became the definitive images of the Luohans. So famous did they become that, when the Qianlong emperor (r. 1736-95) visited on his southern tour of inspection in 1757, he ordered engravings to be taken from the paintings so that they could be preserved. Ironically, these were installed on a small sixteen-sided pagoda, not in a Buddhist temple, but in the Confucian temple there. Another set of copies is preserved as national treasures in the *Sannomaru Shoozokan*, the Museum of the Imperial Collections in Japan.

Politically speaking, imperial patronage was crucial to Buddhism's rise. Sponsorship of the building of temples and monasteries demonstrated formal recognition. Tax exemption gave added value to popular donations. A gift such as a famous Buddhist sutra copied by the Emperor's own brush implied acceptance and conferred authority on the temple to which it was presented. As with Church-State relations in the Christian world, it was a two-way street, a mutually reinforcing relationship. Acceptance of the privileges and gifts was acceptance of the ultimate authority of the Emperor. This was as true of the major dynasties during periods of strong central governance as of the foreign tribes that scrabbled for a foothold during periods of instability. For the latter, patronage was a key part of demonstrating Sinicization and thereby gaining acceptance from the wider populace. Thus, the alien Northern Qi dynasty (386-585) saw lavish sponsorship of the Yungang and Longmen grottoes as a means to enhance their legitimacy. Which is not to say that Buddhism's spread throughout the country was always smooth, or went unopposed by other competing interests.

It was during the Tang dynasty (618-907) that Buddhism encountered its first serious resistance. Officials at the imperial court became increasingly concerned both at the influence that Buddhist monks were exercising over the emperor and the cost of continuing patronage. Incensed that the Emperor wished to waste money on a ceremony to witness the arrival in the capital of a finger-bone of the Buddha, one of his senior officials penned a scathing attack on the monks and bluntly criticized the Emperor's behaviour. In his *Memorial on Bone Relics of the Buddha*, Han Yu (韓愈; 768-824) put the spotlight on Buddhism's alien origins:

> "Buddha was a man of the barbarians who did not speak the language of China and wore clothes of a different fashion His sayings did not concern the ways of our ancient kings, nor did his manner of dress conform to their laws. He understood neither the duties that bind sovereign and subject, nor the affections of father and son."

14

The Emperor, Xianzong (宪宗; r. 805-620), took personal offence and ordered Han Yu's execution. Fortunately for the latter, a formal apology coupled with petitions from his colleagues saw this commuted to exile in Chaozhou (潮州), near the coast of Guangdong Province, some one thousand four hundred kilometres from the capital. A temple there, erected in his honour by the people of the town, reflects their high regard for this upright and capable man. **(Fig.5)** A couplet on the steps leading up to it records his own somewhat rueful contrition:

Fig.5 Han Yu paid for his opposition to Buddhism with exile in Chaozhou. Author's photograph

"For any career achievement comes from diligence, failure from frivolity;
For any action success comes from thought, ruin from thoughtlessness."

Han Yu became a leading figure in the revival of Confucian thought within the bureaucracy and his anti-Buddhist views, in particular that monks and nuns were economically unproductive and therefore a drain on the economy, gained currency after his death. A later Tang emperor, Wuzong (武宗; r. 840-846), took them to heart and, angered by what he regarded as the monasteries' evasion of taxes, unleashed a campaign of persecution and iconoclasm that caused the destruction of some

4,600 monasteries and 40,000 temples. Evicted from their places of study and worship, nearly half a million monks and nuns became peasants and, as peasants, became liable to pay taxes on both grain and cloth. The Emperor was nothing if not even-handed and treated Christians no differently.

As we will see later, this period of persecution is a significant marker in trying to fix the age and origins of the Luohan statues. When they first appeared for sale in Europe, their distinctive three-colour glaze prompted some experts to suggest that they dated from the Tang dynasty. Others thought them more likely to be the products of the later Ming dynasty.

As we shall also see, this argument over dating has swung back and forth for over one hundred years and a key question, if those who favoured the earlier date were right, is how the statues had escaped destruction. An in-between date is equally problematic. When popular uprisings precipitated the fall of the Tang, the barbarians were already at the gates. By the time Harold took an arrow in his eye at Hastings and England became a French colony, they had occupied much of northeast China where the statues were found and, in the eyes of many western scholars, these alien occupiers lacked the technical skills and aesthetic sensibilities required for the creation of such works of art.

That may or may not be unjust, but in order better to understand the initial confusion over dating, we need first to look at what little the West knew about early Chinese art in general, and pottery and ceramics in particular, when the statues went on the block in Paris and Berlin. We will look also at how its appetite and interest both grew and gradually became better informed.

2

Context and Cast

"…all the authorities are agreed that no porcelain pieces are now known which are earlier than the Song dynasty."
William Burton 1906[5]

THE FRENCH do not have a word for *sancai* (三彩), three-color glaze, which is strange when you consider that they were the first Europeans to take seriously the study of Chinese art, and particularly porcelain. They have names for all the other glazes; in fact, the international language of porcelain is French. The Anglo-Saxon world happily adopted their carefully elaborated taxonomy, and not just *Blanc de Chine*, but *clair de lune, sang de boeuf, café au lait, rouge de fer* and the various *familles, jaune, noire, verte etc.*[6] Viewed from a different perspective, these terms are actually grid references that define the extent of exploration of the genre at that point in time. Thus, the fact that there is no word for *sancai* (三彩) tells us that this was still *terra incognita* in 1862, when Albert Jacquemart, assisted by Edmond Le Blant (1818-1897), provided French collectors with the first academic frame of reference for their studies with his monumental *Histoire*

---

5   Burton, William, *Porcelain, a sketch of its nature, art and manufacture*, B.T. Batsford, London, 1906.
6   Credit for most of the lexicon of glazes should go to Louis Gons (1846-1921).

artistique, industrielle et commerciale de la porcelain. Edmond de Goncourt (1822-1896) did not exaggerate when he credited Jacquemart with founding *"la science de la Porcelain de l'Extrême Orient."*

The European collections of the 18ᵗʰ Century, unsurprisingly, were dominated by export ware, that is porcelain mass-produced for export as distinct from the higher quality wares fired in the imperial kilns. A handful of grey-green *longquan* (龍泉) pieces aside, the earliest were the blue-and-whites of the late Ming dynasty (1368-1644), while the majority were those of the Kangxi reign (1662-1722), and the more elaborately decorated polychromes of the same reign, particularly *famille verte* and *famille rose,* together with *celadons* and *Blanc de Chine.* There were radically fewer monochromes, always excepting *turquoise* for which Marie Antoinette had a particular passion. To this day, such pieces are more easily found in France than elsewhere. Chinese porcelains, such as those in the Wallace Collection that made their way from Paris to London with aristocrats fleeing the guillotine in 1789, reflect not just prevailing taste but what was available in the market. While that market was restored once the French Revolution had run its course, the mix had not really changed and it was that mix and those preferences that were inherited by French collectors of the 19ᵗʰ Century and, in the absence of any new discoveries, that informed its connoisseurs and scholars.

The first fresh external stimulus to European art in the 19ᵗʰ Century came not from China but from Japan. America's Commodore Matthew Perry had forced the opening of Japanese ports in 1853 and, in 1854, even before the ink was dry on the treaty, an exhibition of Japanese art was held at the Old Watercolour Society in London. Thus, began an encounter whose influence was to be felt in European graphic arts and design for a century or more. The Japanese were quickly invited to exhibit at the International Exhibition in 1862, and for a while *Japonisme* was the fashion of the day. Art dealers all over the continent rose to the challenge of meeting this new demand. Artists and designers responded to the exotic stimulus across all media, fascinated by the novel lines and tones of Japanese woodcut prints and the power of its simplicity. The graphic arts aside, in France, Galle, Lalique and Tiffany all owed a debt to this Oriental influence, as did dealers such as Samuel Bing, who actively promoted the new flavour and the work of European artists who embraced it. Indeed, it could be argued that *art nouveau* would not have taken off without it. Few French Sinophiles remained unmoved but, resisting the tide, the connoisseur Edmond De Goncourt proclaimed, "All the ancient art of Japan is a poor dutiful imitation of Chinese art."

However, the pendulum would shortly swing back to things Chinese, not least because of interest generated by treasures looted from the Yuanmingyuan (圓明園), the Old Summer Palace, in 1860.[7] And, at almost exactly the same time, the centre of gravity of their appreciation, collection and study would shift from the francophone to the anglophone world.

Before it did, Henri Cernuschi (Enrico Cernuschi) (1821-1896), Italian patriot, French banker and economist, unsettled by the dramatic events of the Paris Commune, embarked on an extended world tour from September 1871 to January 1873, in the company of a young art critic, Theodore Duret. This was no idle tourist trip. Incredible though it may seem today, during their

---

7　The Yuanmingyuan, or Old Summer Palace, was despoiled by British and French troops in October 1860. Unlike the British official trophies, which disappeared into Royal and regimental museums, those presented to Emperor Napoleon III and his wife Eugenie were put on public display from February through April 1861. Private loot began to appear in French auction houses towards the end of that year and, as demonstrated by Lea Saint-Raymond and Christine Howald in *Tracing Dispersal: Auction Sales from the Yuanmingyuan loot in Paris in the 1860s*, initially almost all was bought up by dealers.

visit to the Far East Cernuschi amassed some 5,000 works of art, primarily Japanese, but including a notable collection of Chinese bronzes. On his return, the mansion that he built near Parc Morceau to house the collection became a centre of *Japonisme*, and its glorious four-metre high bronze Buddha Amida a focal point that provided Parisians with their first experience of monumental Buddhist sculpture. On his death in 1896, Cernuschi left both mansion and collection to the City of Paris as a museum.

A decade before Cernuschi went walkabout, another equally voracious collector, and Confederate sympathiser, had fled Baltimore for Paris at the outbreak of the American Civil War, reaching that city in 1861 just in time to witness the arrival of art and antiques from Japan and plunder from China. William Thompson Walters (1819-94) had made his fortune from rye whiskey and railways and had begun collecting American and European art to decorate his Baltimore townhouse. A visit to the London International Exhibition with his son Henry the following year proved something of an epiphany and they later recalled their "surprise and pleasure" on first encounter with Oriental art there. It was the start of a love affair with Chinese porcelain that led them via visits to the major European collections in London, Paris, Versailles and Dresden, and the kilns at Sevres and Meissen, to a pioneering exploration of both the beauty and the science of porcelain: 'There can be no question that the Chinese have established their pre-eminence in this artistic development, compared with all that has been accomplished up to the present time; therefore the Collection will be found to be made up largely of the products of that remarkable people."[8]

Humble from the start they recalled, "It is probable that we have as yet but an imperfect knowledge of the age, history and

---

8   Walters, William and Henry, *The Oriental Collection of W.T. Walters,* Baltimore 1884, v.

meaning of much that appears in the collections of Oriental porcelain, and until some European, residing in China, well versed in the subject, and well acquainted with the Chinese language, has obtained access to the stores of native collectors, we shall be to a certain extent working in the dark."[9] They were fortunate to find just such a man in the form of a physician at the British legation in Beijing.

In between treating his patients, Dr. Stephen Bushell (1844-1908) had become passionately interested in Chinese porcelain. He took it upon himself to attempt a translation of the earliest comprehensive Chinese work written on the subject, Zhu Yan's (朱琰) *Tao Shuo* (陶說), a rambling collection, in Bushell's words, of "extracts from a vast field of native literature, loosely strung together and accompanied by a running commentary by the author." Although he completed the task in 1891, it was not published until 1910, two years after his death. In the meantime, at the behest of Walters-father-and-son, he applied his scholarship to the production of a history of East Asian ceramics to accompany a catalogue of their pieces. *Oriental Ceramic Art: Illustrated by Examples from the Collection of W.T. Walters* was published in 1896 and, more than a century later, is still regarded as both a work of extraordinary erudition and a mine of information on both ceramics and mythology, notwithstanding Margaret Medley's later acerbic comment that one of the translations was "...so full of errors as to be virtually useless".[10] However, those looking for examples from the earlier dynasties would have found little advance on the European collections of a century earlier.

The fact is that the earlier periods were not so much under-represented in European collections as virtually invisible. For

---

9   Walters, Op. Cit., p. 4.
10   Medley, Margaret, *Yuan Porcelain and Stoneware*, London, 1974; p. 8, referring to Stephen Bushell's translation of *Jiang Qi Taoji Fu* (蔣祈陶記附), Jiang Qi's memorandum on porcelain.

example, George Salting's (1835-1909) vast collection of Chinese porcelain, which he bequeathed in its entirety to the Victoria and Albert Museum, contained almost nothing from the early dynasties. Such pieces were simply unobtainable in his lifetime. Access to Chinese works such as the *Jingdezhen Tao Lu* (景德鎮陶錄), which was translated into French by Stanislas Julien in the middle of the century (1856)–a remarkable feat of scholarship for a man who had never visited China–meant that curators and connoisseurs were aware of the forms and palettes of earlier dynasties, but it was in large part a theoretical appreciation.[11] Western art historians had had to take on trust from Chinese texts that the Tang dynasty (618-907) was a Golden Age, reinforced only by what Japanese sources and derivations were able to corroborate.

As William Burton wrote in 1906, "Contemporary European students would fix the date for the invention of porcelain to the latter part of the T'ang dynasty (618-907). This, to say the least of it, is a date of respectable antiquity, but when we enquire as to the evidence on which such an opinion is founded, we are referred only to Chinese writings; and when we ask for authentic specimens, all the authorities are agreed that no porcelain pieces are now known which are earlier than the Song dynasty (960-1179), while the Song productions have become so scarce that they are hardly to be procured by the most princely purse, even in China itself."[12] Dr. Berthold Laufer's *Chinese Pottery of the Han Dynasty*, just one of the fruits of the three years that extraordinary scholar spent in China at the behest of the American Museum of Natural History, did not appear until 1909.

It was only with the construction of the railways–the Qing government began to grant rail concessions to foreigners from

---

11 Stanislas' translation was not bettered until Geoffrey Sayer's appeared almost a century later in 1951.

12 Burton, Op. Cit.

1895–that significant new finds of Tang tombs led first to a trickle and then to a flood of ancient artifacts as clandestine excavations followed in the wake of accidental discoveries. Up until that point, the mix and pattern of private collecting had not really changed and it was that mix and those preferences that Loo Ching Tsai (盧芹齋; pinyin: *Lu Qinzhai*), more commonly known as C.T. Loo, would have encountered when he first arrived in Paris in 1902 (**Fig.6**).

Fig.6 C.T. Loo (1880-1957), dealer extraordinaire. Public Domain

The orphaned child of a poor peasant family, he had been fortunate to find work in the house of a rich merchant, and when Zhang Renjie (張人傑) (**Fig.7**), the son of his wealthy benefactor, was appointed Third Counsellor at the Chinese Embassy in Paris, Loo traveled with him. Once established there, doubtless in breach of all diplomatic protocol, the son harnessed his commercial instincts to the cause of revolution. Ton Ying, the small importing business he opened on Place de la Madeleine, where the young C.T. Loo learned his trade, dealt in tea, raw silk, porcelain, lacquer, furniture and sundry antiques, and its clientele was blissfully unaware of the contributions these purchases were making to the activities of the revolutionary, Sun Yat-sen (孫中山).

C.T. Loo was plainly aware of this secret side to the business and, his interests being commercial rather than political, he was probably frustrated by it. If the business was to grow,

Fig.7 Zhang Renjie (1877-1960) raised funds for revolution while posted to Paris. Public Domain

Fig.8 Edgar Worch (1880-1972), Parisian German oriental antique dealer. After P. Schmitz 2013

profits needed to be reinvested and, as the young man became acquainted with Dikran Kelekian, Paul Vignier, Edgar Worch (**Fig.8**) and the other Parisian antique dealers of the time, his eyes would certainly have been opened to the greater potential for profit in art and antiquities than curios. Indeed, it is entirely possible that he early on began to import things of interest to them on his own account, for in 1908, hard on the heels of the discovery of the Dunhuang scrolls, Loo opened his own small gallery, Lai Yuan et Cie, on Rue Taitbout in the 9th arrondissement, and in 1911, on his first visit back to his homeland, followed up by opening offices in both Peking and Shanghai.

The 19th Century was the time when European scholars first began to take an interest in Oriental religion and the discoveries at Dunhuang (敦煌) represent a high watermark. The German philosopher Arthur Schopenhauer (1788-1860), albeit not a convert, had been the first Western intellectual to affirm significant tenets of Eastern philosophy. Others followed curiously in his footsteps aided by the translations of the omnivorous sinologist Stanislas Julien, whose history of porcelain was mentioned earlier. The French industrialist Emile Etienne Guimet (1836-1918), an inveterate traveller, was commissioned by the Minister of Public Instruction in 1876 to embark on a study of the religions of the Far East. Along the way, he assembled a collection of Chinese and Japanese porcelain, as well as religious statuary, which formed the core of his museum. Opened in Lyon in 1879, it was transferred to Place d'Iena in Paris ten years later. Known officially as the *Musée National des Arts Asiatiques*, unofficially it is still far better known as *Musée Guimet*. On three separate occasions in the 1890s, Guimet invited Japanese and, latterly, Tibetan monks to perform elaborate Buddhist ceremonies in the museum. These were hugely popular and guests included the left-wing political leader, Georges Clemenceau (1841-1929), who had become interested in Buddhism after meeting the Japanese nobleman and future politician Saionji Kinmochi. Clemenceau eventually became obsessed with the religion, but history does not relate whether he was present in March 1905, when Mata Hari debuted her allegedly Javanese dance routine at the Guimet.[13]

The religious statuary was something of a novelty. Little "Laughing Buddhas" and small Guanyin (Goddess of Mercy) figurines had been popular items among the *Blanc de Chine* export ware and were believed to bring good luck. Soldiers' loot, almost by definition, had to be portable and rarely strayed beyond decorative items in precious materials that were easier to convert into cash. Their Generals' gifts to monarchs might be larger scale, but the "monumental" items favoured mythical

---

13   Aldrich, Robert, *Vestiges of Colonial Empire in France*, Palgrave Macmillan, 2005, p.283.

beasts rather than meditative monks. Thus, aside from a large gold dagoba reliquary and some embroidery, there is little in the plunder presented to Empress Eugénie, now preserved at Chateau Fontainebleau, that is overtly religious.

Missionaries and merchants were familiar with "Heathen Idols" of every description, but the reports of the former were biased, and the latter embroidered, and the ordinary European or American was aware of devotional deities only from such second or third-hand travellers' tales. For most, the Cernuschi's towering Amitabha and the Guimet's smaller, multi-armed, gilt-bronze Hindu statues and Indo-Chinese and Japanese sculpture would thus have been their first real encounter with Oriental objects of worship. Initially, most of it would have made little sense, but it would at least have helped flesh out the imagery of Sir Edwin Arnold's poetic narrative epic *The Light of Asia–the Great Renunciation*, and Kipling's more colloquial *Buddha of Kamakura*.[14] Aesthetically, however, what must first have struck those imbued with the Hellenistic sculptural tradition would have been the apparent serenity in the multiple versions of a curiously stylized, not-quite-human countenance.

On the other side of the Atlantic, inquisitive intellectuals and adventurous aesthetes followed paths similar to those of their European cousins. Wealthy families on the Eastern seaboard of America were no strangers to the China trade, so it is hardly surprising that some of their sons and daughters should head to the East. Even so, Edward S. Morse's journey was to say the least unusual. An avid childhood collector of snails and shells on the Portland coast, he was expelled from every school he attended. Despite an absence of formal education, he became an acknowledged expert, helped found *The American*

---

14   Published in 1879 and 1892 respectively.

Naturalist and went to Japan in search of brachiopods in 1877 only to find himself appointed professor of zoology at Tokyo Imperial University. Whether he was aware of the linguistic link between porcelain and shells is unclear, but he assembled both a remarkable collection of, and expertise in, Japanese pottery and porcelain. His example touched two others of his countrymen.

From Salem Massachusetts, Ernest Fenollosa (1853-1908) wound his way via study of philosophy and sociology at Harvard to art school, and then at the invitation of Edward Morse to the Imperial University of Tokyo in 1878. Immersion in Japan's art and culture led him to Buddhism. The third member of Japan's "Boston Triumvirate" was a wealthy third-generation scion of a Boston family that had made its fortune in the China trade. A physician and son of a physician, William Sturgis Bigelow (1850-1926) tired of medicine and took time off to travel to Japan in 1882 in the company of Morse and Fenollosa. He stayed for seven years, studying the country's art and culture and securing the permission of the Japanese authorities to photograph the treasures of its temples that were normally locked in storerooms and closed to outsiders. He, too, converted to Buddhism. Isabella Stuart Gardiner, who visited the triumvirate with her husband in 1883, and whom Bigelow nicknamed "The Serpent of the Charles", did not, but she did install a "Buddha Room" in her home, where Fenollosa's former student, the Japanese scholar Okakura Kakuzo, would sometimes perform a tea ceremony for her guests.

Talks on Buddhist topics by travellers and explorers became popular at geographic clubs, and learned papers began to appear in the transactions of learned societies. For example in 1898, the Journal of the Royal Asiatic Society published a ground-breaking essay by the traveller T. Watters entitled *The Eighteen Lohans* of *Chinese Buddhist Temples*.[15] Academic, popular and political interest were all further fired by the three perilous expeditions undertaken by Sven Hedin (1865-1952) to unexplored regions of Chinese Turkestan and Tibet between 1894 and 1908. And, finally, the scrolls brought back from the Silk Road oasis of Dunhuang (敦煌) by Aurel Stein (1862-1943) in 1907, supplemented by others documented *in situ* or retrieved by the French polyglot Paul Pelliot (1878-1945) the following year, (**Fig.9**) dramatically increased Western understanding of the historical development of Buddhism and its spread from the Indian sub-continent via Central Asia to China, Korea and Japan. That knowledge would be rounded out by the great French sinologist Edouard Chavannes (**Fig.10**) who, over a six-year period commencing in 1909, catalogued many of China's great cave sites on his *Mission archéologique dans la Chine septentrionale*. Accompanied by Victor Segalen (1878-1919), military doctor, archaeologist, ethnographer, philosopher and photographer, he was only just in time. (**Fig.11**) As the Qing dynasty declined and law and order broke down, a process of pillaging began that was to decimate the sculptural population of the great grottoes. Tianlongshan (天龍山) was just one of the victims, as noted by Michael Ondaatje in *Anil's Ghost*: "Cave 14 was once the most beautiful site in a series of cave temples in Shanxi (山西) province....This was the place of a complete crime....All the statuary had been removed in the few years following its discovery by Japanese archaeologists in 1918, the Bodhisattvas quickly bought up by museums in the West (and East)."[16]

Our Confederate sympathiser-in-exile, William Walters and his son Henry were the advance guard of that pre-Roosevelt

---

15 Watters T., "The Eighteen Lohans of Chinese Buddhist Temples", in *Journal of the Royal Asiatic Society*, vol. 30, (1898), pp. 329-47.
16 Ondaatje, Michael, *Anil's Ghost*, p. 12. Established during the Eastern Wei dynasty, the cave prospered under Emperor Xuanzong between 714-40 CE. One of its statues can be found in Tokyo National Museum. Publication by Yamanaka in the 1920s of an illustrated book of the grottoes' contents is sometimes blamed for its ransacking.

Fig.10 Edouard Chavannes (1865-1918) and his wife in Japan. Public Domain

Fig.9 Paul Pelliot (1878-1945) poring over scrolls in Cave 163 at Dunhuang. Public Domain

Fig.11 Victor Segalen (1878-1919) conducting academic research in northern China in 1914. Public Domain

generation of industrialists who built commanding positions in railways, steel, petroleum, chemicals and finance and then began buying the world and endowing the North American continent's great museums. The Metropolitan Museum of Art was founded in 1870 by a group of businessmen, financiers, artists and thinkers to bring art and art education to the American people. John Pierpoint Morgan (1837-1913), the greatest banker America had ever known, became its President. Boston celebrated the nation's centennial by opening its Museum of Fine Arts on 4 July 1876, and would ultimately benefit from the gift of some 40,000 objects of Japanese art brought back home by William Bigelow, when he finally returned. A close family friend of another Boston Brahmin, Congressman Henry Cabot Lodge, Bigelow took a shine to the latter's younger son, John Ellerton Lodge, and used his influence to secure him a job at the museum. The same influence steered the younger man towards Oriental art and he would eventually become curator of the Asiatic Department, a position he held from 1915 to 1933. Boston was followed only three years later by the Art Institute of Chicago, under the generous guiding hand of another banker philanthropist, Charles L. Hutchinson (1854-1924).

Further south and a decade later, the "Penn" was founded, funded by prominent Philadelphian financiers and businessmen. Few bother to remember the Penn's cumbersome, more formal title as the University of Pennsylvania Museum of Archaeology and Anthropology, but it serves as a useful reminder that this extraordinary post-Civil War investment would yield huge dividends in a new generation of highly motivated archaeologists, anthropologists, ethnographers, art historians and curators.

The Brooklyn Museum was founded in 1895. In 1901, the American Museum of Natural History sent the anthropologist and latterly distinguished sinologist Dr. Berthold Laufer on a three-year expedition to China during which he accumulated an extraordinary range of objects ranging from ancient bronzes and Han ceramics to musical instruments, puppets, costumes and household items. Cleveland opened in 1905 thanks to two local industrialists Hinman Hurlbut and John Huntington, the same year as was established the Seattle Fine Arts Society that surgeon Richard Eugene Fuller would later transform into a museum. Planned earlier, but slower in realisation came Philadelphia's Museum of Art, in 1923, and ten years after that the Nelson-Atkins Museum in Kansas City, the improbable home of one of the world's finest collections of Asian art.[17]

In parallel with the investment in public institutions ran an equally extraordinary assembling of private collections. The West had long cast envious eyes on Chinese porcelain, but loot from the Yuanmingyuan opened its eyes to a much broader range of decorative art and seemingly impossible craftsmanship.

William Walters was the omnivorous pioneer and he was followed by some equally hungry, albeit more selective collectors like Isabella Stewart Gardner (1840-1924), Benjamin Altman (1840-1913), J.P. Morgan (1837-1913), Charles Freer (1854-1919) and John D. Rockefeller Jr. "Junior" (1874-1960). Initially, the impact on the market for Asian art and antiques was slight, but in the years following the Civil War, it quickly gathered momentum. Interestingly, it was the Japanese dealer Sadajiro Yamanaka (1866-1936) who first sensed the changing current (**Fig.12**). Well ahead of the pack, Yamanaka arrived in New York in 1894. He opened his first shop in Chelsea, New York the following year, selling the collections of impecunious Manchu princes both there and in London. He opened branches in Boston (1899), London and Osaka (1900), had an agent in Paris (1905), an office in Beijing (1917), and another branch in Chicago (1928). The enterprising English fur trader, George Crofts (1871-1925), who had arrived in Tientsin, present-day Tianjin (天津), in 1899, also spotted an opportunity when work on a railway cutting unearthed a trove

---

17 The Nelson-Atkins derives its double-barreled name from its original sponsors, publisher William Rockhill Nelson and Kansas City school teacher Mary McAfee Atkins, whose wealth came from her husband's real estate business.

Fig.13 George Crofts (1871-1925), fur trader become antique dealer and patron of the ROM in Toronto; Courtesy of the Royal Ontario Museum

Fig.12 Sadajiro Yamanaka (1866-1936) in Tianlongshan Grottoes, Shanxi–"place of a complete crime..." Public domain

of burial objects (**Fig.13**). He developed both a personal interest in Chinese art and antiques and a profitable sideline, sourcing for wholesale dealers such as S.M. Franck & Sons in London. A much later meeting with Charles Currelly, Director of the Royal Ontario Museum in Toronto would yield extraordinary benefits for that institution and an honorary doctorate for the fur trader.

Quite coincidentally, the year that Yamanaka opened his shop in New York was the year that the Qing Government began issuing concessions to foreign firms to build railways. Wary of dominance by any single Western power, it parceled out the concessions to several different European nations, as well as America and Russia. With the railways came an equally varied group of financial backers and foreign engineers. One of the latter, a Frenchman by the name of Joseph Charignon (1872-1930), had already spent three years in Turkey before being posted to China in 1898 to work on the line connecting

Kunming in the southeast of the country to Hanoi and the port-city of Haiphong in present-day Vietnam (**Fig.14**). This traversed extraordinarily difficult terrain, but the young Charignon, who was something of a polyglot and polymath, profited from the experience by studying the costumes and customs of the local peoples in his spare time. During the subsequent construction of the line southwards from Peking to Hankow, present-day Wuhan on the Yangtze River, his talents attracted the attention of senior Qing officials. Thus, he was appointed an adviser to the Qing Government in 1908 and subsequently to the Nationalist Government. In this capacity, in 1914, he produced a plan for the development of a comprehensive Chinese railway network. He was the first Frenchman to take Chinese nationality, adopting the name Sha Hai'ang (沙海昂). To the extent that he collected anything, it was restricted to books. Not so his young Belgian colleague, Jean Jadot (1862-1932), who would later make a name for himself in the Congo and be appointed governor of the Belgian Bank, Société Générale. While working on the same line linking Peking to Hankow, he developed a liking for ancient bronzes.

Another engineer, a Swede by the name of Orvar Karlbeck (1879-1967), worked on the railways from 1906 to 1927, starting on the southern section of the British financed Tianjin-Pukou Railway (津浦鐵路) in the Huai (淮) Valley. (**Fig.15**)[18] There he found and started collecting small ancient bronze belt hooks and mirrors. Eventually, sensing a commercial opportunity, he began sourcing antiquities for serious European collectors, and on one occasion, to the astonishment and admiration of his scholarly Chinese acquaintances, received a visit from no less a personage

---

18   Karlbeck, Orvar "Selected Objects from Ancient Shou-Chou", *Ostasiatiska Museet* (*Bulletin of the Museum of Far Eastern Antiquities*), Vol. 27, Stockholm, 1955, p. 41.

Fig.14 Joseph Charignon ((1872-1930), French polymath railway engineer in the uniform of a Lieutenant of Artillery, Hanoi, 1914. Creative Commons

than the Swedish Crown Prince, Gustav Adolf![19]

Construction of the railways triggered the accidental excavation of Tang (唐) dynasty (618-907) tombs and it was not long before their contents began to appear in the market place, where they caused a sensation. The glories of the Tang were no myth; tangible proof had been found and museums and collectors were eager for more. The clandestine digging that followed was an archaeologist's nightmare, as tomb after tomb was unscientifically stripped of its magnificent furnishings and sold to Japan and the West without any record to assist later research. The pioneering collector in England was William Cleverly Alexander, a banker who collected Japanese woodcuts and who had early on recognized the genius of the expatriate American artist, James McNeill Whistler. His collection was included in the first exhibition of the Tang dynasty finds organized by Dr. Hercules Read of the British Museum in 1910.[20] *"Early Chinese Pottery and Porcelain"* was staged by the Burlington Club, which in those days was a society of collectors and connoisseurs rather than of brash Oxford graduates intent on trashing

---

19 Johansson, Perry, *Saluting the Yellow Emperor: A Case of Swedish Sinography,* Brill, 2011, p. 106.

20 In his preface, Read acknowledged the part played by railway construction in opening the eyes of the West to China's earlier wares.

Fig.15 Orvar Karlbeck (1879-1967), Swedish engineer and procurer of antiquities for royalty and the aristocracy. Courtesy of Freer / Sackler

respectable restaurants.[21] It was a great success and marked the rise to prominence of a man who was to become the internationally acknowledged expert on Chinese ceramics for the next quarter century.

A graduate of Jesus College, Cambridge, with a first in Classics, Robert Lockhart Hobson (1872-1941) had entered the British Museum in 1897, where he developed a reputation both for systematic, fact-based cataloguing and seeing objects of art where others saw only craft work. Initially, his studies focused on English pottery and porcelain, but a natural curiosity led him to take an interest in the museum's Chinese collection and he was among the first to witness the arrival in England of the Tang dynasty pieces. The catalogue for the 1910 exhibition was largely his work and much admired for the quality of its scholarship. In 1921 he was made Keeper of the Department of Ceramics and Ethnography, and in 1934 Keeper of Oriental Antiquities and Ethnography, a position which he held until his retirement in 1938. He was a founder member of the Oriental Ceramic Society, which was established in 1921 and succeeded its first President, the great collector George Eurmorfopoulos, serving from 1939 to 1942.

In the United States, the Tang debutantes had their coming-out at a comparable exhibition at Knoedler's, a leading dealer in old masters in New York, in 1914. Most types of early ceramics were represented albeit few were of the first quality, the exceptions being some "numbered" *Jun* (鈞) ware pieces, at

---

21 The Burlington Fine Arts Club, to give it its full name, had previously held two exhibitions, the first in 1895, the second in 1896, but both of these primarily featured blue and white porcelain.

that time believed to be from the Song dynasty, (宋; 960-1279) and the Korean celadon. The same year, two more *Jun* (鈞) ware pieces appeared in the first exhibition of Chinese art staged in Sweden. These belonged to Countess Wilhelmina, a great collector and cataloguer, a pioneer in the exploration of pre-export Chinese ceramics and, in due course, a member of the "Syndicate" supplied by Oscar Karlbeck, the Swedish engineer turned scholar and dealer whom we encountered earlier.[22]

The exhibits in New York were on loan from a Mr. C. L. Freer, who had obtained them in Japan (**Fig.16**). Charles Lang Freer (1854-1919) was the first serious American collector to visit the Far East. From humble beginnings in New York, he had built the Peninsular Car Company, America's largest manufacturer of railway carriages, and had started collecting art in the 1880s. He made his first visit to Asia in 1894, spending eleven months traveling via the Suez Canal to Sri Lanka, India, Singapore, Hong

Kong, Shanghai and Tokyo. Later, when stress-related health problems decided him to retire at the turn of the century, he elected to combine travel with collecting.

Like W.C. Alexander in England, Freer had been impressed by Whistler's work when viewing some etchings in New York, and on his first visit to London in 1890, he introduced himself to the artist. They became fast friends, spending much time traveling together, until Whistler passed away in 1903. The art historian

Fig.16 Charles Lang Freer (1854-1919), pioneering American collector of Oriental art. Creative Commons

22   Kerr, Rose, "Countess Wilhelmina's Chinese Treasures: the Hallwyl Museum, Stockholm", a lecture on 23 October, 2014, *Bulletin of the Oriental Ceramic Society of Hong Kong*, No. 16, 2013-15, p. 73-5. Apart from Countess Wilhemina, the "Karlbeck Syndicate" included HRH Gustav VI Adolf of Sweden, Carl Kempe, the Rohsska Museum in Gothenburg, the British Museum, the Berlin State Museum and the British collectors Charles and Brenda Seligman, Oscar Raphael, Henry Oppenheim and George Eumorfopolous.

Ernest Fenollosa (1853-1908), whom Freer met in 1901, became his muse and adviser. He began collecting voraciously and eventually gifted his entire collection to the Smithsonian, including the famous "Peacock Room" that he had purchased anonymously from the Whistler estate in England and shipped home in 1904. By the time he paid his second visit to China and Japan, an eight-month trip in 1906-7, completion of the Trans-Siberian Railway and its link to Beijing through Port Arthur, present-day Lushun (旅順), via the Chinese Eastern railway had transformed travel. What used to be a long and arduous two to three-month sea voyage to Europe was now a quick and comparatively comfortable three-week rail journey. By this time, his name was also better known and he was treated as a serious collector.

On his next visit, first to Europe and then China, in 1909, it is likely that Freer called on established dealers like Dikran Kelekian, Marcel Bing (son of Samuel) and Charles Vignier in Paris. Assuming he did, the latter would have shown him the beautiful Northern Qi dynasty (550-577) Bodhisattvas from the grottoes at Xiangtangshan (響堂山)–the "Mountain of Echoing Halls"–260 miles south-southwest of Beijing that had been acquired by C.T. Loo. These were among the first life-size stone sculptures to make a journey to the West, and they did it in style on the Trans-Siberian. Freer did not buy one, nor did he meet Mr. Loo, who had only just opened his first shop in Paris on the Rue Taitbout. It would be another five years before they met by chance, one cold December 1914 day, on a train from Toronto to New York. In the unexpected but enthusiastic conversation that followed, Freer persuaded Loo that, in future, America, not Europe would drive demand for Asian art and antiquities. Loo opened his New York gallery the following year and not long thereafter sold Freer's friends, Eugene and Agnes Meyer, the Bodhisattva that Agnes gifted to the Freer in 1968. He sold three others to the Penn.

On his 1909 trip to China, Freer also called on the Chinese connoisseur Duanfang (端方) (1861-1911) in Tientsin (天津) (**Fig.17**). Unusually for a Han Chinese, Duanfang was a Manchu bannerman, who became a senior politician and, at the time they met, he was Governor of Zhili Province (直隸), roughly the equivalent of today's Hebei (河北), but embracing both Beijing and Tientsin. He was a determined supporter of reform, including equality of treatment between Manchu and Han, and had earlier been sent on an official mission to Japan, the United States, Britain, France, Germany, Austria and Scandinavia to research their constitutional arrangements. On his return, he advocated China following Japan's Meiji example. A keen collector, he purchased Egyptian antiquities while abroad. Tragically, as Director General of Railways, while on his way to put down an uprising in Sichuan, he was beheaded by mutinying troops, who returned the corpse to his family, but demanded a ransom for his head so that he could be buried whole. Improbable though it might seem, it fell to Orvar Karlbeck, who was a friend of the family, to make the grisly exchange.[23] Sometime later, Duanfang's treasured Shang and Zhou (商/周1766-1121-255 BCE) bronzes were bought from the family by the American scholar John Calvin Ferguson (1866-1945) on behalf of the Met in New York for some 20 million taels of silver, or circa $100,000.

Following his meeting with the ill-fated connoisseur extraordinary, Freer traveled the 600-mile length of the Yangtze River from Hubei (湖北) to Shanghai. Unlike most other contemporary American collectors, Freer wanted to see China's history on the ground, On his final visit in 1910, he visited the great grottoes at Longmen (龍門石窟), however a stroke in May

---

23   Lawton, Thomas, *A Time of Transition: Two Collectors of Chinese Art*, 1991, pp.62-63.

1911 put paid to further travel and thenceforth he purchased from Asian dealers in America.

One of the reasons that collectors like Freer and his peers were able to buy both Japanese and Chinese antiques so cheaply in Japan was that, in turning towards modernity and the West, the Japanese were neglecting their past. For example, Kojiro Matsukata (1865-1950), the Western-educated–he was a graduate of Rutgers University–president of Kawasaki Shipbuilding spent

Fig.17 Duanfang (1861-1911), Han Chinese Manchu Bannerman, reformer and connoisseur. Public Domain

his fortune pursuing a lifelong dream to build a collection of Western paintings and sculpture for Japan (**Fig.18**). He succeeded famously and his collection formed the core of what is now the Japanese National Gallery. However, as we shall see, even he could be persuaded to buy ancient Chinese works of art, as also Yasujiro Tsutsumi (1889-1964), the founder of the Seibu business empire, which included both property development and railways. (**Fig.19**) Railway barons were not a uniquely North American phenomenon.

Another collector that Freer may have met was of a rather different stripe and one of the more colourful members of Beijing's expatriate community. Johan Wilhelm Normann Munthe (1864-1935) (**Fig.20**) was born in Bergen, Norway, and received two years training at the Military School for non-commissioned cavalry officers before heading for China. Arriving in 1887, he walked into a job in the Chinese Customs Service thanks to a relative,

Fig.18 Kojiro Matsukata (1865-1950), collector of Western painting and sculpture who purchased one of the Luohans. Public Domain

Fig.19 Yasujiro Tsutsumi (1889-1964), self-made property tycoon, collector and Speaker of the Japanese House of Representatives 1953-54. Public Domain

Iver Munthe Dase, who was already living there. However, during the first Sino-Japanese War, he offered his services to the Imperial Army. His reckless bravery and dramatic handlebar moustache brought him to the attention of General Yuan Shikai (袁世凱) and they became good friends. (**Fig.21**) In 1900, he joined the international troops during the Boxer Rebellion, working as an interpreter and guide for the Russian forces. One year later he became Major General and adjunct to General Yuan, who had steadfastly opposed the Dowager Empress' desire for punitive attacks on the foreign forces. Munthe remained in Yuan Shi-kai's service as chief of security for the foreign legations, and chief designer and modeler of medals and decorations, until the would-be-emperor's death in 1916.

Unlikely though it seems for a man of action, Munthe developed an interest in Chinese art and antiques and built up a large collection of some 780 paintings and 270 album prints, in addition to jades, porcelain and stone sculptures. He had the latter scrubbed clean to remove all traces of pigmentation and displayed

Fig.20 Johan Munthe (1864-1935), Major General, adjunct to Yuan Shikai, designer of military decorations and collector of antiquities. Public Domain

Fig.21 Yuan Shikai (1859-1916), the General-who-would-be-Emperor. Public Domain

them in his garden, along with seven marble columns that previously adorned the Old Summer Palace, the *Yuanmingyuan*.[24] As one visitor related: "On our knocking we were admitted by a servant into a quiet and sombre garden of breath-taking beauty, the chief feature of which was an avenue of tall trees leading toward the house with large stelae and sculptured figures of stone placed between the trees on either side of the path–stelae and figures which I was to learn later, dated back two, three and even four thousand years."[25] Possibly concerned at the precariousness of the political situation in China, Munthe early on decided to gift all 2,550 artifacts, to his good friend in Bergen, Johan Bogh, the director of the *Vestlandske Kunstindustrimuseum*, the West Norway Museum of Decorative Art. However, he delayed their

---

24 In February 2014, the KODE Art Museum in Bergen, Norway, with the assistance of the Chinese businessman, Mr. Huang Nubo, and Beijing University, arranged for the return of the columns to China for permanent display at the university.

25 Charles Arrot, an American who visited Beijing in 1925 while on a world tour, was invited by Munthe to photograph his collection, *ms* with Vestlandske Kunstindustrimuseum, quoted by Gillman, Derek, "General Munthe's Chinese Buddhist Sculpture", in Skourpski, Tadeusz, ed., *The Buddhist Forum*, Vol. IV, p. 105.

departure and they were still in Beijing in 1925, when the German art historian Otto Fischer inspected them.[26]

The China where Munthe lived and worked, and which Freer visited was in a state of precipitous decline. The Taiping Rebellion (1850-64) had cost an estimated 20-30 million lives, the bloodiest conflict in human history. The imperial forces that eventually overcame the rebels numbered nearly a million soldiers, including a small regiment of Chinese soldiers led by foreign mercenary officers known as the Ever-Victorious Army. Subsequent attempts at internal reform such as the "Self-strengthening Movement" did not go as far as Japan's internal reforms and were handicapped as much by the presence of foreign enclaves as entrenched internal political rivalries. Following China's defeat in the First Sino-Japanese War (1894-5), the young, well-intentioned but weak Guangxu emperor (光緒; r.1875-1908) launched a programme of cultural, political and educational reform, but a parallel plan forcibly to remove the Empress Dowager Cixi (慈禧) from power was betrayed by General Yuan Shi-kai, who was supposed to take control of the Tientsin garrison. Cixi countered with her own *coup d'etat*, placing the emperor under house arrest within the imperial garden known as Zhongnanhai (中南海), until his death, and ruling as regent in his place. The emperor's closest advisers, the "six gentlemen" of the One Hundred Days' reform were summarily tried and executed and their coffins placed in the *Fayuansi*, (法源寺) a Beijing temple dating from the Tang dynasty (618-907) that would thereafter be known as the "Martyrs' Shrine".

Cixi's subsequent role in the so-called "Boxer Rebellion" remains a matter of debate, but the Boxer's 55-day siege of the

---

26   An attempt to sell the collection to the Los Angeles County Museum collapsed over suspicions cast on the authenticity of a number of the items. Eventually, the collection was returned to Bergen, where it is now on display at the Vestlandske Kunstindustimuseum. Munthe was buried in Beijing in 1935.

Legation Quarter, during which the young French scholar Paul Pelliot behaved with exemplary courage, was to have disastrous consequences, and not just for the great library of the Hanlin Academy (翰林院), which was torched.[27] Foreign intervention followed in the form of the Eight-Nation Alliance that fought its way into the capital–the Empress Dowager fled to Xi'an (西安) with the Guangxu emperor in tow–relieved the siege, summarily executed all suspected Boxers and indulged in unrestrained pillage. Not that plunder was a military monopoly. Every afternoon except Sundays, auctions of looted goods were held outside the gate of the British legation and Lady Ethel MacDonald, wife of the Ambassador, was amongst the keenest of bidders. The Beitang (北堂), the Catholic Cathedral where Alphonse Favier, the French Bishop, had gallantly defended thousands of Chinese Catholics during the uprising, became a mart for stolen goods. In its aftermath, the Bishop himself was accused of having looted the mansion of a Qing minister, Yuen Chang (袁昶; 1846-1900), who had been executed by the Empress Dowager for opposing attacks on the embassies. At the end of August, when the gates of the Forbidden City were thrown open, few members of the Diplomatic Corps showed any restraint in collecting elegant souvenirs.

It fell to the long-serving Inspector General of China's Imperial Maritime Custom Service, Sir Robert Hart (1835-1911), to broker the Boxer Protocol with Viceroy Li Hongzhang (李鴻章), settling on terms that, while onerous, allowed the Dowager Empress to continue her reign. (**Fig.22**) Not that it was for long, or that peace broke out internally. Despite sweeping reforms, popular discontent continued to bubble across the empire, exacerbated by matters as extraordinary as Francis Younghusband's bloody

---

27   Pelliot was awarded the *Legion d'Honeur* for his gallantry during the siege.

invasion of Tibet, and as mundane as the bankruptcy of provincial railway companies. On 13 November 1908, the Guangxu emperor died of suspected arsenic poisoning, followed a day later by the Empress Dowager. She died within hours of her installing the last Qing dynasty emperor, the child Puyi (溥儀).[28] Three years later, the dynasty was overthrown, and three years after that a gunshot in Sarajevo plunged the Western world into war.

In the dying days of the dynasty, chaos and confusion ruled in the capital, everything had its price. (**Fig.23**) The golden rule for buyers and sellers of art and antiquities being no different from that for other investors–"Buy with the cannons, sell with the bells."–opportunists abounded.[29] When the British Orientalist Archibald Sayce visited Edmund Backhouse in Beijing in 1912, the latter told him that the "Chinese were very nervous and were selling off their old treasures for nominal sums." Sayce accordingly treated himself to "a wonderful harvest" of porcelains and Song (宋; 960-1279) paintings, noting: "It is an opportunity which will never recur."[30] Even so, that avid collector, John Pierpont Morgan must have been just a little surprised to learn that, on 8 March 1913, an unsigned cable had reached his

Fig.22 Viceroy Li Hongzhang (1823-1901), late Qing diplomat who negotiated the Boxer Protocol with Sir Robert Hart. Public Domain

---

28 The academic consensus is that the Empress Dowager died of natural causes following a stroke. The Shunde Museum in Guangdong province prefers the notion that she was assassinated and credits one of its native sons with the deed. Liang Tiejun (梁鐵君) (1853-1908) of Meicun, Yingtan district, was a follower of the reformer Kang Youwei (康有為) and is described by the museum as a *"Hero of Modern Times"*, who was later killed for a *"breach of confidence"*.

29 Aphorism attributed to Nathan Rothschild.

30 Trevor-Roper, Hugh, *A Hidden Life: The Enigma of Sir Edmund Backhouse*, 1976, p. 93.

Fig.23 Lions in transit–one of a pair of "Fu Dogs" en route to Toronto.
Courtesy of the Royal Ontario Museum © ROM

office from Francis H. McKnight, an American diplomat in Beijing, advising that the Imperial family, no longer in power, was prepared to sell the Palace collection in its entirety for an estimated US$4 million. China's new President, Yuan Shikai, had allegedly agreed subject to approval of the National Assembly, which had been elected only one month before, and full details were provided by Shi Xu (史旭; 1852-1921), the loyal Taibao (太保), or Grand Guardian of the Imperial Household through the messy transfer of power. Morgan and family were in Egypt at the time and exchanges of cables on the potential transaction followed them to Rome, where on 31 March he died.[31] It was in these extraordinary times that the extraordinary group of Buddhist statues known as the "Yixian Luohans" first appeared in the art market.[32]

---

31   Lally James J., J.P. Morgan (1837-1913): "An Early American Collector of Chinese Porcelain", a lecture given on 26 November 2007, *Bulletin of the Oriental Society of Hong Kong*, No. 15, 2015.
32   Perzynski refers to the place where he claims the Luohan were hidden as Ichou, the prefecture later transliterated as Yizhou, and which later still became Yixian, when it was re-classified as a county.

3

PERZYNSKI'S PROGRESS

"All these Buddhas came from far away."[33]
— *Friedrich Perzynski*

STEVEN SPIELBERG is supposed to have modeled Indiana Jones on the American archaeologist Langdon Warner (1881-1955).[34] (**Fig.24**) He might just as easily have chosen Friedrich Perzynski, who contrasted his arrival in Ichou (易州 now Yixian 易縣) with the expatriates that hunted pheasant there, noting wryly, "I do have two loaded revolvers and ammunition, climbing ropes and an axe, but I am hunting for Gods and not game!"

Jagd auf Gotter–Hunt for the Gods–is riveting reading, and contemporary curators and art historians were all captivated by Perzynski's account of his "discovery" of the caves at Yixian (易縣) when it was published in 1913. At the same time, they were dissatisfied that it lacked detail, and disappointed that it was not more rigourously academic. Most of their successors have suffered from the same schizophrenia, and that is a

---

33   Unless otherwise indicated, all text in quotation marks in this chapter is taken from Friedrich Perzynski, *Jagd auf Gotter*, in *Von Chinas Gottern*, Munich, 1920, as translated by Richard Smithies with the assistance of Ron Bidmade and Elizabeth Allistone.

34   The Chinese regard Warner as villain rather than hero for pillaging frescoes from the cave walls at Dunhuang. In 1924, experimenting with a new type of adhesive, he removed, but damaged 26, and only fragments of six of these are now in a condition to be displayed.

tribute to the power of Perzynski's pen. It is a very unusual, multi-layered piece of writing. The breathless description of his daring adventure is peppered with poetic passages on the surrounding countryside, philosophic reflections on the decline of a great civilization and historic allusions, while emotional tirades against looting of artifacts are counterbalanced by seductive references to the pleasure of owning unique artistic treasures. It is also a reflection of the man.

Fig.24 Langdon Warner (1881-1955), American archaeologist and Monuments Man. Photo Courtesy of Harvard Fine Arts Library

Friedrich Perzynski (1877-1965) was born on 20 August 1877 in Berlin to a less-than-successful merchant of that great city. His father's financial problems led to young Friedrich having to leave school at seventeen and take employment with a dealer specializing in fine books and prints. This was a period when the European art world, in particular the graphic arts, were strongly influenced by the twin currents of *art nouveau* and Japonisme, Japan having opened to the West only in 1868. Perzynski fell under the spell of the Japanese prints he encountered in his work and, after only four years, left the business to teach himself Japanese, write a novel and, in 1903, publish a book on *ukiyo-e* entitled *The Japanese Colour Woodcut*. He followed this up in 1904 with a monograph on its renowned practitioner Katsushika Hokusai. He was among the very first Europeans to research the genre and in 1905, impressed by his unusual expertise, Gustav Pauli, director of the *Kunsthalle Bremen,* the Bremen Art Museum, commissioned him to go to Japan and buy prints and books for the museum.

That experience, acquired at the age of only twenty-eight,

allowed Perzynski to set himself up as an independent dealer, sourcing for and advising both private collectors and museums. What is less well-known is that he extended his range of interests to include Chinese art and particularly porcelain, as is attested by the series of four articles on classification that he contributed to the *Burlington Magazine* between 1910 and 1913.[35] In 1912, he embarked for China and it was on this trip that he had his memorable encounter with the *sancai* (三彩) Luohans. But this was not the only adventure he had. His intellectual curiosity and the extent of his travels around China are both evident from a collection of essays entitled *Von Chinas Gottern: reisen in China* that he published in 1920, and which included a re-print of his by then famous account of his hunt for the Luohans. Nor were the Luohans his only trophies. The Freer Gallery of Art, for example, has a Northern Wei dynasty standing Bodhisattva, which Perzynski brought to Berlin in 1914 and is believed to have sold to the collector Paul Kempner.[36]

With the outbreak of the First World War, his language skills led naturally to recruitment by the *Nachrichtenstelle fur den Orient*, the German Intelligence Bureau for the East. However, once peace was restored, he returned to his career as a dealer in Oriental art, including sourcing textiles for Paul Cassirer in Berlin. He also continued to pursue his artistic and intellectual interests. In 1924, he was allowed, exceptionally since he had no first degree, to complete a doctorate at the University of Hamburg, presenting as his dissertation the massive two-

---

35 Perzynski, Friedrich, "Towards a Grouping of Chinese Porcelain I", *The Burlington Magazine* 1 October, 1910, Vol. 18 (91), pp. 20-41, and parts II to IV, Dec 1910, Mar 1911 and Mar 1913 respectively.

36 Freer Gallery of Art, Acc. No. F1952.15, which Stanley Abe established came originally from the Gongxian Cave 1, niche 1, Henan Province. See also Otto Kummel, *Chinesische Kunst: Zweihundert Hauptwerke der Austellung der Gesellschaft fur Oatasiatische Kunst in der Preussischen Akadmeie der Kunst*, Berlin, 1929. The Freer purchased it from C.T Loo, who bought it from Edgar Worch in 1944.

volume work subsequently published as *The Masks of the Japanese Schaubune*. Perzynski was one of the founding members of the *Arbeitsrat fur Kunst*, the Workers' Art Association established by Bruno Taut (1880-1938), Walter Gropius (1883-1969) and Erich Heckel (1883-1970). He also loaned several pieces to the 1929 Chinese Art Exhibition in Berlin, but, finding himself increasingly out of sympathy with the political changes of the following years, he chose to leave Germany in the 1930s, moving, like his friend Harry Graf Kessler, first to the south of France and then Mallorca. On 27 March 1942, he set sail from Lisbon on the *Cabo* bound for Argentina, where he settled in Buenos Aires. Despite poor health and increasingly straitened circumstances, he kept up a considerable correspondence with publishers and poets, musicians and museum curators until his death from pancreatic cancer on 11 August 1965, aged 88.[37]

Let us now re-wind the tape to Perzynski's arrival in Beijing in 1912, aged thirty-five, by then an experienced dealer in Japanese art. He had a good eye. The German art historian Otto Fischer, who met him later in Beijing, granted him that, observing, "Perzynski buys up rare and select articles. He possesses an unerring taste, a sense for the extraordinary, for the aesthetically beguiling."[38]

Equally, he was a keen observer of the momentous changes occurring around him and their impact on ordinary people: "They have abandoned the building of the mausoleum for the Guangxu Emperor (光緒; r. 1875-1908). The cruelest poverty reigns among them....We pass by the grave, the moonlight shining through the roofs of the halls where building has barely begun. Hewn stones lie around, tiles and logs, neatly stacked in piles. Once it begins

---

37   Walravens, Hartmut, *Friedrich Perzynski (1887-1965) Kunsthistoriker, Ostasienreisender, Schriftsteller: Leben–Werk–Briefe*, Melle, Wagner Edition, 2005.
38   Fischer, Otto, *Wanderfahrten eines Kunst-freundes in China und Japon*, Stuttgart, Deutsche Verlags Anstalt, 1939, p. 308.

to get colder and all the gods have been sold, they will come and steal the wood from the Emperor's mausoleum for their hearths. Frost and hunger destroy all reverence."

The revolvers were not just for show; these were troubled times. A dynasty had died a lingering death. There had been popular uprisings all over the country, and some military mutinies. A new republican government had been declared, but the transition was anything but smooth. Power in the military sense rested with Yuan Shikai (袁世凱), but day-to-day administration continued to rely on the good will of the traditional bureaucracy, now unpaid but patiently waiting to see who would eventually take charge. Hence the concern mentioned several times in Perzynski's account that his *laissez-passer* had not yet arrived, his cable to the German Consul in Tientsin and his decision not to call upon the Commandant of the Western Tombs at the Yamen until the safe conduct arrived.

It was shortly after he arrived, in the summer of 1912, that art dealers in Beijing showed him the torso of a glazed pottery Luohan (**Fig.25**). "The owners feasted their eyes upon my profound amazement as they showed it to me. I had never seen anything like it. At the time we called him a Priest, for he had, despite the traditional long ears, the striking pictorial quality of a portrait. His eyes, with their dark shining pupils, looked as if into another world. He lived, he spoke, he dreamed." Perzynski was alerted to its possible source by a Japanese acquaintance, who in his words "claims to have been the first to have discovered the commercial value of these demi-gods of the Buddhist pantheon." Not named in Perzynski's account, he was later identified as the dealer Terasawa Shikanosuke.[39] Perzynksi followed up on his tip-off by making two visits to Yixian (易縣), the first in the summer

---

39   Harada Yoshito, "Chokureishoekiken kyuzai to rakan ni tsuite" in *Toa kobunka kenkyu*, November 1940, pp. 299-305.

of 1912, the second in November of the same year.

Yizhou (易州), as the principal town was then called, lies 96 kilometres southwest of Beijing. It would not have been a difficult journey as the Peking-Hankou railway had been completed in 1906 and a spur line installed for the convenience of members of the imperial family visiting the nearby *Qing Xiling* (清西陵), the Western Tombs of the Qing. On his first visit, which seems to have been more of a reconnaissance, Perzynski was taken up the steep-sided Emeisigou (峨嵋寺溝), the Emei Temple valley,

Fig.25 Perzynski's "Priest", Liao dynasty (907-1125), previously in the Museum fur Asiatische Kunst, Berlin. Photo by Friedrich Perzynski

westward beyond the Guangxu mausoleum to a Guanyin Pavilion (觀音閣) high above a ruined temple. He did not see any Luohan statues there, but he did find two steles. Although he had some difficulty deciphering them fully, he gleaned from one that, in 1624, local devotees had funded repairs to and re-gilding of the Guanyin (Goddess of Mercy) statue in the pavilion, while from the other, which he thought dated from the beginning of the seventeenth century, he transcribed a poetic description of the setting:

> "*Longmensi is an old temple. Like some mighty screen, the mountain enfolds it.*
> *Shan tze tung lies not far from here, to the east, while in the west,*
> *The mountain descends steeply to the plain. It is silent here.*

Of all the mountains, this is deemed to be the most holy and renowned place.
Yet dread grips he who ventures here, and his skull shatters as he climbs in fear.
From the valley, clouds and mist ascend and human voices are seldom heard.
Trees spread their limbs and crows caw in their midst.
Woodcutters come and go, and wild monkeys chase one another through the trees."

From this, he deduced that the *Longmen Temple* (龍門寺), the Dragon Gate Temple, was the ruined temple below. Incised on the same stone tablet, Perzynski also found the intriguing words: "*Alle diese Buddhas kommen von weither / All these Buddhas came from far away*", on which he appears to have hung high hopes of finding the Luohans, and successive generations of scholars a variety of theories about both their origins and dating.

Before returning to Beijing, Perzynski planted some seed money with agents, tasking them to inform him if they heard any rumours about Luohans. This seems to have paid off because shortly thereafter he was rewarded with a report from one of them that two statues were hidden under the courtyard of a Manchu house. The agent was instructed to view and, if possible, buy a statue, and he reportedly managed to see one, which was broken into several pieces, just before he was arrested by the local Commandant, the guardian of the Western Tombs. As Perzynski tells it, the sellers promptly disappeared in several different directions taking both the fragments and his money with them.

Poorer for the loss, but undeterred, Perzynski next sent a scholar friend to make further enquiries, but taking elaborate security measures: "We agreed upon a secret number code which he wrote upon his chest." Again this seems to have paid off because a coded telegram duly arrived informing him that his friend had tracked down the fragments, including the "goddess's face", but they were in a dangerous place, while, slightly more confusingly, the second "complete painting is still in its old place and has been carried away." And so, our hero entrained on his second visit to Yixian, armed to the teeth and accompanied by a photographer.

He was not a little nervous and not without cause: "One after the other, the many Peking curio dealers who had come trooping along when they heard of the discovery, were taken into custody until a cloud of fear spread among the inhabitants and out into the remotest parts of the region." So, not wishing to attract too much attention to himself, Perzynski elected to stay at a Lamaist temple, the Yongfu Monastery (永福寺), where he was advised Chinese princes were accommodated on their visits to the tombs. He also had it put about that he was convalescing from an illness and wished to hike in the hills, "seeking inner refreshment", despite which "there was disturbing news the next morning. I learn that the authorities have been continuously collecting information on the purpose of my journey and that soldiers have searched the temple by night. The Commandant of Qing Hsiling (清西陵), the Western Tombs, has forbidden the inhabitants of Ichou to sell me any of the lohan." The previous day a hunter had brought him the foot of the enormous two-metre Guanyin statue that he had seen in the summer. Fortunately, he had returned it to the hunter the same evening. However, a day that began with elation ended in frustration.

They had set off in cold clear air, their "long procession of baggage carts" scarcely unobtrusive, attracting "embarrassingly interested glances" from the local soldiery as they passed the barracks, their donkeys driven by "Moslems with quite un-

Fig.26 The range of hills above Yizhou that Perzynski christened Achtlohanberg, Eight Luohan Mountain. Photo by Friedrich Perzynski

Chinese features." The track gradually petered out as they approached the range of hills that Perzynski called *Achtlohanberg*, or Eight Luohan Mountain, and they were forced to pack their provisions and cooking kit on the backs of their porters before proceeding further (**Fig.26**). The ground was slippery and the path overgrown, brambles constantly snagging their clothes. It was also very steep: "Often we are forced to scramble up on all fours." The first cave that their guide pointed to high above them was too small for the statues and in any case, "Only chamois can make their way up here!"

Angrily assuming that the guide was deliberately leading them astray, Perzynski decided to make for the Guanyin Pavilion to see if the foot he was given really came from her. A hot and sweaty half-an-hour scrabble later they reach the shrine hewn into the cliff face and, true enough, the statue had been vandalized.

Fig.28 The Yongzheng Emperor's Mausoleum. Photo by Friedrich Perzynski

(**Fig.27**) Surveying the damage, Perzynski mused gloomily "So now we sit amidst the ruins of the cave, lamenting a China that in gnawing poverty thus destroys its noblest art treasures." After climbing back down to the valley floor they decided to walk over to the Yongzheng emperor's (雍正; r. 1723-35) tomb (**Fig.28**) "to give the impression that I am simply on a world tour." Back in his rooms, he wondered bitterly

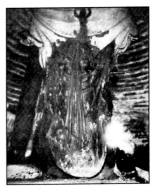

Fig.27 Vandalized statue in the Guanyin Pavilion above Yizhou. photo by Friedrich Perzynski

whether the Commandant feared competition, suggesting that he might be one of those involved in the trafficking of looted art.

The following day found him in better spirits as a Lama had promised to meet them and lead them up Eight Luohan Mountain. "…our donkeys arrive at the door. The cook and the boy merrily gallop on ahead…I sing loudly and quite out of tune."

Yet only a short while later he was cursing just as loudly

because the Lama failed to show at the appointed time and place. Perzynski sent someone to find him and had started to stride on alone when a peasant volunteered to guide them up a pathless slope that in places required the use of ropes. "Oh for the Tai shan (泰山) in Shantung (山東) Province, where one can climb to the summit up elegant stone steps, and where I groaned that Buddhism dispenses its blessings with so much discomfort."

Looking down from the crest of the ridge they saw the village of *Xiagaosi* (下高寺), whose inhabitants they were told had tried to get a Luohan down to the valley only to smash it to pieces in the process. If that was supposed to raise his hopes, the first cave that they reached that day would have been a disappointment, containing nothing but "…a sorry looking altar upon which squat three roughly painted idols as in any simple village shrine." A

little further along the ridge, the dejected Perzynski lagging behind the guide and his scholar friend saw them suddenly disappear into some scrub. Following them through a great hole in the cliff, he found himself standing in a deep cavern (**Fig.29**).[40]

An inscription on a stele in the antechamber revealed it to be the *Shanzidong* (睒子洞), the Shanzi Grotto mentioned on one of the

Fig.29 The entrance to Shanzidong, the Samaka Grotto above Yizhou. Photo by Friedrich Perzynski

---

40   Hsu Hsian-ling, Eileen. *Monks in Glaze: Patronage, Kiln Origin, and Iconography of the Yixian Luohans*, Brill, 2016, pp. 20 and 23, gives the measurements of this cave as 38 metres deep by 6.5 wide, with an entrance 8 metres high by 4 across.

Fig.30 The interior of the Shanzidong cave. Photo by Friedrich Perzynski

stone tablets at the Guanyin Pavilion.[41] Still more exciting, he spotted some shards lying on the floor "I look down at them and begin laughing like a child–Lohan!" Another stele dating from the Kangxi reign (康熙; 1662-1722) commemorated the later renovation of the Buddhas, but the cave itself was a shambles as is evident from Perzynski's photograph of its interior. **(Fig.30)** He did, however, see an unglazed statue of a Laughing Buddha, and also found what he believed to be a Yuan dynasty ceramic incense burner on the altar that crumbled at his touch. Even so he was becoming more suspicious: "As twilight falls, we make our way down by another, better track and it becomes clear to me that our guide, innocent as he seems, has done all in his power to slow down my day's work."

In a teahouse at the bottom of the hill, a monk introduced

---

41   *Shanzi* (睒子) is the Chinese rendering of *Samaka*, the name of the bodhisattva-become-man, son of blind parents, in a story of one of *Sakyamuni's* previous incarnations. Accidentally slain by the king, *Samaka*, revives when the latter immediately and sincerely repents.

them to the owner of one of the Luohan heads, who promised to dig it up and show it to them no later than the next day. By nightfall, it had not appeared.

On his third hike up Eight Luohan Mountain, Perzynski visited three more caves guided by a gap-toothed pheasant hunter. The first two turned out to be larger than they looked from a distance and the guide told them that each had previously housed two of the Luohans. A little higher up, he pointed out a third cave where another Luohan was being removed when the thieves were surprised by soldiers. In the panic and confusion that ensued, it was tipped over the cliff and smashed to smithereens. They clambered up a precipitous eighty-degree slope getting giddier by the minute until the guide hauled Perzynski over the lip of the grotto. It took him a few minutes to grow accustomed to the gloom, but when he did he saw that the cave was big enough for five to stand in and, to his great satisfaction, fragments of a Luohan were scattered all around: "…a portion of the chin, a few fingers reflectively touching the temple and a sunken eye without a pupil."

They climbed down and, ravenously hungry, made for the by-now familiar tea-house on what Perzynski has nicknamed Guanyin Mountain to eat their lunch in silence. By the time they have finished, a motley assortment of locals had arrived at the temple, amongst them a group who claimed to have in their possession a seated Luohan with a beard. They had had to move it around to stay ahead of the authorities and had buried it for safety near Baoding (保定) some twenty miles to the south. Unwilling to endure the discomfort of a long journey in a cart, Perzynski detailed his cameraman to follow them and take photographs of the statue before he made up his mind. In fact, he already had: "My mission is accomplished. It is impossible for me to buy anything here now (but) I have sat in the cave where one of the Luohan had once reposed."

To both his relief and that of his friend, his passport arrived in the morning so they finally felt confident that they could go to the local government office, and pay their respects to the Commandant. Expecting a jumped-up arrogant military type, Perzynski was pleasantly surprised to be met by a scholarly, silver-whiskered mandarin.[42] He also enjoyed regaling his readers with a detailed description of the circuitous diplomatic route taken by his friend on the way to broaching the subject of the Luohans, playing up Perzynski's scholarly achievements and even exaggerating his age from 35 to 49. He should not have bothered; the Commandant was candid: "Yes the Lohans have given him some serious problems. Thieves have taken them from their places of concealment, smashing most of them in the process. But he has had all the fragments collected together and the last bits have been brought down the mountains. A few of the thieves have been caught and clapped in jail for ten years. All the commemorative tablets have been copied and sent to Peking, where they are now displayed. He would be glad to have copies made for me and also to show me the Lohan in his possession."

And so he did, and Perzinski stood facing "the trunk of a Lohan. His head has been knocked off at the neck, as has part of a shoulder blade and the feet. In his hand he holds a scroll. The head is leaning against the wall next to the torso. With its yellowing ivory tone, it looks like the head of a man who has been executed."

The fragments of the other Luohans filled several baskets, and yet more baskets held smaller fragments and sculptures that Perzynski gauged dated from the Ming dynasty (1368-1644). Before they took their leave, the Commandant confided that he

---

42 Richard Smithies' translation of Perzynski's account, as reproduced in the Addendum to Hsu, p.203, inexplicably omits a short paragraph describing the Commandant.

could not keep the Luohan at the Yamen and was thinking of giving it to a temple. Perzynski's friend is not slow to understand the hint and quickly advised him that he might then purchase it from the temple.

The cast of characters Perzynski introduces while relating his adventure is truly stellar. An illiterate "Lamaist priest expelled from his monastery for theft' was his first contact. A "Mohammedan with the eyes of a thief" led him to the Guanyin Pavilion. The "defrocked Lamaist priest," whose "nose and mouth almost meet and forehead mirrors his delightful spiritual depravity," put in a second appearance promising, but failing to show him the head of the Luohan previously seen by his agent. When at last he was introduced to the owner of the head, he found that he had "the appearance of a manure-carter or butcher dealing in donkey meat." Although the latter promised to dig the head up and show it to Perzynski the following day, he failed to deliver. A "pheasant hunter, who opened his mouth to show a gap in his teeth" guided him on his third hike and, back at the teahouse, "all sorts of unshaven individuals arrive"; and a youth "with filthy fingernails" acted as spokesman for these "unshaven knights of plunder", who claimed to have buried the bearded Luohan near Baoding (保定). Finally, to complete the cast, as they board the train for Beijing, they were accosted by "a gentleman of some forty years of age, with curiously cunning eyes and shining cheeks", who offered them two more Luohans that he knew were hidden in the hills. And so, promising the man "mountains of gold", they departed for Beijing.

It was all splendid cloak-and-dagger stuff. It vividly captured the unsettled atmosphere of these troubled times, but one can understand why researchers have been frustrated by the lack of more academic detail. That lack of detail is, however, consistent with the one third-party comment we have on Perznyski's character.

The art historian Otto Fischer, who visited Beijing in 1925, observed that Perzynski "has been here previously and knows the labyrinthine ways of the art market, he obviously has already discovered many an object which he jealously hides away in case and closet."[43]

Like all dealers, Perzynski was secretive–I have been unable to find any photograph of him–and lamentations about China's decline and the looting of priceless works of art notwithstanding, Perzynski the dealer is never far from the surface in *Hunt for the Gods*. He notes early on that, "In the absence of any government restrictions, China's Gods have become a lively trade article."

Yet a few lines later, he waxes lyrical on the obsessive joys of collecting and possession. "A person who has never had a painting or sculpture, that threw new light on the psyche of a whole period, alone in his possession, protected from covetous eyes, even the eyes of friends, can hardly imagine the intoxicating sense of power that comes over the discoverer as he contemplates his find. Possession of a legion of slaves is a meagre reward compared to the awareness of being master of the most radiantly transformed spiritual expression of that which inspired the elite of an entire age and which was cast by the medium of the artist, out of elemental chaos into a precisely defined form."

But as his frustration with the lies and prevarications of the populace builds, the lyricism evaporates: "My heart yearns for a Lohan and my banknotes burn in my pocket."

Indeed, he considered his mission accomplished and returned to Beijing only after he had determined that it was not possible to purchase any statues in Yixian. It was the tip-off from Terasawa Shikanosuke that had propelled him there in the hope that he could

---

43   Fischer, Op. Cit., p 308.

cut out the middlemen, the dealers in Beijing who had shown him his first Luohan. As a recent arrival in Beijing, it was perhaps naïve of him to imagine that he could. The established dealers and their agents on the ground, be they the muscle that rescued treasures from wherever they were concealed, or the conniving officials who greased the wheels of secret transportation, would have had no interest in letting him in on their game. This finally became obvious to him–"Everywhere I turn, I meet with passive resistance or a smile that betokens refusal, and promises that go un-kept"–just as it is obvious to us from his subsequent pattern of acquisition and sales. Only one-and-a-half Luohans passed through his hands; the bust shown him in Beijing and another that is mentioned nowhere in his adventure, but is illustrated in *Jagd auf Gotter.* **(Fig.31)**

Perzynski had been duped and, although he nowhere names him, he vented his spleen spectacularly on Terasawa Shikanosuke: "A Japanese claims to have been the first to have discovered the commercial value of these demi-gods of the Buddhist pantheon–one of those jackals who scour the continent of Asia, under every conceivable pretext, to tailor a comfortable and durable jacket for themselves out of the skin of the poorest. No American is more cunning, no German more brutal, no Englishman more unscrupulous than this human pestilence, which the island kingdom, gripping

Fig.31 The "Younger Monk" now in the Metropolitan Museum, New York. Photo by Friedrich Perzynski

the Asian continent as with a dragon's claw, discharges like pus from its teeming populace. And no physiognomy is more base, more clearly etched by all the evils of covetousness and perfidy than that of the Japanese emigrant who seems to have the slogan 'survival of the fittest' written in monumental characters on his belly." Such a vicious diatribe would make little sense if his mission had been successful. Either his wallet or his pride had been hurt, and of the two, the latter seems more likely. Possibly, a complex bidding process had begun amongst the "owners" of the Luohans as Perzynski described them, and the established dealers anxious to get them quickly to market. Perzynski, the new kid on the block, was an unknown quantity and they wanted him out of the way, so they sent him on a wild goose chase around the Western Tombs.

If that was their intention, they succeeded, for both Edgar Worch and George Crofts beat Perzynski to market. Worch's exhibition at the Musée Cernuschi in Paris in June 2013 launched the Luohans on the world stage and both of his statues were snapped up by American museums, the Penn and Boston's Museum of Fine Arts. Croft worked less publicly, but no less successfully, sourcing for the specialist wholesale dealer, S.M. Francks & Son, who placed one in the British Museum and the other, a little later, in the Royal Ontario Museum in Toronto. Perzynski was not able to stage his exhibition at the *Kunstgewerbemuseum* in Berlin until November, some five months after Worch, so he was well behind the pack and needed something extra for his marketing campaign. That something extra was *Jagd auf Gotter*. In retrospect, it was a stroke of genius, and also in retrospect those who had sent him on a wild goose chase had reason to be grateful to him. As noted earlier, dealers are notoriously secretive about their sources, and Otto Fischer confirmed that Perzynski was no exception. What prompted

Perzynski to break with normal practice was his realization that his adventure might provide a provenance that would be attractive to curators and collectors alike.

The aesthete in him knew that the Luohans were extraordinary works of art. Unlike other extant ancient Chinese statues, they had been sculpted from life, indeed so brilliantly sculpted that the monks still live and breathe as they focus on their inner beings. Their origins were shrouded in mystery and the historian in him recognized a riddle, a riddle in five parts: when were they made, where were they made, whence had they come, why had nobody seen them before and why were there only eight instead of sixteen or eighteen? The penultimate question was perhaps the most puzzling, given Chinese scholars' penchant for praising objects of beauty seen on their travels, amongst which must be numbered the sixteen Luohans of the Yanxiadong grotto (煙霞洞) at Hangzhou (杭州).[44] However, the salesman in Perzynski saw that he could use his exploration of the caves in Yixian to suggest plausible solutions to all five parts of the riddle.

At one level, Perzynski's tale paints a vivid portrait of time and place. It provides authentic context. At another level, it entices curators and collectors with the romance of high art preserved from destruction at the hands of invading barbarians. At another, it is purely suggestive, subtly posing questions that hint at what history has hidden from human memory. Its author would have us believe that his mission was to establish where the mysterious statues had come from and he provides his proofs very cleverly, layer by layer.

His first trip, the reconnaissance, sets the scene with the discovery of the two steles at the Guanyin shrine. The poetic description of the remote and rugged landscape, the antiquity

---

44 Jin Shen, "Tan Hebei Yixin Bafowa Liaodai Sancaitao luohan", *Wenwu chunqiu*, 2003, no. 2, China Academic Journal Electronic Publishing House.

of the Longmen Temple, the holiness of the Shanzi Grotto and the link it establishes between them provide the perfect Shakespearean *mis-en-scene* for the tantalizing opening line: "All these Buddhas came from far away".

The enormous Guanyin statue, two metres tall not including its one-metre high and two-metres wide rocky base, set Perzynski puzzling: "In what gigantic kiln did they fire this colossus and how did they manage to get it up here?" The question is rhetorical; he wishes simply to demonstrate that the difficulties of moving such large and fragile terracotta sculptures over such forbidding terrain were daunting, but not insuperable. As for getting them down, "Moslems, followed by ruffians of every description loaded these clay colossi on long bamboo poles and carried them down into the valley where they were buried." Blaming the minority Moslems, the imported labourers on the Imperial tombs made redundant by the collapse of the dynasty, absolved the local Chinese population, whose reverence for such sacred relics, it is implied, would not have allowed them to loot the shrines. However, he had not yet figured out where the Luohans originally came from: "Were they from Honan, the most artistic of China's provinces, brought by pious pilgrims? Did they want to save them from the Mongol incursion in the thirteenth century and hide them in these totally inaccessible caves?"

There follow the highs and lows of Perzynski's three hikes up Eight Luohan Mountain on his November trip. He re-visited the Guanyin on the first after a fruitless climb up to another cave–"Perhaps we are climbing the wrong mountain!"–to remind his audience that it is there and to reveal that it too has been targeted by booty hunters. He needed also to explain his visit to the Yongzheng (雍正; r.1723-35) mausoleum not just as a necessary subterfuge, but as a means to introduce the propitious geomantic nature of the location. A site selected for imperial tombs was surely already deemed sacred.

The next two hikes followed a similar pattern: high spirits in the morning, frustration and suspicion during the day followed by a ray of hope at day's end. On the second, Perzynski lost heart when he found only sorry looking village idols in one cave. He straggled dejectedly behind his companions, only to rejoice at reaching the Shanzi Grotto mentioned in the inscription and finding a few Luohan shards on the floor and a Yuan dynasty incense burner on the altar.

Resting after his exertions, he suggested a solution to another part of the riddle. The Guanyin Statue had demonstrated that the heavy Luohans could have been carried up to the caves and hidden there, but Perzynski still needed a reason. "I ask myself question after question. Why and how were these colossal statues brought up these heights so far from the world? No, these caves were used as hiding places. Time and again I think of the iconoclastic eras such as the time of the Mongol invasions or during the ninth century, when imperial persecution decrees resulted in the destruction of tens of thousands of Buddhist temples and the annihilation of so many splendid art treasures."

Another stele reinforced the sense of antiquity: "We discover a new monument made of stone, which recounts renovation of the altars at the time of the Zhengde Emperor (正德; r. 1506-21) at the beginning of the sixteenth century. What had been restored then must have existed for centuries before."

He reserved the penultimate proof for the third hike, but before he saw it, his guide offered the first hint as to why so few of the Luohans had survived. They had been scattered between several caves and, in at least one case, a Luohan had been tipped over a cliff and destroyed when the looters were surprised by the local militia. No matter, this was the day when Perzynski confirmed to his own satisfaction that the Luohans really had been hidden in the caves because he saw the unmistakable fragments of fingers and a part of a face, and again wondered "How were these statues carried up here? I ask myself this question again and again."

No Luohan resembling the description of these remnants subsequently emerged, but the reference a little later to a bearded Luohan ties in with the statue purchased by Boston's MFA, whose hirsute Indo-European features prompted queries about its provenance. Likewise, the final proof seen by Perzynski in the Yamen the next day, a Luohan holding a scroll in its hand, which matches exactly the statue of the older of the two monks in the Metropolitan Museum in New York. It was left to the aristocratic Commandant to tie up the loose ends: yes, bandits had been taking the Luohans from where they were hidden and many had been broken in the process. He had put the perpetrators in jail and collected up all the bits and pieces. He had also copied the inscriptions from the steles and sent them to Beijing to be displayed. Who could ask for a more authoritative provenance, even if it was still unclear where the Luohans had come from before they were stashed in the caves at Yixian?

Look a little closer, however, and the loose-ends begin to fray again, leaving more question marks hanging over the steles themselves.

Perzynski saw two at the Guanyin Pavilion on his first day of hiking in the hills. He saw two more at the Shanzi Grotto on day three. Yet less than forty-eight hours later, at the Yamen, the Commandant told him not only that transcriptions had been made of all the memorial tablets, but that the tablets had already been sent to Beijing. Not impossible, but still a most impressive feat of logistics, if true. However, as we shall see, eighty years later, the two steles that Perzynski found at Shanzi Grotto were still there, which suggests that either the Commandant was exaggerating his efficiency or, perhaps, Perzynski was putting words into his mouth. Either way, the Commandant's reported statement officially disposed of the evidence in a way which, while seeming to protect it, also very conveniently discouraged further enquiries. It is significant that in a letter to Allen Whiting, Director of the Cleveland Museum, Perzynski later stressed that he was the "only person who has all the stone inscriptions around the Lohan caves."[45] And yet, as far as we know, he neither shared them with, nor showed them to anyone during his lifetime, and none were found with his papers thereafter.

A close reading of *Jagd auf Gotter* reveals several other inconsistencies and inaccuracies. Possibly Perzynski was in too much of a hurry to mount his exhibition to arrange for careful editing. Nevertheless, they are interesting, not least the somewhat curious choice of photographs that accompany the text. There are seven in all and they appear in the following order: a panoramic shot of the mountain range above Yixian; a difficult-to-interpret photograph of the vandalized Guanyin (Goddess of Mercy) statue; the arch at the entrance to the Yongzheng mausoleum; a cliff-side showing the mouth of the Shanzi Grotto; a shot of its jumbled interior; a Luohan which he exhibited in Berlin and sold to the Met in New York, but which is not mentioned anywhere in the text; a close-up of the same (**Fig.32**); and, finally, the head-and-shoulders bust of the Luohan first shown him in Beijing, which he sold to the collector Herz "Harry" Fuld, and which was believed destroyed during World War II. (**Fig.33**)[46]

Still more interesting, and frankly puzzling given that he

---

45 Letter to Frederic Allen Whiting, Director of Cleveland Museum of Art, in 1936; see Walravens Op. Cit., 2005, p. 146.

46 Tragically, Harry Fuld was one of those German Jews whose businesses and art collections were targeted by the Nazi Party. Both were confiscated shortly after his death in 1933. His art works were auctioned and his Luohan bust was eventually acquired by the *Museum fur Ostasiatische Kunst* in Berlin, which was damaged by Allied bombing in the closing years of the Second World War.

took a photographer with him on his adventure, is that there are no photographs of the steles he claimed to have seen, nor of the shards and fragments of the Luohans seen in Shanzi Grotto and one other cave, nor of the Luohan, scroll in hand and head on floor, that he saw in the Yamen. Recall that his photographer was conveniently absent, having been sent off to photograph the bearded Luohan allegedly buried near Baoding (保定). Similarly oddly, Perzynski appears to have taken no rubbings of the stele inscriptions, and the reader is left to assume that he accepted the Commandant's kind offer to make copies for him. In short, the most serious general anomaly is the absence of any visual evidence to support the "proofs" that he proffered.

Fig.32 Close-up of the "Younger Monk" now in the Metropolitan Museum, New York. Photo by Friedrich Perzynski

The atmospherics of his account have the ring of authenticity, of someone who had definitely walked the ground, tramped the hills, seen the dawn and the dusk, smelled the cooking smells and lived in fear of arbitrary arrest. But there is also much hearsay and much that is contradictory. For example, he early on claims that the dealers had no idea where the Luohans had actually come from, and yet later he tells us that all the Beijing curio dealers who descended on Yixian when they heard of the

Fig.33 Harry Fuld, German Jewish businessman who purchased Perzynski's "Priest", and whose collection was confiscated by the Nazis. Courtesy of Institut fur Stadtgeschichte, Frankfurt am Main

statues were thrown in jail. He describes the caves as "totally inaccessible" yet complains when one of his guides leads him and his companions down an easier route than the one they had climbed on the way up. He also reports that "Moslems, followed by ruffians of every description loaded these clay colossi on long bamboo poles and carried them down into the valley where they were buried," and later volunteers the otherwise irrelevant boast of his guide that "his brother can carry a weight of 200 catties down these mountains."

Staying with the topography, there is also one very basic error. The poetic depiction of the landscape on the stele at the Guanyin Pavilion inexplicably describes the mountains as descending west to the plain, whereas in fact they fall towards the east. Of course, it could be just a slip of the pen in transcription or translation, but we cannot know because we cannot check it against the original.[47]

One piece of hearsay that is particularly extravagant is the oral tradition quoted from an old Lama, according to which the great itinerant 7th Century monk Xuanzang (玄奘; c.602-664) had been so inspired by the Yixian landscape that he had founded a temple there. Recalling the recent discovery of the library of scrolls at Dunhuang (敦煌) in northwestern Gansu province, Perzynski fantasizes, "This discovery would be finer than Marc Aurel Stein's findings, more valuable for our understanding of East Asian Art than all the scientific expeditions so far." This was good salesmanship as the Dunhuang discoveries were both current and sensational, but it would appear that Perzynski, apart from wishing to convince his readers that he had got closest to the source of the Luohans, was also anxious to extend their antiquity. A similar motivation seems to inform the other

---

47 To further confuse matters, the translation of the descriptive verse on the stele in Hsu's *Monks in Glaze* mis-reads "Ost" in the preceding line as "West"!

hypotheses that he injects and repeats at different points in the narrative on the provenance of the Luohans and the reasons they might have been hidden in the heights above Yixian despite the enormous effort required to transport them there. These were not something suggested to him by his Chinese contacts or gleaned from his reading of the steles, these were his own suppositions. These were ideas that he introduced, musing to himself (and his readers), while resting on the mountain.

The masterstroke, however, was his re-christening of that mountain range itself. He gave it a new name, a name that appears on none of the steles he reported seeing–these refer to "Emo Mountain", "White Jade Mountain" or "Hundred Flowers Mountain"–nor on any map, nor in the 1747 local gazetteer.[48] *"Achtlohanberg"*, Eight Luohan Mountain, is entirely Perzynski's invention, a lie cleverly introduced in a frustrated aside that no one at the temple would admit to having climbed it, and then repeated several times in his tale, including in Chinese translation: *Bafoshan* (八佛山). Why eight and not sixteen or eighteen, which are more normal numbers when counting Luohans? Because, by the time he wrote his sales catalogue, he already knew that there were only eight on the market and he wanted to emphasize their rarity value. In the process he did something that none of the other dealers managed to do, he succeeded in creating a legend, a legend which, later on, those same dealers were more than happy to hide behind, and which has mesmerized scholars for more than a century.

Perzynski republished *Hunt for the Gods* in 1920, including it in a collection of essays entitled *von Chinas Gottern: Reisen in China*. By that time, he must have been confident that his account had

---

48 Perzynski, Op. Cit., *Achtlohanberg* appears first on p. 138, and again on pp. 139, 140, where he interchanges with *Bafowa* or Eight Buddha Mountain, p.145, p.147 and p.150, where it becomes the *sogenannten Achtlohanberges* "so-called Eight Luohan Mountains".

been accepted and the legend had become lore. In challenging it a century later, this author is acutely conscious that Perzynski is no longer alive to defend his reputation. Since his account is so central to the mystery surrounding the origins of the luohans, and the controversy that this book will provoke, a full English translation of the essay is provided as an addendum so that readers may judge for themselves.

4

Dating Dilemmas

"Never has East Asian sculpture imparted a more grandiose, immediately recognizable form to the passionate struggle for spiritual enlightenment than that which, in contrast to the Buddhas and Bodhisattvas, is expressed in the Arhat."
Otto Kummel, German art historian[49]

IT WAS NOT what they were used to, but it took their breath away. The unveiling of the first two Luohans at the Musée Cernuschi in June 1913 was met with a mixture of amazement and uncertainty. Curators and critics, accustomed to seeing only idealized or stylized representations of Buddhist icons, were surprised by images so clearly taken from life. More than that, they looked in awe at the manifestation of spiritual struggle.

"It is no conventional deity which sits before us. The features are so human as to suggest an actual portrait, but for the supernatural enlargement of the ears in Buddhist fashion. The contracted brows bespeak deep concentration: the eyes, dreamy yet wide awake, look through and past us into the infinite; the nostrils are dilated in deep breathing; the lips compressed in firm yet compassionate lines. It is the embodiment of the Buddhist

---

49   Kummel, Otto "Die Austellung der Samlung Perzynski im Berliner Kunstgewerbemuseum", in *Ostasiatische Zeitschrift*, N.F. 2, January-March, 1914, p. 458.

idea of abstraction and aloofness; yet it lives in every line, the personification of mental energy in repose."[50] Their uncertainty, with one exception, had all to do with dating.

Almost alone amongst curators of the day, Robert Hobson, later to become Keeper at the British Museum, while rhapsodizing about the Luohan's aesthetic merits, maintained his objectivity.[51] (**Fig.34**) In introducing the museum's new acquisition (**Fig.35 and Plate II**), he commented, "It is only natural that there should have been differences of opinion on the age of the three Lohans, seeing that they are in many ways unique. Ming (1368-1644), Yuan (1260-1368) and Sung (960-1279) were all hinted at in turn by Parisian critics, and the suggestion of Tang (618-907) origin was received with more surprise than credence. And yet on

Fig.34 *Robert Lockhart Hobson (1872-1941), first among curators to appraise the importance of the Luohans. Courtesy of Lafayette Ltd.*

Fig.35 *Luohan, stoneware with sancai glaze from Hebei, China; Liao dynasty (907-1125); 103 cm; Acc. No. 1913,1221;* © *Trustees of the British Museum*

50   Hobson, R.L., *Chinese Pottery and Porcelain: An Account of the Potter's Art in China from Primitive Times to the Present Day*, London, 1915, Vol. I, p. 36.
51   The other exception is the archaeologist Carl Whiting Bishop, then Assistant Curator in Oriental Art at the University of Pennsylvania Museum, whose description of the newly arrived Luohan statue in the September 1914 *Museum Journal* reads like an autopsy report.

both artistic and technical grounds this last is well supported, and what circumstantial evidence there is point in the same direction."[52]

So far so polite, but the great cataloguer was clinically merciless in demolishing the other theories: "Those who suggest a Sung or Yuan date for the Lohan overlook the fact that the Sung and Yuan glazes, as far as we know them at present, are all of the high-fired feldspathic order, and that the soft lead glazes of the T'ang pottery seem to have been in abeyance from the end of that period until their revival on the Ming earthenware. So that on technical grounds the Lohan should belong either to the T'ang or to the Ming dynasty. The latter is practically ruled out by artistic considerations, for there is no parallel in the conventionalized Ming statuary with such works as these."[53]

In case it is not obvious, Hobson's preoccupation with accurate dating was not just a matter of professional pride. Both as curator and cataloguer, Hobson recognized that this was the first key to unlocking the riddle of the Luohans' origins. The spread of dates between the Tang and Ming dynasties is a whole millennium, from 618 to1644. Battle lines were being drawn one thousand years apart, and one gets the distinct impression that Hobson felt affronted by such amateurish appraisals. He was as certain as any man can be that the Luohans were high art from the Tang.

Hobson referred to *three* Luohans, and it is apparent from the context that these comprised the two exhibited at the Musée Cernuschi plus his own. At the time he penned *A New Chinese Masterpiece in the British Museum*, he had had the opportunity to inspect all three, but had only seen illustrations of those later

52   Hobson, R.L., "A New Chinese Masterpiece in the British Museum", *The Burlington Magazine*, XXV, May 1914, p.69.
53   Hobson, Op. Cit., 1914, p. 70.

Fig.36 Dr. Otto Kummel (1874-1952), Director General of the State Museums in Berlin and pre-WW II collator of the infamous catalogue of art works targeted by the Nazis. Courtesy of Bundesarchiv Bild183-L08363

exhibited in Berlin, in a note by Dr. Otto Kummel published in the *Ostasiatische Zeitschrift* in March 1914. (**Fig.36**) The latter fares no better than the French under Hobson's scalpel.

"Dr. Kummel in conclusion states that Mr. Perzynski places their date '*ohne gross Uberzeugung*' (trans. without great conviction) in the 10th Century, but that he (Dr. Kummel) cannot believe that they were made before the date of the highest development of the Arhat-ideal, i.e. before the beginning of the Sung period. As the Sung period began in 960 the difference should be easily adjusted. For the rest the precise significance in Dr. Kummel's dictum is difficult to seize, but he will find an equally grand conception of the Arhat in the standing figures of '*K'an king ssu*' grotto at Lungmen, which is not later than the 8th Century."[54]

Fig.37 Leopold Reidemeister (1900-87), German archaeologist and art historian. Public Domain

Leopold Reidemeister loyally defended his former boss' theory in 1937, but went on to suggest the possibility of a Liao dynasty (907-1125) dating by reference to some pottery shards unearthed in Manchuria.[55] (**Fig.37**)

Hobson had also read Perzynski's account of his "venturesome

---

54 Hobson, Op. Cit., 1914, p. 70. Hobson's reference is to the Kanjing-si, the Sutra Reading Temple, in the Eastern Hill at Longmen, where twenty-nine life-sized Luohans are carved in realistic relief.

55 Reidemeister, Leopold, "Kermaische Funde aus Jehol und die Lohan von I-Chou", *Oastasiatische Zeitschrift*, Neue Folge XIII, Heft 5, 1937, pp. 161-8.

pilgrimage" to Yixian in the Neue Rundschau and apparently enjoyed it, recalling "At the entrance of the cavern Mr. Perzynski found a fragment of a Lohan, which he recognized at once as T'ang pottery; and I must confess that I experienced no little satisfaction in reading this part of the narrative which showed that the opinion of the man on the spot corroborated my own. Unfortunately, Mr. Perzynski arrived too late, for he found nothing but broken pieces of the figures and eight empty niches in which they had stood."[56]

This is a little odd because nowhere in his account of his visits to the caves does Perzynski recognize any shards or fragments as "T'ang", nor does he mention "niches", never mind eight empty ones. Perhaps in his initial elation with the museum's new acquisition, Hobson's memory played him false.[57] Either that or he fell early victim to Perzynski's powers of subtle suggestion, for it is only when describing his first sight of the bust shown him in Beijing that Perzynski noted the "three delicate colours–green, yellow and brown–the *sancai* (三彩) of the Tang period." Hobson would not be the last to be so seduced.

In any case, by the time he came to write his 1925 monograph on the British Museum's Luohan, Hobson had shrugged off most such subliminal effects. Reading between the lines, while he stuck to his guns on the Tang dating, he seems, after mature consideration, to have taken Perzynski's embellishments with a far larger pinch of salt than previously, "...with regard to the dating of these Lohans little help can be obtained from local sources...after all, local tradition on such a remote occurrence can hardly be considered seriously. The question of dating, then, must be decided on stylistic and ceramic grounds."[58]

---

56   Hobson, Op. Cit., 1914, p. 70.
57   Hobson, Op. Cit. 1914, p. 70. He repeats the mis-remembrance in a footnote on page 35 of *Chinese Pottery and Porcelain*, which was published the following year.
58   Quoted by Marion Wolf, "The Lohans from I-chou", *Oriental Art* 15, No.1, 1969, p.56.

In the years that followed, research on the two different aspects of the dating conundrum proceeded along roughly parallel tracks but at varying speeds, with the result that conclusions have occasionally been shunted both backwards and forwards. For convenience, the stylistic and technical journeys are set out separately below.

As regards the latter, Hobson was the first to remark on the statues' technical sophistication, "...high as the figure ranks as sculpture, it is far more remarkable as pottery. To fire such a mass of material without subsidence or cracking would tax the capabilities of the best equipped modern pottery, while the skill displayed in the modeling is probably unequalled in any known example of ceramic sculpture."[59]

He was also the first to venture a preliminary analysis of the statue's material composition: well-fired white pottery that was soft enough to powder under the blade of a knife; coated overall with soft lead glaze in three colours, leaf-green, an ochreous yellow and an almost colourless white that had weathered: slightly brown and minutely crackled on its exposed upper surfaces; and with the pupils of the eyes highlighted in black clay. Thus far the technique was that of the Tang, but no further. The tomb statuettes of that dynasty were shaped in moulds to facilitate multiple replication. "The Lohan on the contrary are individual works of art each modeled by the hand of a master and instinct with the fire of his genius. Compared with the tomb figurines they are as the moon among the lesser lights."[60]

Not all curators were as lucky as Hobson, who happily noted that the British Museum's Luohan stood on its original rocky stand and, barring very minor restorations, was in near pristine condition. The Luohan acquired by the Museum of Fine Arts in

---

59   Hobson, Op. Cit., 1915, Vol. I, p. 37.
60   Hobson, Op. Cit., 1914, p. 70.

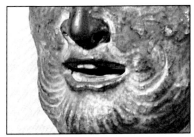

*Fig.39 "…gap-toothed…"; detail of Fig. 38
The beard and missing tooth are sometimes
taken as identifiers of Subinda (Nandimitra)
the fourth Luohan*

*Fig.38 "…one with a beard…buried
at Baoding…" Luohan, stoneware with
sancai glaze from Hebei, China; Liao
dynasty (907-1125); The Luohan in the
Museum of Fine Arts, Boston, with its
original head. © museum of Fine Arts,
Boston*

Boston was one of those that had been exhibited by Worch in Paris. It was particularly unusual in that the Luohan's features were distinctly Indo-European rather than Chinese, hirsute and oddly, but deliberately, gap-toothed.[61] (**Fig.38**) Whether it was the full beard he sported, or the missing tooth that first prompted the curator, John Ellerton Lodge, to take a closer look is unclear, but careful examination, including a delicate incision into the joint between head and neck, raised a suspicion that its head might not have been original. (**Fig.39**) Okakura Kakuzo had been in Beijing on MFA business in 1912, but there is no indication that he had seen the Luohan then and, in any case, he could not be consulted because he had passed away the following year. In a note to the Director dated 27 March 1915, Lodge wrote "…the head is made of a red clay, entirely different from the mixture of white and red clay of which the body appears to be formed, indicating that the

---

61   The Luohan named Subinda is often portrayed as gap-toothed.

head and body may not be contemporary."[62]

Lodge subsequently raised the matter with Yamanaka and Co. in New York, through whom the MFA had purchased the statue. The firm's manager there, Mr. D.J.R. Ushikubo assured him that the statue was exactly as displayed in Paris, but that he would do his best to check on provenance on his next visit to Beijing. A few months later he reported: "I tried to secure full information in regard to the Lohan figure of the Boston Museum. Fortunately, I have had an interview with Mr. Terazawa (sic), who brought the figure with a few Chinese partners... The number of figures he brought out are three: one figure perfect, after a hard task; and the other two by breaking on account of their packing, etc. It was almost impossible to carry life-size figure in perfect condition such a long journey and obliged to break the heads, bodys (sic.) and stands and carry back only the heads and bodys (sic.), leaving behind stands at that time. By this statement it is certain that the repairings (sic) were made at Peking when the separate parts of the body arrived, and it is now clear that the head and the body of the Lohan which is now in the possession of the Boston Museum are of the same age."[63]

This general corroboration of Perzynski's explanation for the heavy restorations of some of the Luohans was apparently accepted by the museum, but we will return to this exchange in a later chapter. The MFA was pleased to receive the Luohan's missing rocky base not long thereafter. For one reason or another, however, one of the MFA's curators was never really happy with its Indo-European physiognomy and eventually commissioned

62 Lodge, J.E., to the Director, March 27 1916, folder and box unidentified, AAOA-MFA; see Daisy Wang Yiyou, *The Loouvre from China: A Critical Study of C.T. Loo and the Framing of Chinese Art in the United States, 1915-1950*, a dissertation presented to the faculty of the College of Fine Arts of Ohio University in partial fulfilment of the requirements for the degree Doctor of Philosophy, 2007, p.88.
63 Letter to Lodge, September 6, 1916, folder and box unknown, AAOA-MFA; see Wang Yiyou Daisy, Op. Cit., p.112, footnote 245.

the sculpting of the replacement head that sits on the statue's shoulders today. (**Fig.40 and Plate I**) This has more in common with its brethren in other museums, being more Chinese in appearance, and so it should since, anecdotally, the man who modeled for it was a cook from Boston's Chinatown.[64]

The Metropolitan Museum of Art in New York had contracted with Perzynski to buy the complete Luohan in his Berlin exhibition, but the First

Fig.40 Luohan, stoneware with sancai *glaze from Hebei, China; Jin dynasty 12th Century; H 102.7 cm excluding base; Francis Bartlett Donation of 1912, 15.255. Photograph © 2021 Museum of Fine Arts, Boston*

World War delayed delivery until 1920. The first curator of its Department of Far Eastern Art was an unusual appointment. The Dutch impressionist painter, Sigisbert Chretien "Gijs" Bosch Reitz, had started life as a businessman before taking up a brush and later visiting Japan and making a comprehensive study of its art. (**Fig.41**) Welcoming the safe arrival of the youthful-looking Luohan in the museum's Bulletin, he, like Hobson before him, commented with great satisfaction that this statue had only very minor restorations. (**Fig.42 and Plate VII**) True, its head had been broken off at some point, but it had been reattached and fastened in place with metal rivets of the sort commonly found in Ming porcelain repairs. Bosch Reitz was also the first to notice that the Luohans had been constructed on a metal framework, which had not melted on firing because the soft lead glaze did not require

---

64   Jin Shen, Op. Cit. p. 67,

Fig.41 Sigisbert Chretien "Gijs" Bosch Reitz, the Dutch impressionist painter who became the first curator of Far Eastern Art at the Met in New York. Public Domain

Fig.42 The Met's "Younger Monk"; luohan, Liao dynasty (907-1125), ca. 1000. Stoneware with three-color glaze; H 104.8 cm excluding base. Metropolitan Museum of Art, New York; Fletcher Fund 1920, Acc. No. 20.114

a very high heat. Like Hobson, Bosch Reitz was satisfied with the Tang dating on the basis of the "usual T'ang glazes".[65] Like Hobson, he was also both curious and meticulous.

This careful attention to detail shines through his paintings, and also shows in his very succinct tallying of the statues that had so far surfaced. In addition to the Met's, he listed those in the British Museum, Boston's MFA, the University Museum in Philadelphia (as the Penn was then known), the ROM in Toronto and the Matsukata Collection, and then goes on to say: "...four others are owned by private collectors and dealers. In all ten are known besides a great many small fragments, several hands and feet and baskets full of broken pieces."[66] At time of writing, he would have been aware of C.T. Loo's persistent attempts to

---

65   Bosch Reitz, Sigisbert Chretien, "A Large Pottery Lohan of the T'ang Period", *Bulletin of the Metropolitan Museum of Art*, 16, January 1921, p. 15.

66   Bosch Reitz, Ibid., p. 15.

sell the Met a second older monk, as well as the torso sold by Perzynski to Harry Fuld, but he offered no hint as to the location of the remaining two. It is evident from this detail, however, that he had made his own enquiries, and his conclusion was that originally the statues would have formed part of a set of sixteen, of which ten had survived.

Not content with this, he helpfully provided some additional observations about the survivors: "Of the ten Lohans known, five only have their original heads, one has the mask only, three have heads of reddish clay covered with a carefully applied slip and green glaze–these heads have been fired upside down–one has no head at all."[67]

These are significant details and, again, it is clear that he had been communicating with his fellow curators and probably dealers as well. He happily confirmed that the Met's Luohan had its original head, and it is not difficult to identify the other four. The heads on those in the ROM and the Matsukata Collection match his description of those fired upside-down (**Fig.43 and Plate V; Fig.44 and Plate IV**), and he obviously knew about the third in Boston's MFA. So, eight again, leaving only two to puzzle over: one with a "mask only"; and the other "no head at all". At the time he was writing, the Luohan now in Kansas City's Nelson-Atkin's museum had not yet been resurrected, so we must look elsewhere for them, but we do not have to look very far. The first is probably a head in Cleveland, which was later discounted, while the headless one was still sitting in General Munthe's garden waiting for Otto Fischer to give it a thumbs-down when he visited in 1925. In fact, in his account of the visit, he mentions two, one of them dated 1339, and both much more coarsely fashioned than the

---

67   Bosch Reitz, Ibid., p.16..

Fig.43 Figure of a luohan, reportedly from Yixian, Hebei Province, China; moulded earthenware with sancai glaze, Liao-Jin Dynasty, 11th century; H 104 cm. excluding base; 914.4.1. ROM2005_1592_1; Courtesy of the Royal Ontario Museum © ROM

Fig.44 "...leaning slightly to the left as if easing a cramp.", Luohan, Liao dynasty (907-1125); H 104.2 cm. By kind permission of the Sezon Museum of Modern Art, Karuizawa

eight already abroad.[68]

Two years later, Cornelia Harcum at the ROM agreed with her colleagues in London and New York that the Luohans were "extraordinary examples of the ceramic art of the Tang dynasty."[69] (**Fig.45**) Like Hobson she picked up on the difference between tomb figures that had been moulded and mass produced, and the Luohans that had been individually modeled. Indeed, it is apparent that she had made reference to Hobson's work and closely paraphrased his assessment that such large masses of clay would have required great skill on the part of the Tang potters to fire successfully. Likewise, Horace "Howard" Furness Jayne (1898-1975), the first curator of East Asian art at the

---

68   Fischer, Otto, *Wanderfahren eines Kunst-freundes in China und Japan*, Stuttgart, Deutsche Verlags Anstalt, 1939, p. 308.

69   Harcum, Cornelia, "*Chinese Pottery Statue of a Lohan*", *Bulletin of the University of Toronto*, 1923, pp. 1-3.

Philadelphia Museum of Art and then Director of the University of Pennsylvania Museum of Archaeology and Anthropology, who judged the latter's Luohan "among the noblest examples of Chinese sculpture ever brought to light," adding for good measure that "no portrait statue of any age or land can rival the museum's figure."[70] (**Fig.46 and Plate III**) When he proudly loaned it to the International Exhibition of Chinese Art in London in 1935, the catalogue entry listed the Luohan as "T'ang Dynasty".[71]

Coincidentally, the only early twentieth century comment by a Chinese scholar that the author has so far found, was written by a contemporary of Jayne's at the University of Pennsylvania. Liang Sicheng (梁思成; 1901-72), the father of modern Chinese architecture, studied there from 1924 to 1928 under the Boxer Indemnity Scholarship Program, together with Lin Huiyin (林徽因; 1904-55), the poet-architect who would become his wife. (**Fig.47**) The Penn museum's Luohan, and its brethren seen later in New York, left a lasting impression, as is obvious from his description of it in his *History of Chinese Sculpture*: "...their appearance is that of real people, the pleating of their garments is

Fig.45 Cornelia Harcum (first half 20th Century), who migrated from her native Baltimore to work at the ROM in Toronto. Courtesy of Royal Ontario Museum © ROM

---

70   Jayne, Horace F., in *The Chinese Collection of the University Museum* in *Handbook of the Principal Objects*, Philadelphia, 1941, p. 50.
71   Jayne, Horace F., Op. cit. p. 50.

Fig.46 Seated luohan, Liao dynasty (907-1125); H 104.1 cm. excluding base. Courtesy of the Penn Museum, object no. C66A

true to life...Whether it is in the elegance of their pose, or the sincere concentration of their knitted brows, each has its own individual character and personality. These are not just casually imagined carvings, but sculptures taken from life. They are so wonderfully modelled that they can be compared with Roman statuary. They are portraits created by very careful observation of expressions, and not just of the countenance, but of the whole structure of the body and drape of fabrics. Not one of them is unreal; all are true to life. At the third level of observation, the effect is most accurate and so subtle that it creates a faithful illusion of life and in this they are not second to the finest masterpieces of the Italian renaissance."[72]

Among the other treasures in the Penn Museum that Howard Jayne agreed to loan to the 1935 International Exhibition in London was a stone panel from the Tang emperor Taizong's (太宗; 626-49) tomb, carved with one of his favourite steeds, *Saluzi*, "Autumn dew", a bay charger that he had ridden at the siege of Luoyang (洛陽) and in seven other battles. Small wonder then, that a Chinese scholar such as Fu Zhenlun (傅振倫; 1906-99)

---

72 Liang Sicheng, *History of Chinese Architecture*, 1985, China Architecture and Building Press:"......其貌皆似真容，其衣褶亦甚寫實。......或容態雍容，......或蹙眉作懇切狀，要之皆各有個性，不徒為空泛虛縹之神像。其妙肖可與羅馬造像比。皆由對於平時神情精細觀察造成之肖像也。不惟容貌也，即其身體之結構，衣服之披垂，莫不以寫實為主；其第三量之觀察至精微，故成忠實表現，不亞于意大利文藝復興時最精作品也".

should subsequently have lamented the dispersal of Chinese antiquities to museums and private collections around the world.[73] China had been re-unified under Chiang Kai-shek only seven years before, and Sun Dianying's (孫殿英; c.1887-c.1947;) looting of the Eastern Tombs that year was only the latest and most egregious example of warlords turning ancient artefacts into modern arms and soldiers' pay.

Fig.47 Liang Sicheng (1901-72), a graduate of the University of Pennsylvania, who strove to preserve China's built heritage. Public Domain

In 1940, the Japanese scholar, Harada Yoshito, published his own findings on the Luohans, "originally in Yixian", confirmed that Perzynski's un-named Japanese acquaintance was Terasawa Shikanosuke, and concurred with Hobson on his Tang dating.[74] In fact, nobody seems to have queried Hobson's technical ceramic analysis until 1944, when Bosch Reitz's successor at the Met, the ever arrogant Alan Priest (1898-1969), took a very different view. (**Fig.48**)

Priest spent much of the Warlord era of the 1920s scouting for antiquities in Beijing. Taking up residence in a Chinese mansion and waited on by a bevy of pretty house boys, he mixed business and serious research with Chinese opera and other more hedonistic pleasures and pursuits. He was a textiles specialist rather than a ceramicist, but in his 1944 volume on Chinese sculpture in the Met, Priest radically revised the Luohans' dating from Tang (618-907) to Ming (1368-1644).[75] There is some

---

73   Fu Zhenlun, "Zhongguo yishu gunji zhanlan canguan ji (Record of Viewing the International Exhibition of Chinese Art)", in *Beiping gugong bowuyuan nian kan*, 1936.

74   Harada Yoshito, "Chokureishoekiken kyuzai to rakan ni tsuite" in *Toa kobunka kenkyu*, November 1940, pp. 299-305.

75   Priest, Alan, *Chinese Sculpture in the Metropolitan Museum of Art*, New York, 1944, Catalogue Numbers 73 & 74.

Fig.48 Alan Priest (1898-1969), long-serving curator of the Met NY's Far Eastern collections, in retirement in Kyoto, Japan. Courtesy of the Metropolitan Museum, New York

suspicion that he "borrowed" this view.

The same year saw the publication of a book by the expert ceramicist and dealer Warren Cox, which included a detailed analysis of the Met's two Luohans. In a footnote beneath Cox noted: "I am gratified to see that, after having written the above and having told Mr. Alan Priest, curator of Far Eastern Art of the Metropolitan Museum of Art, that it was my intention to publish the figures of seated lohans as Ming, he in his recent book on Chinese sculpture has said, *'These figures were called T'ang when they first appeared, and most of the owners up to this moment have stuck to that dating. A careful comparison with T'ang and Ming glazes shows the glazes of the Museum's Lohans to be far closer to Ming, as the sculpture itself seems closer to the Ming, we suggest the later date.'* I had not told Mr. Priest how or why I thought both the glazes and the modeling were, not closer to but actually, Ming."[76]

Alan Priest's curatorial showmanship was unfortunately coupled with slipshod scholarship. Researchers delving into the Smithsonian's archives have found page after page of corrections to the articles and catalogue entries casually drafted by him and then passed to his assistant for checking. This cavalier

---

76   Cox, Warrren E.,*The Book of Pottery and Porcelain*, New York, 1944, pp. 530-31.

Fig.49 Aschwin Lippe, Prinz zur Lippe-Biesterfeld, the German art historian whose expertise supported Alan Priest's showmanship at the Met NY. Courtesy Dutch National Archives

attitude is well captured by a stinging rebuke in a memo from the aristocratic German art historian Aschwin Lippe, Prinz zur Lippe-Biesterfeld (**Fig.49**), who worked for him after the Second World War. Responding to Priest's carping at the "yap and snarl of scholars as to who painted what and when," he reminds him bluntly that making such appraisals "is our job and what we are paid for."[77]

Four years after Priest carelessly punted the Luohans from Tang to Ming, further scrutiny by William Young (1906-2000), the pioneer of scientific analysis, conservation and restoration at Boston's Museum of Fine Arts, booted the ball straight back the other way. The museum had previously discovered a number of coins embedded in earth in the innermost folds of its Luohan's

---

77   Lippe, Aschwin, *Friendly Notes Part II*, Smithsonian Archives of American Arts, quoted in Meyer, Karl E., and Blair Brysac, Shereen, *The China Collectors–America's Century Long Hunt for Asian Art Treasures*, 2015, p. 289.

robes, the latest of them dated 1103/04, but that could have been "salting" and had been deemed, scientifically, to prove nothing.[78] Young's rigorous examination of three typically Tang shards from Nara, in Japan, and "two indisputable T'ang and two Ming samples…along with a sample from the lower part of the museum's Lohan" was more scientific. It involved spectro-photometry, spectro-chemical analysis and tests for hardness, as well as for the lead and lime content of clays and glazes. In concluding his report, he noted, "it is possible to detect, with a fair degree of certainty, differences between Ming and T'ang material. It also indicates that the Lohan figure belongs to the T'ang period."[79] When Warren Cox published a revised edition of his book some thirty years later, a decade after Priest's passing, he retracted his Ming dating with good grace, stating modestly: "Actually, I was wrong."[80]

The statues are all slightly more than life-size, averaging around 50 inches / 234 cm in height, and weighing in at around 450 lbs / 204 kg including their separate rocky stands. Restoration work by the ROM in the 1980s confirmed that they were built from pottery slabs of coarse clay clothed in a thin layer of finer white, onto which the *sancai* (三彩) glaze was painted. It also confirmed Bosch Reitz's earlier observation that the slabs were reinforced with iron rods to prevent sagging during firing, and that the clay had perforations to assist drying and permit steam to escape that might otherwise have built up and caused distortions.[81] Clearly they had been made in kilns that specialized

---

78 Hobson, Op.Cit. 1925, p. 6 footnote, cites Stewart Kershaw of the MFA, Boston as his source.
79 Young William J., "Notes on Sho-so-in, T'ang and Ming Pottery", *Far Eastern Ceramic Bulletin*, Cambridge, Mass., Vol. I. No. 1. July 1948, pp. 57-66.
80 Cox, Op. Cit. 1979 revised edition, p. 531.
81 Young, Op. Cit., although the reinforcing for the Berlin bust now in the Hermitage may have been bamboo, according to Derek Gillman's second-hand report of remarks by Dr. Maria Menshikova at SOAS in March 2014.

in architectural work, glazed tiles, pillars, decorative dragons and other mythical beast finials. Equally clearly, they were not run-of-the-mill products. Their varied postures are entirely natural, as is the flow of their garments. It is obvious that they were sculpted by skilled artists before glazing and their glazing is of the finest quality. While their garments and mode of dress differ in style, the pattern in the fabrics is identical and there is virtually no blurring between colours. This, taken with the combined effect of the extraordinarily life-like expression of faces and postures, place them as products of an imperial workshop, i.e. workshops used to carrying out Court commissions.

In fairness to those who urged for a Tang dynasty dating, it should be stressed that the notion of that period of Chinese history being an "Augustan Age" had been absorbed second-hand from materials that the Japanese themselves traced to Tang influence, a point acknowledged by Hobson. Art historians in the West had virtually no first-hand experience of sancai (三彩) and other Tang ware until the digging of railway cuttings in the early part of the twentieth century disturbed Tang tombs, and the furnishings recovered from them began to provide tangible proof. So it was not simply a knee-jerk reaction of the "if-it-is-sancai-it-must-be-Tang" sort. Nevertheless, even experts like Hobson, while acknowledging that Tang sancai (三彩) were typically secular rather than sacred and destined for tombs rather than temples, did not deem that distinction sufficient reason to question their judgment on dating. We will come back to this point later. However, it should be emphasized that more recent research by the Chinese scholar Jin Shen has demonstrated convincingly that sancai (三彩) glaze was indeed not used for temple sculpture until the Northern Song (960-1126), when shortage of bronze prompted use of substitutes.[82]

As far as is known, none of the Luohans was subject to thermo-luminescence testing until 1987, when the MFA in Boston, apparently still fretting about its non-original head, sent samples of both body and head to the Research Laboratory for Archaeology and the History of Art in Oxford, England. The results were inconclusive but indicated that the head had been fired "in antiquity", while the body seemed to be younger and at least part of it had been fired closer to the Ming than the Liao dynasty.[83] When the Penn Museum had theirs tested in 1997, the readings showed a mid-point of 1210 CE, plus or minus 200 years. Stuart Fleming, the Penn's conservator, subsequently tightened this to plus or minus one century. A similar test on the younger Luohan in New York's Met likewise narrowed the range to 1210 CE plus or minus 100 years, which suggested a Liao (907-1127) or Jin (1115-1234) dynasty dating.[84]

This scientific evidence was reinforced by the 1983 discovery of the Longquanwu (龍泉務) kiln at Mentougou (門頭溝), in what are now the western suburbs of Beijing. Chief among the finds excavated there in 1985 were three half-life-size Buddhist sculptures: a white ceramic Buddha, and two *sancai* (三彩) bodhisattvas. Marilyn Gridley's meticulous stylistic analysis of the statues convincingly narrowed the range to 10th-11th Century.[85] Much as Chinese scholar, Fu Zhenlun (傅振倫) and colleagues involved in the dig would have liked to pinpoint Longquanwu (龍泉務) as the kiln where the Luohans were fired, Gridley's analysis was not sufficient for that, but it was enough

---

82   Jin Shen, Op. Cit., p. 65

83   Hsu, Op. Cit. p. 159 with footnote 74, quoting a letter dated 2 April, 1987 addressed to Richard Newman, research scientist at the MFA Boston.

84   Stuart Fleming's letter of 25 October 1997 to Jennifer White, Curator at the Penn Museum, quoted in Hsu, Op.Cit., p. 220, End Note 7.

85   Gridley, Marilyn, "Three Buddhist Sculptures from Longquanwu and the Luohan from Yixian", *Oriental Art*, vol. 46, no. 4, 1995, pp. 20-29.

to demonstrate that the Liao potters had the requisite technical expertise.[86] In fairness, Gridley also noted that no *sancai* (三彩) Buddhist sculptures had so far been found at kiln sites in Liaoning (遼寧) or Chifeng County (赤峰) in Inner Mongolia.[87] It would be another two decades before further technical analysis by Nigel Wood and others matched the clay used in the production of the Luohans to a small deposit just to the west of Beijing.[88]

The West knew almost as little about early Chinese sculpture at the beginning of the 20th Century as it did about *sancai*. Indeed, Perzynski the autodidact mocks his contemporaries: "Back home, people are writing books about Chinese art, and an authority such as Bushell leaps boldly over eight centuries in his treatise on Chinese sculpture, because he has nothing to recount from that period." So, it was an extraordinary intellectual leap for a man, such as Hobson, who had dedicated the best part of his early career to English pottery and had only lately turned his attention to the Orient, to proclaim excitedly in 1914, "It seemed to us as if the veil had been lifted and the forerunner of the Japanese temple masterpieces stood at last revealed."[89] It was his informed eye that was the first to see the connection between the vividly life-like Luohans and Japanese statuary, citing by way of example: the Yuima in the Hokkeji nunnery, which was ascribed to the middle of the 8th century; the portrait figure of the priest Ryoben (RIP 773) in the Todaiji monastery; and the portrait figure of Chisho Daishi (RIP 891) in the Onjoji monastery. "All have

---

86   Zhao Guanglin, "Longquanwu yaozhi diaochaji (Account of the Investigations of the Longquanwu Kiln Site)", *Yandu*, 1987, No.5, p. 32.

87   Gridley, Op. Cit.,1995, p. 28.

88   Wood, N., Doherty, C., Menshikova, M., Eng, C., and Smithies, R, "A Luohan from Yixian in the Hermitage Museum: Some Parallels in Material Usage with the Longquanwu and Liuliqu Kilns near Beijing", *Bulletin of Chinese Ceramic Art and Archaeology*, No.6, Beijing, December 2015, pp.34-35.

89   Hobson, Op. Cit, 1914, p. 69. The BM had purchased its luohan from S.M. Frank & Co. the previous year, shortly after Worch displayed his in Paris, and before Perzynski's exhibition in Berlin.

similar sculptural qualities, the same 'life movement' which is the ideal of T'ang art, and means not only life in motion but life in repose"[90]

For Hobson, the key was that the Luohans were portraits taken from life: "It is no conventional figure following a tradition of centuries, but the product of a young and vigourous art with freshness and originality in every line." The following year, with the publication of *Chinese Pottery and Porcelain*, he pursued the same theme: "So rare are examples of this style, that, unless we turn to painted pictures or frescoes such as have been brought back by the recent expeditions in Turfan, we must look in the temples of Japan, not, indeed, for similar Chinese work, but for the Japanese masterpieces in bronze, wood and lacquer of the same period, which avowedly followed the Chinese art."[91] The Luohans were the missing link, he believed, between late Tang statuary and the Japanese *chinzo*, the portraits of distinguished Zen monks and such a transmission of art via a religious route closely parallels the emergence of the cult of the luohan following the persecution of Buddhism in 841-845 and the coincident development of Zen Buddhism.[92]

On seeing the face of the elder Luohan in the Yamen, Perzynski, with his early grounding in Japanese art history had commented, "I think of the Japanese *Noh* masks of the *Yase-Otoko*, emaciated by involuntary asceticism." The *yaseotoko*, or "emaciated man" masks, whose lean flesh scarcely disguised the structure of the skull, were used in *Noh* theatre to represent those who have disobeyed the Buddhist dictate not to take life and were now ghosts suffering in Hell. So, it is hardly surprising that Leopold Reidemeister later made the same connection as

90   Hobson, Op. Cit., 1914, p, 69.
91   Hobson, Op. Cit., 1915, p. 36-37.
92   Smithies, Richard, "The Search for the Lohans of I-Chou (Yixian)", *Oriental Art* 30, 1984, pp. 261, referencing Wen Fong, "The Lohans and a Bridge to Heaven", p. 43.

Hobson, and illustrated his essay with a statue of Kokei, the end-12th Century Patriarch of the Hosso School from the Kofakuji temple in Nara (**Fig.50**).[93] However, as we have seen, he also suggested another link in the chain of transmission by connecting the Luohan to *sancai* (三彩) pottery that he had discovered in Jehol, or present-day Chengde (承德). Referring back to Perzynski's inscription, '"*Alle diese Buddhas kommen von weither,*" ("All these Buddhas come from afar"), he closed his case with a flourish: "*Wir mochten hinzufugen von Jehol!*" ("We should add "from Jehol"!)[94]

Fig.50 Kokei's end-12th Century statue of the Patriarch of the Hosso School in the Kofukuji Temple in Nara, Japan. Public domain

As we saw in Chapter One, the Buddhist monk, poet and painter, Guanxiu (貫休; 832-912) had painted portraits of the Luohans after they had appeared to him in a dream, and his caricatures had achieved considerable fame. The artists who sculpted the terracotta Luohans may or may not have been aware of Guanxiu's iconic grotesqueries but, if they were, they chose to ignore them. They concentrated instead on the twin task of creating a true-to-life impression of living Luohans, while capturing the inner struggle of the meditative process, the toll taken by asceticism on the physical being and the serenity of its spiritual outcome. These were real people, respected religious ascetics who had freed themselves from this world, but whom

93   Reidemeister, Op. Cit., 1937, Abbr. 12, Tafel 28, p. 169
94   Reidemeister, Op. Cit., 1937, pp. 161-8.

this world wished to immortalize in the kilns. As real people, they demonstrated that a spiritual outcome was within the reach of ordinary men. And perhaps they had been just sufficiently of this world stubbornly to have continued their example to their followers in the face of persecution by Emperor Wuzong (武宗; r. 840-846) of the Tang.

It was Basil Gray (*pace* Leopold R.) who first gave voice to the thought that the spirit of Tang art lived on even as that great dynasty died, "That the T'ang style did not cease abruptly with the fall of the dynasty is clear."[95] (**Fig.51**) Referencing archaeological surveys by the Japanese in Manchuria, he noted that in addition to Northern Song dynasty, Ding (定) wares and celadons, a considerable quantity of *sancai* (三彩) and yellow and green glazed monochromes in the Tang style had been unearthed and placed in the Mukden Museum. He drew particular attention to two *sancai* (三彩) covered boxes there in the Tang tradition,

"but rather more advanced in style", one being decorated with an incised hare, the other a freely drawn flower, motifs that were unknown on Tang wares. This insight has been more than borne out by subsequent finds in the territories occupied by the Liao (遼) and it is clear that, at least in the kilns, technical mastery was retained and new twists were given to old themes, for example scalloped rims with alternating upward peaks between downward curves.

Fig.51 Basil Gray (1904-89), Islamic art specialist, who became acting- Director of the British Museum. Courtesy of julia&keld

The   difficulty   for   those   who

---

95   Gray, Basil, *Early Chinese Pottery and Porcelain*, London, Faber & Faber Ltd., 1953, p.14.

supported a Liao (遼) dynasty dating (907-1127) was how to overcome a peculiar prejudice amongst Western scholars against the nomadic and pastoral tribes who had nibbled away at China's northern border as the Tang imploded. The Tang had been a "Golden Age", when China was open to the world, when ideas, techniques, fashions and faiths had been exchanged directly with its neighbours. They, the scholars, found it difficult to conceive of transmission via non-Tang third parties. Thus, generally speaking, the Tangut, a Tibetan people who established Xi Xia (西夏) or Western Xia (1038-1227), the Khitan, who became the Liao (遼; 907-1125), and the Jurchen, who displaced them as the Jin (金; 1115-34), have had a bad press amongst Western historians. Reischauer and Fairbank are more polite than most, carefully clothing the word "barbarian" in inverted commas, but they are still dismissive: "Except for architectural monuments such as temples and tombs, the Khitan people seem to have left little cultural heritage."[96]

So, we should be grateful to Marilyn Gridley for laying the myth of the "barbarian" Liao (遼) eloquently to rest in the 1990s.[97] The conquering Khitan (契丹) coveted Chinese art and culture just as much as territory. They even had a special term for the Chinese artists and artisans whom they brought back north: "*shu shan*" (precious coral). Those kidnapped in this way were re-settled in new communities named after their place of origin. One such place mentioned earlier is Longquanwu (龍泉務), named after one of the Quyang (曲陽) kiln towns, Longquan, in Dingzhou (定州), famous for their white "Ding" wares.[98] A mid-tenth century Liao raiding party took the potters back with them and settled them beneath the Western Hills of their southern capital

---

96   Reischauer, Edwin O., and Fairbank, John K., *East Asia The Great Tradition*, Boston, 1958, p.254.
97   Gridley, Op. Cit., 1995, pp. 20-29.
98   "Beijing Longquanwu yao fajue baogao (Archaeological Report of the Longquanwu kilns in Beijing)", in *Beijing shi wenwu yenjiaosuo*, 2002, ed., Beijing.

Fig.52 Protective structures around the Yungang Grottoes. Author's photograph.

Fig.53 Decorative detailing from an earlier dynasty preserved in later restoration at Yungang Grottoes. Author's photograph

in Hebei, today's Beijing. The "*wu*" suffix denoted a business or taxable undertaking.[99] If they were "barbarians" before they crossed the border, the Khitan/Liao (契丹/遼) assimilated very quickly thereafter and, as Reischauer and Fairbank indicate, they were generous patrons of religion and the arts. Amongst much else, they funded extensive repairs to the grottoes at Yungang (雲崗), building protective wooden "temple" structures around the exposed stone Buddhas (**Fig.52**). The originals burned down, but their replacements still display animistic detailing from the earlier date (**Fig.53**). They sponsored the construction of the great twin Huayan Monastery (華嚴寺) in their secondary capital Datong (大同). The Lower Huayan Monastery was completed in 1038 and is still much as it was then, complete with its original wooden sculptures. Its Upper counterpart, however, had to be re-built in its entirety after it burned down in 1140.

The Liao also refurbished the Lingyan Monastery (靈巖寺) in Shandong (山東), which incorporates a hall of thirty-six painted clay Luohans in animated postures and with vividly expressive

---

99   Hsu, Op. Cit., p.50 with footnote 87.

faces. The great wooden pagoda of Fogong Temple (佛宮寺) in Shanxi (山西) **(Fig.54)** was built by the Liao Emperor Daozong (道宗; r. 1052-1101) in memory of his grandmother, who came from the area. At one stage the Khitan/Liao stretched as far south as Kaifeng (開封), occupying that city for a short while before retreating back across the Yellow River, and for much of their reign they occupied all of Shandong, Hebei and Shanxi. They were thus

Fig.54 All wooden pagoda at Fogang Temple in Shanxi. Author's photograph

guardians of the great pilgrimage grottoes at both Yungang (雲崗) and Xiangtangshan (響堂山).

In his 1998 essay, the Chinese scholar Jin Shen (金申) noted that the shift away from the increasingly stylized iconography of the Tang to life-like sculptures, from the ethereal to the human, first shows itself in the Yanxiadong (煙霞洞), or Cloud and Mist Grotto in Hangzhou during the Northern Song (960-1126) **(Fig.55)**. A lovely rotund and seemingly lazy, painted clay Luohan, also Northern Song, in the Guanyin Pavilion of Qinglian Temple (清蓮寺) at Jincheng (晉城) in Shanxi **(Fig.56)** provides another example. However, Liao statuary has a vivacity that distinguishes it from these and lifts it above them, suggesting that under their new masters, the artists were given greater license than before. They may have borrowed Chinese artists and artisans, but in doing so, the Liao facilitated a new flowering of the arts. Their sculptures build on Tang traditions and give it new life. Their forms move to a different rhythm. Their features have a new character. They breathe. They live.

Fig.55 Luohan in Yanxiadong, Hangzhou, Five Dynasties (907-966) to early Northern Song (960-1129). After Ding Mingyi, 2000, pl. 15

Fig.56 A lovely lazy stucco luohan from the Guanyin Pavilion of Qinglian Temple at Jincheng, Shanxi province; Northern Song dynasty (960-1279). After Li Song, 2005, pl. 8

A few examples should suffice to illustrate the point, starting with the Luohan acquired from C.T. Loo by the Nelson Atkins Museum in Kansas City in 1933. The artists' sculptural skills extended across all media. Thus the magnificent gilt bronze Guanyin in the Penn that was retrieved from a river bed in Mukden, Manchuria, modern day Liaoning (遼寧), though quite how it got there is unclear. Thus the wooden Guanyin (觀音), seated in the posture known as "Royal Ease" (*maharaja lalitasana*) in the Honolulu Museum of Art, which was allegedly taken from a Tang dynasty temple called "*Chang-chiao ssu*" (sic) on the upper regions of the Yellow River in an area that was occupied by the Tanguts. No temple of that name has so far been identified but, coincidentally, it was purchased by the same Japanese industrialist, Matsukata Kojiro, who acquired one of the Luohans. In the view of the author, it has little in common with Tang statuary and rather more with the extraordinary Liao dynasty Guanyin

(觀音) in the Nelson Atkins Museum (**Fig.57**). Carved from a single tree trunk, the latter must rank amongst the world's most beautiful sculptures. Little wonder that Laurence Sickman (**Fig.58**) should have shifted gear from eloquent to lyrical when describing it: "An almost uncanny impression of movement, as though the gods were stepping forward with an easy, stately pace, or had just taken their seats on the lotus throne, is produced by the great agitation and restless movement of the garments and encircling scarves. These latter accessories are especially important in creating an almost spiral movement in three dimensions as the long, broad ribbons trail over the arms, loop across the body and curve around the

Fig.57 Guanyin of the Southern Sea, Liao-Jin dynasty (907-1234). Wood with polychrome, 95 x 65 in. By kind permission of the Nelson-Atkins Museum of Art, Kansas City, Missouri William Rockhill Nelson Trust, 34-10

back. In the actual carving the folds are deep, with sharp edges, so that the maximum contrast is obtained between highlight

Fig.58 Looking for bargains–Laurence Sickman in Luoyang, China, 1932. Laurence Sickman Papers, MSS 001, The Nelson-Atkins Museum of Art, Kansas City, Missouri

and shadow. Frequently the ends of garments and scarves are caught up in whorls and spirals obviously derived from the calligraphic flourishes of painting."[100]

A little less exalted, but Liao dynasty stoneware statues of Luohan, found at a village in northeastern Inner Mongolia in 1986 (**Fig.59**)[101], echo the sculpted-from-life vivacity of their wooden carvings, as do several dried lacquer heads from the same period. In many cases, the final coating of the latter has worn away (**Fig.60**), but one in the Nelson-Atkins Museum (**Fig.61**), retains sufficient to demonstrate the extraordinarily life-like effect achieved by the artists. Similar examples, possibly part of a set, may be found at the Seattle Museum of Art, the MFA Boston and the Art Institute, Chicago. When looking at them, one can understand why Basil Gray should have drawn a parallel with the terracotta Luohans,[102] and why the latter would have reminded Perzynski of the *yase-otoko* masks.

The earliest known dried lacquer Buddhist sculpture can be

---

100 Sickman, Laurence, and Soper, Alexander, *Art and Architecture of China*, Pelican History of Art, 1956, p. 101-2. .

101 Exhibited Tongliao City Museum; excavated in 1986, Hulunqi, Nailingao Sumuzhu, Wulibuge Cun.

102 Gray, Op. Cit., 1953, p.15, where he notes their provenance as a temple in Hebei, south of Beijing. See Seattle Museum of Art, Eugene Fuller Memorial Collection, Acc. No. 40.96.1-.2; the MFA Boston, Acc.No. 50.193; and the Art Institute of Chicago, Acc. No. 1928.258.

Plate I, *Luohan, stoneware with* sancai *glaze from Hebei, China; Jin dynasty 12th Century;*
H 102.7 cm excluding base; Francis Bart lett Donation of 1912, 15.255. Photograph
© 2021 Museum of Fine Arts, Boston

Plate II, *Luohan, stoneware with sancai glaze from Hebei, China; Liao dynasty (907-1125);*
103 cm; Acc. No. 1913,1221; © Trustees of the British Museum

Plate III, *Seated luohan, Liao dynasty (907-1125); H 104.1 cm. excluding base.*
Courtesy of the Penn Museum, object no. C66A

Plate IV, "…leaning slightly to the left as if easing a cramp.", *Luohan, Liao dynasty (907-1125); H 104.2 cm. By kind permission of the Sezon Museum of Modern Art, Karuizawa*

Plate V, *Figure of a luohan, reportedly from Yixian, Hebei Province, China; moulded earthenware with sancai glaze, Liao-Jin Dynasty, 11th century; H 104 cm. excluding base; 914.4.1. ROM2005_1592_1; Courtesy of the Royal Ontario Museum © ROM*

Plate VI, *The Met's "Older Monk"; luohan, Liao dynasty (907-1125), ca. 1000. Stoneware with three-color glaze; H 104.8 cm. excluding base. Metropolitan Museum of Art, New York, Frederick, C. Hewitt Fund 1921, Acc. No. 21.76*

Plate VII, *The Met's "Younger Monk"; luohan, Liao dynasty (907-1125), ca. 1000. Stoneware with three-color glaze; H 104.8 cm excluding base. Metropolitan Museum of Art, New York; Fletcher Fund 1920, Acc. No. 20.114*

Plate VIII, *Luohan, Chinese, from Yixian, Hebei Province, Jin Dynasty (1115-1234). Stoneware with sancai glaze; H 118.1 cm excluding base. The Nelson-Atkins Museum of Art, Kansas City, Missouri: Purchase William Rockhill Nelson Trust, 34-6*

Plate IX, *The Luohan Tamrabhadra; Liao dynasty (907-1125); H 105 cm excluding base. Courtesy of Musée Guimet; Photo © PMN-Grand Palais (MNAAG, Paris) / Thierry Olivier*

Plate X, *Perzynski's "Priest" following restoration - bust of Liao Dynasty sancai Luohan from Yixian; H 54 cm. The State Hermitage Museum, St. Petersburg, Inv. No. VF-3930; Photograph © The State Hermitage Museum, St. Petersburg. Photo by Alexander Lavrentyev*

Plate XI, *"…slung stylishly over shoulder like a cricketer's jersey." Detail of 914.4.1.: Figure of a luohan, moulded earthenware with sancai glaze, Liao-Jin Dynasty, 11th century, reportedly from Yixian, Hebei Province, China; ROM2016_15019_11. Courtesy of the Royal Ontario Museum © ROM.*

*Fig.59 Head of Louhan, Liao dynasty (907-1125);
stoneware. Courtesy of Tungliao City Museum,
Inner Mongolia*

*Fig.60 Head of Luohan,
Chinese, Liao-Jin Dynasty (907-
1234). Dry lacquer with traces of
gilding and paint, 12¼ x 8 x8¼
inches (31.12 x 20.32 x 21 cm).
By kind permission of the Nelson-
Atkins Museum of Art, Kansas
City, Missouri: William Rockhill
Nelson Trust, 31-84*

*Fig.61 Head of Luohan, Chinese,
Liao-Jin Dynasty (907-1234).
Dry lacquer with traces of gilding
and paint, 11½ x 6½ x 6½ inches
(29.2 x 16.5 x 16.5 cm). By kind
permission of the Nelson-Atkins
Museum of Art, Kansas City,
Missouri: William Rockhill Nelson
Trust, 33-9/2*

found in the Honolulu Museum of Art.[103] It bears an inscription giving the name of both the donor and the artist, and a cyclical date equivalent to 1099. Its features are unremarkable, but its costume is unusual in that the upper and lower hems of the *kasaya* are secured just below the left shoulder by means of a string and ring attachment to the upper hem of the garment. This sort of fastening, a modification to prescribed dress, was not known before the Song dynasty (960-1279). None of the terracotta Luohans have such a device, which modestly strengthens the argument for an earlier dating.

A number of specialists, notably A. B. Griswold, have studied the posture, gestures, robes and accessories of Buddhist statuary.[104] Intuitively, the Luohans' robes should tell us something about the monastic sect to which they belong, and possibly their status. Griswold puts it more categorically: "It is certain that the dress in sculpture often carries a sectarian message, if not a polemic." He may well be right. Unfortunately, however, while the clues may be there, the code that would enable us to decipher them is lost in the mists of time. A monk's garments, his *kasaya* (袈裟; *jiasha* in Chinese) were stipulated in the Theravada Vinaya, and comprised an inner robe covering the lower part of the body, a robe covering the upper part, and a cloak, the latter often being loosely termed the *kasaya*. In the cooler climate of northern China, a sleeved garment was substituted, not without some controversy, for the second garment, albeit it would often be worn off one shoulder. Nature provided the dyes for robes and in the Indian subcontinent, colour for an ordained monk's robes ranged from red and yellow to blue and black. In China, while red robes were common when Buddhism first arrived, later

---

103   Honolulu Museum of Art, Accession no, 4818.
104   Griswold, A.B., "Prolegomena to the Study of the Buddha's Dress in Chinese Sculpture (Part II), with Particular Reference to the Rietberg Museum's Collection", *Artibus Asiae*, 1965, p. 335-348.

during the Tang dynasty, monks typically wore robes of grayish-black, earning them the nickname "Black Robes".

Marilyn Gridley described how the detailing of the Luohans' *kasayas* is sufficient to distinguish the patchwork of fabric stitched together from narrow strips of scrap cloth. An obvious symbol of poverty, this was also a deferential reference to the Buddha, who was usually depicted wearing a patched cloak. Gridley also notes that five of the Luohans, the two in the Met and those in the British Museum, the MFA in Boston and the Hermitage, wear Indian-style garments, while those in the Nelson-Atkins, the Penn and the ROM wear a Chinese-style sleeved robe under the *kasaya*. (She was aware of the existence of only eight statues at that time.) What is more striking about the whole set, however, is the use of the three-colour *sancai* (三彩) palette. If grayish-black was the norm, this can hardly be an accident, or merely attributable to the availability of such glazes. Indeed, there are distinct similarities with the, albeit faded colours in paintings of Luohans in the Mogao Caves (莫高窟) at Dunhuang (敦煌) that have been dated to the Xixia (西夏; 1038-1227), the Tangut contemporaries of the Khitan / Liao.[105] The *sancai* robes make a bold statement, speaking of some new departure, and must surely reflect accurately the colours and devices of the sect to which the monks belonged.

Just as the postures and gestures of each of the Luohans are all different, so too the way they wear their robes and the patterning of their garments. For some the decorative devices appear in the main body of the fabric; for others it is in the borders or seams. Hobson noted that the tan-brown borders of the robe worn by the stern Luohan in the British Museum are edged in green and ornamented

---

105 Matsumoto Eiichi, *Study of Dunhuang Painting Images*, Tokyo, Bunka Gakuin Tokyo Kenkyujo, 1937, Cave 97, and Wang Huimin, "On the Inscription of Paintings of the Sixteen Arhats in Dunhuang" in *Dunhuang Research*, 1998-04, on-line.

with white quatrefoils and plum blossoms. The latter were popular in woven fabrics of the Liao and symbolized endurance, which seems appropriate for monks who had weathered the worst of winters in the great anti-Buddhist persecutions of the late Tang dynasty. The triple-pointed motifs in the fabric of several of the other Luohan are less obvious.

Dr. Hsu's notion that the artisans used the Chinese character for mountain, 山 (*shan*) as a coded indicator of the statues' destination is a tad fanciful.[106] If the motif is indeed *shan*, however, why not a reference to Mount Meru, the sacred five-peaked mountain of Buddhist cosmology, or, more pragmatically, a humble monastic genuflection to Muyeshan (木葉山), the most sacred mountain of the sect's new patrons, the Khitan? Or maybe, rather than a mountain, they represent a stylized Day Lily, symbol of spotlessness and purity? Or perhaps they are "flaming orbs" of enlightenment? On other statues, the glaze has run and the decoration is less distinct. More cloud-like than anything else, the original motifs might have been endless knots or conch shells. It is hard to tell, but clearly, like the lines in the monks' faces, the patterns in the cloth were copied from "life". The clues are there for all to see and would have been read and understood by contemporaries. Unfortunately, absent the discovery of a "Rosetta Stone", we lack the means to decipher them accurately today.

Gray noted the dried lacquer sculpted heads mentioned earlier as closer comparators than Reidemeister's 12th Century wooden examples from Shanxi and their Kamakura derivatives. Citing a headless marble Buddha dated 1032 in the Freer Gallery for further comparison, he argued strongly that the Luohans could not be later than the 11th Century. While venturing Liao dynasty

---

106   Hsu, Op. Cit., p. 191.

origins, he robustly rebutted Reidemeister's reference to the Jehol shards noting that the Luohans were "altogether superior in body and glaze to the wares found on the Manchurian sites."[107]

Writing in 1956, Sickman followed Gray's lead, remarking on the similarity with 12th Century wooden sculptures in the modeling of the garments, "the same realistic treatment of the soft, heavy materials and the same deep folds with sharp edges." Intriguingly, he notes that a similar Luohan had been reported in the mid-9th Century Foguang Temple (佛光寺) in Wutai Shan (五台山). He offers no source for this information, but continues with his commentary on the origins of their style, focusing on the two Luohans in the Met, "The facial types are purely Chinese; the heads show a knowledge of bone structure and anatomy rarely displayed in so clear a manner. The high cheek-bones and heavy Mongoloid fold above the eyes and the thick lips of the young Lohan all describe a type to be met in north China to-day. With his hands folded in his lap, his head thrown slightly back and an expression of intense concentration, he is as though practicing some Yogi breathing exercise conducive to meditation. In contrast, the elderly Lohan holding a sutra scroll in his left hand might well be a learned lecturer about to discourse on the doctrine. In these pottery Lohans there is no over-statement, no caricature, but a well-modulated, rational and sober expression of a religious concept–the possibility of salvation that is offered to all and the dignity of renunciation. The personal and emotional character of later Buddhism could not be better expressed."[108]

Like Gray, Sickman made the connection with the life-size lacquer heads, "They all possess a strong portrait quality and are modelled with great sensitivity. The characterization delves beneath the mere features and penetrates to a deeper,

---

107   Sickman and Soper, Op. Cit., pp. 101-2.
108   Sickman and Soper, Ibid., p. 102.

psychological portraiture expressive of spiritual states of being."
He saw clearly the sculptural stylistic link: "It may be that the
strikingly individual and portrait-like figures of Lohans that have
survived in north China are, in fact, only examples of established,
traditional types." Osvald Siren would later make a similar
connection while searching for the origins of a bust in a different
medium, the marble bust in the Rietberg Museum (**Fig.62**).
Noting that "the psychological undercurrent or approach to the
motif was of the same kind as in the Lohan statue," he went on
to argue that the sculptural comparators he had chosen "may be
characterized as remainders of a sculptural art which was based
on T'ang traditions and was re-kindled in remarkably free forms
with fresh vigour. They are in other words, excellent parallels of
the realistic trend in Chinese sculpture which seems to have been
of importance in the Liao period."[109]

Fig.62 *Bust of uniformed military officer, Chinese, from northwest Hebei Province, Liao dynasty (907-1125); marble, larger than life-size. Courtesy of the Rietberg Museum, Zurich*

From the mid-1960s the academic
and curatorial consensus gravitated
towards the Liao period, as carefully
summarized by Marion Wolf.[110] First,
Peter Swann put into plain words what
others had hinted at, that the Tang style
had been carried forward and developed
in the lands under Liao rule, where
Tang traditions of portraiture continued
"at their finest and a series of large
figures of Lohans in typical T'ang three
colour glaze has survived," adding for
good measure, "...technically, they are
masterpieces; artistically,... they have

---

109 Siren, Osvald, "The Chinese Marble Bust in the Rietberg Museum", *Artibus Asiae*, 1962, pp. 18-19.
110 Marion Wolf, Op. Cit., pp. 51-7.

an immediate personal impact; religiously they reflect a belief in an all-embracing personal salvation..."[111]

Then, as the Metropolitan Museum prepared to open its new Sackler rooms in the mid-1960s, Aschwin Von Lippe (1914-88), curator in the Department of Far Eastern Art, penned a precise state-of-play of the technical and sculptural aspects of the dating controversy:

"Reidemeister (1937) regards the Lohans... as part of the so-called Khitan or Jehol pottery which was produced in Jehol from T'ang times through the Liao, possibly even the Chin period. As sculpture he links them up with the Lohan of 1158[112], and with the Six Patriarchs of the Hosso School by Kokei in the Kofukuji in Nara from the end of the twelfth century....Analysis of the material and glaze undertaken in Boston confirm the Lohan as belonging to T'ang pottery...All this seems to justify dating the Lohan between A.D. 1000 and 1100, or from the tenth to the twelfth century."[113]

Another carved marble Luohan dated 1180 in San Francisco's Asian Art Museum reinforces this comparison.[114] Thus the caption under an image of one of the Luohan in the Met's Bulletin for May 1965 read: "*Life-sized glazed pottery Lohan of the Liao-Chin dynasties.*"

By the 1990s, the stylistic consensus had been solidly underpinned by the archaeological finds at Longquanwu (龍泉務). Indeed, the cumulative evidence of this new creative impulse led Jacques Giès, the Guimet's curator, triumphantly to declare that the Luohan statues "confirm that northern China, under the so-

---

111 Swann, Peter C., *The Art of China, Korea and Japan*, Frederick A. Praeger, New York, 1963, pp. 125, 143.

112 A carved marble Luohan dated 1186 then in the Rockefeller collection and now in Boston's Museum of Fine Arts.

113 von Lippe, Aschwin, Catalogue card No. 20.114, Metropolitan Museum of Art, New York.

114 A carved marble Luohan dated 1180 in the Asian Art Museum, SF, Accession No. B60S208.

called 'barbarian' foreign dynasties, was the centre of a flourishing Buddhist culture that had deserted the 'legitimist' China of the Song."[115] He might have added that they kept open the West-East corridor first driven by the Tang for the transmission of both worldly and otherworldly ideas. There is a lovely little Japanese temple in Fukuoka, the Jotenji (1242), which celebrates the return of its founder, Shoichi Kokushi, from "Song" China with the recipes for *udon* and *soba* noodles, and *manju* bean jam!

One by one, each of the museums fell quietly into line. While almost all continued to source the statues categorically, "reportedly" or "probably" to the caves at Yixian, old cards describing the Luohans as Tang dynasty (618-907) were replaced by new ones giving a Liao dynasty (907-1125) dating, or in a few cases a slightly more conservative Liao / Jin dynasty (907-1234) dating. Some supported this via reference to the discovery of the Longquanwu kilns, among them Donna Strahan and her colleagues at the Met, who boldly placed the Luohan very precisely in the reign of the emperor Shengzong (聖宗; r. 982-1031).[116] Their logic is slightly curious in that it assumes that the Longquanwu potters only gradually mastered the skills required to make massive statuary. If, as they argue, the three smaller statues found there represent prototypes, then the Luohans, being larger, must post-date them. Larger always follows smaller, and never vice versa? Be that as it may, for some two decades, until 2016, the Liao-Jin dating went unchallenged.

115 Giès, Jacques, *Revue du Louvre*, February 1998, pp. 13-14.
116 Strahan, Donna; Leidy, Denise Patry et al., *Wisdom Embodied: Chinese Buddhism and Daoist Sculpture in the Metropolitan Museum*, 2010, pp. 112-16.

5

STILL FISHING IN PERZYNSKI'S POND

"...models not only fix the mesh of the nets that the analyst drags through the material in order to explain a particular action, they also direct him to cast his net in select ponds, at certain depths, in order to catch the fish he is after."

Graham T. Allison[117]

ACHTLOHANBERG, Perzynski's sly re-christening of the mountain range bordering Yixian as "Eight Luohan Mountain", has survived unchallenged for far too long. Eight is a rather unconventional multiple for Luohans, but it was probably his best guess as to the number of statues that would eventually reach the market. Thus, first two are exhibited in Paris and one-and-a-half in Berlin. Then one is found for the British Museum and another for the ROM. Another goes to Japan and the Met buys a companion for the one it bought in Berlin. By 1920, the number had already reached seven-and-half, and Bosch Reitz, the curator at the Met in New York, had satisfied himself that there were actually ten not including fragments, albeit there was some confusion about

---

117   Allison, Graham T., *Essence of Decision–Explaining the Cuban Missile Crisis*, Little Brown, Boston, 1971, p.4

Fig.63 Luohan, Chinese, from Yixian, Hebei Province, Jin Dynasty (1115-1234). Stoneware with sancai glaze; H 118.1 cm excluding base. The Nelson-Atkins Museum of Art, Kansas City, Missouri: Purchase William Rockhill Nelson Trust, 34-6

a couple of candidates.[118] So, by the time Laurence Sickman found number nine for the Nelson-Atkins Museum, Perzynski's "*acht*" should have been looking a little suspect **(Fig.63 and Plate VIII)**. Not so; as late as 1993, when Marilyn Gridley wrote her dissertation, the myth still had a firm hold and she devoted several pages to justifying her belief in it, on both iconographic and stylistic grounds.[119]

She starts with two bald statements: "Eight individual sculptures came to the West after being removed from the cave in 1912 or earlier. Seven of those survive today."[120] Was she not aware of one going to the East? No, she had heard rumours, but describes them in a footnote as "never been confirmed".[121]

This is most odd since we saw in the last chapter that Bosch Reitz at the Met had publicly recognized the one in the Matsukata Collection as early as 1921, and knew enough about it to comment on its non-original head. This was later picked up by both Cornelia Harcum at the ROM and Bosch Reitz' successor

---

118   Bosch Reitz, Op. Cit., p. 14: "*...four others are owned by private collectors and dealers. In all ten are known besides a great many small fragments, several hands and feet, and baskets full of broken pieces.*"
119   Gridley, Marilyn, *Chinese Buddhist Sculpture Under the Liao; Free Standing Works in Situ and Selected examples from Public Collections,* International Academy of Indian Culture and Aditya Prakashan, New Delhi, 1993.
120   Gridley, Op. Cit., 1993, p. 183.
121   Gridley, Op. Cit,. 1993. p. 212, footnote 386, indicates that she may have allowed herself to be misled by a postscript in Richard Smithies' 1984 article.

Alan Priest.[122] Gridley does, however, acknowledge: "The number of Lohans in the original set at *I-chou* is a question of iconography which has never been satisfactorily answered. Eight is an unusual number for a group of Lohans..." only to continue "but I believe the *I-chou* sculptures may originally have been a set of eight."[123] She goes on to note that "one of the main tasks of the Lohans, then, is to protect the Law in the four quarters of the world, or the eight directions", and one unconvincing page later concludes: "Another reason for believing there may have only been eight to begin with is that the final count, now that several sculptures have been eliminated for various reasons, is eight. And those eight, as the above stylistic analysis has shown, are an integrated group of four pairs." A true believer, she was fishing in Perzynski's pond and Graham Allison would say that she had chosen her catch before she chose her net. She is not alone.

One of the last hold-outs among the supporters of the Tang dynasty dating was the independent scholar Richard Smithies. Indeed, Marilyn Gridley singled him out for special mention. Noting the seeming consensus recorded by Marion Wolf, she expressed her surprise that, "In 1984, Richard Smithies reopened the case with some startling and controversial propositions. He argued that they (the Luohans) were made in the early 10th Century in one of the traditional *sancai* production centres, either Chang'an (Xi'an–西安), or Taiyuan (太原)."[124]

This stubborn clinging to the Tang is a pity because, among more modern writers, Mr. Smithies has brought a rare passion to his research and has done more than most in excavating and collating the minutiae of the Luohans' story. This author would be the first to gratefully acknowledge his debt to Mr. Smithies for

---

122 Harcom, Cornelia, Op. Cit., 1923, p.4; and Alan Priest Op. Cit., 1943, Catalogue Number 70.
123 Gridley, Op. Cit., 1993, pp. 210-12.
124 Gridley, Op. Cit. 1995, p. 20.

all this spadework and, in his defence, would note that the essay referred to by Marion Wolf was published a year before the kilns at Longquanwu (龍泉務) had surrendered their secrets.

The title of Mr. Smithies' research essay, his first on the subject, is telling: *The Search for the Lohans of I-Chou (Yixian).*[125] He is totally convinced of Perzynski's hypothesis that the Luohans were hidden in the caves above Yixian to protect them from invading barbarian forces and he is eager to establish how they got there and from whence they originally came. Since details of the discoveries at the Longquanwu kilns had not yet been published at the time he was writing, we can forgive him for suggesting the pottery workshops at Taiyuan (太原) as the most likely place of manufacture. Founded under the Tang and sponsored by the state, they would have had the necessary technical skills. His alternative suggestion of the imperial works at Xi'an (西安) is, geographically speaking, a bit more far-fetched. Smithies notes both workshops would have had "close ties with the many monasteries and temples located on the mountain of Wutai (五台山)," and observes that the road connecting Taiyuan to Yixian runs along the valley of the Hu Tuo (滹沱) River to the north of Mount Wutai. Tying these strands together he posits the Luohan statues as an imperial gift of the late Tang to one of the temples at Mount Wutai, which were so revered by the monks there that they determined to hide them rather than risk losing them to the invading Khitan. It seemed to Smithies that "the guardians of the Lohans would have had more reason to fear the covetousness of the Khitan as new converts to Buddhism, rather than their destructiveness." In his view, the monks had to haul the statues east because Taiyuan to the south was still under attack by Song forces and because monks who had travelled the road previously

---

125   Smithies, Richard, "The Search for the Lohans of I-Chou (Yixian)", 1984, *Oriental Art* 30, no. 3, pp. 260-274.

knew of the existence of the caves along the way.

This is all very ingenious but, even if we were to accept an early 10th Century dating, does it hold water? As the crow flies, Taiyuan is 160 kilometres southwest of the temple complex at Mount Wutai, and Yixian is another 160 kilometres to the east. Having no wings, the Luohans would have had to travel considerably further, first following the river valleys for as far as they could by boat or raft, and then transferring to some other form of transportation for the ascent of the holy mountain. For hardy pack animals carrying component architectural ornaments such as roof tiles and finials wrapped in straw that would be perfectly feasible, but the size and weight of the Luohans militate against such a solution. They would have required a wagon or a sledge and much manhandling over steep and narrow rocky tracks. For an imperial gift nothing would have been impossible; no manpower and no effort would have been spared. However, for the monks to smuggle the statues eastwards intact through the Taihang Mountains (太行山) to Yixian would have required a miracle or two. Size and weight alone would have made moving them on the flat a logistical challenge, never mind hoisting them by hand up steep rocky slopes and over the lip of a cave in a sheer cliff. Not impossible, but not something to be undertaken lightly either openly by day or secretly by night.

As to why the statues were never recovered, Smithies argues that the chaos and conflict of the Five Dynasties period (907-960) made it impossible and that knowledge of the existence of the Luohans and the precise place of their concealment was lost with time. What Smithies fails convincingly to explain, however, is why, alone amongst all the treasures made of more precious materials with which the temples on Wutai Mountain were doubtless endowed, the monks would have chosen to spirit away only the terracotta Luohans. Sadly, and somewhat surprisingly, the ROM swallowed Smithies' version and reproduced it almost word-for-word, but without attribution, in its otherwise elegant coffee table volume *Homage to Heaven, Homage to Earth*.[126]

Several years later, in an essay on the Luohan in the Penn Museum, Smithies retreated from some elements of his original hypothesis.[127] He conceded that it had by then been accepted that the statues were made during the Liao dynasty (907-1125) "using techniques developed under the Tang", but oddly makes no reference to either the discovery of the kilns at Longquanwu or Marilyn Gridley's essay on the same. As to where they originally came from, he recalls that both Bosch Reitz and Laurence Sickman thought that they had been installed in the caves as places of pilgrimage, but disagrees with them. He remains convinced that they were hidden there for their protection and quotes Hobson's comment, "the natives apparently had a tradition that the lohans came to that locality in the Yuan dynasty, which may be near the truth, especially if, as suggested, the statues were brought there for sanctuary," conveniently forgetting that this was the elated Hobson of 1914 still partly under Perzynski's spell. There is no other source for this "tradition", and, as we have seen, a decade later, a by now more cautiously objective Hobson pointedly distanced himself from any such local sources.[128]

The problem with Smithies' work, and he is by no means alone in this, was that he was under the same spell. He wanted to believe Perzynski's tale. Thus, in his most recent commentary, while admitting that Perzynski did not see any complete Luohan *in situ*, he concludes that "Perzynski himself actually saw or was

---

126 Far Eastern Department, ROM, *Homage to Heaven, Homage to Earth: Chinese Treasures of the Royal Ontario Museum*, Toronto, 1992, pl. 101.

127 Smithies, Richard, "A Luohan from I-chou (Yixian) in the University of Pennsylvania Museum", 2001, *Orientations* 32, no. 2. pp. 51-56.

128 Hobson, R.L., "A New Chinese Masterpiece" in *the British Museum*, The Burlington Magazine, no. 25, May 1914, pp. 69-73.

reliably informed of at least six luohan before he left Yixian."[129]

Frankly, that is a bit rich, bearing in mind Perzynski's comment early on that "All the inhabitants of Yizhou only seem to think of misleading me." By the end of his visit, judging by the sarcasm with which he greeted his last informant, it is obvious that Perzynski had lost all patience and concluded that reports of other sightings were largely unreliable.

Friedrich Perzynski visited the caves at Yixian in 1912. Given the subsequent controversy over dating, it might seem extraordinary that some seventy years were to pass before any field studies were conducted there. The only person known to have visited in the meantime was the German art historian Otto Fischer in 1925, whose later comments, as we saw in the previous chapter, came without benefit of source. One other person who may have visited was Langdon Warner, who found a Luohan head while scouting in Beijing in late 1916. The head ended up in the Cleveland Museum whose curator,

Allen Whiting, gave an account of its origins to Perzynski some ten years later. (**Fig.64**) Perzynski subsequently wrote to Warner: 'Mr Whiting of the Cleveland Museum told me some days ago, when showing me his Lohan head, that you are the discoverer of the Lohan grottoes at Yizhou. I was quite amused and surprised. He furthermore told me that you got the Lohan head of the Cleveland Museum on the spot. Could you spare the time to explain?

Fig.64 Allen Whiting, Curator of Oriental Art at the Cleveland Museum. Public Domain

---

129 Smithies, Richard, in Hsu Hsiang-ling Eileen, *Monks in Glaze: Patronage, Kiln Origin, and Iconography of the Yixian Luohans*, Brill, 2016, Addendum, p. 206.

You know that I am quite anxious to have a few of your photos (made at Yizhou) which you promised to send. If you would be kind enough to add some remarks on the Lohan head etc, I would be extremely grateful. No need to say that I will mention my sources in my writing on the Lohan of Yizhou."[130]

"Amused and surprised"–I should think so! Surprised that Warner might have claimed credit for Perzynski's "discovery"; definitely, but even more amused that he might have claimed to have found a Luohan head on the spot since Perzynski knew full well that the Luohans had never been there. Viewed in this light the request for photographs is simply a tease and, as far as is known, Warner never furnished Perzynski with any. The head was later judged not to have come from the same group of statues. Ironically, it was one of Allen Whiting's successors as Curator of Oriental Art at Cleveland who candidly confessed, "When a curator comes back and says he discovered an important

Fig.65 Sherman Lee, Curator of Oriental Art at the Cleveland Museum.
Photograph © Mark Duncan

130 Letter from Friedrich Perzynski to Langdon Warner, dated 8 December 1926. I am indebted to Prof. Paul R. Goldin of The Penn for this reference from the Registrar's files at Cleveland Museum.

art work, he really means a dealer discovered it."[131] Perhaps Sherman Lee had this incident in mind. (**Fig.65**)

So why no other independent fieldwork? We need look no further than the fact that, in the 1920s, China was still in the throes of post-revolution internal strife; in the 1930s it was invaded by Japan; and thereafter came civil war. Survival aside, scholars such as Liang Sicheng (梁思成) and Lin Huiyin (林徽因), whom we met in the last chapter, were preoccupied with protecting China's surviving heritage rather than chasing after what had already disappeared. The great International Exhibition of Chinese Art at the Royal Academy in London in 1935-6, co-organized with the Chinese Government, included over eight hundred works from the Chinese National Collections. Inevitably, it also drew Chinese curators' attention to the scale of the seepage of valuable antiquities to the West. Thereafter, however, Chinese scholars had many other distractions and it was not until the 1990s, that research by Zhang Hongyin (張洪印), Director of the Yixian Bureau of Cultural Relics, pin-pointed the location of Perzynski's caves, and corroborated some of his findings. These included the location of the Longmen Temple (龍門寺) and the existence of two of the four steles he claimed to have read.

The first stele found by Zhang Hongyin in his 1997 field studies was one that is not mentioned in Perzynski's account. It was located lying in the grounds of an old Buddhist temple in Louting village (婁亭村) in the valley to the south and west of the caves in the cliff. Dated 1741, *The Record of the Longmensi (Dragon Gate Temple) on White Jade Mountain* was written by Sai'erdeng (賽爾登), Vice Chancellor of the Imperial Academy, who supervised the major repair and renovation of all Buddhist and Taoist sites on *Baiyushan* (白玉山), or White Jade Mountain,

---

131   Rogers, Mary Ann, "Sherman E. Lee", *Orientations*, Vol. 24:7, July 1993, p. 46.

northwest of Yizhou following that area's designation as the site of the imperial mausoleum in 1730. It mentions the Guanyin pavilion, which Perzynski had visited seventy years earlier, but neither Shanzi Grotto. nor other caves, nor any Luohans.[132] It does, however, record the older names of the area: White Jade Mountain was originally *Emoshan* (峨磨山); the temple founded there in the Song or Yuan was thus originally called Emosi (峨磨寺), and echoes survive today in the name of the valley, *Emeisigao* (峨嵋寺溝), several centuries after the mountain turned to White Jade and the temple became the Longmensi. Since Perzynski made no mention of these older names, it would appear that he did not see this stele.

Zhang Hongyin (張洪印) discovered a second stele, a well-preserved marble slab dated 1519, in a niche just below a cave in the cliff. Entitled *Record of the Successful Completion of the Images*, the inscription identified the site as the Shanzi Grotto visited by Perzynski and commemorated the generosity of Song Jun (宋均), a member of the Rear Unit of the Maoshan (茂山) Guard of the Daning (大寧) Regional Military Command, in donating religious statuary to local shrines. The images included a set of thirteen carved and gilt wooden statues, a Buddha and twelve Bodhisattvas, which took some eight years to complete and install in the grotto. Zhang Hongyin located a third stele near the cave, but did not have time either to decipher or to take a rubbing of its inscription. From their general description, these appear to be the same two steles that Perzynski found in this location.

However, Zhang Hongyin did not find the two other steles that Perzynski claimed to have seen near the Guanyin Pavilion, including the one with the Delphic declaration that, "All these

---

132 A full translation of the inscription on this stele and others found by Zhang Hongyin and Eileen Hsu Hsiang-ling is provided in Appendix II.

Buddhas came from far away." When Zhang Hongyin enquired about the existence of other steles, local villagers told him that they had buried several more to save them from the depredations of Red Guards during the Cultural Revolution. However, the fields were then under cultivation and he could not excavate to verify the claim. Zhang Hongyin published his findings, including the inscriptions from the two steles he had deciphered, in 2003.[133]

Despite finding neither inscriptions nor shards dateable to earlier than the Ming dynasty (1368-1644), he apparently saw no reason to question the legend, now well-established, that the Luohans had at some point been hidden in the caves.[134] More surprisingly, despite the very obvious stylistic differences between the Luohans and Ming examples, he allowed himself to be persuaded by the evidence of the shards and the 1519 stele that they belonged to that dynasty.

The next person to walk the ground, aided by Zhang Hongyin's helpful sketch map of the area (**Map 2**), was Dr. Eileen Hsu Hsian-ling, who visited Yixian in 2008 and again in 2011, and subsequently surprised the academic world by challenging the curatorial consensus on the Luohans' Liao dynasty dating in her book *Monks in Glaze: Patronage, Origin and Iconography of the Yixian Luohans*. There is so much else that is good in *Monks in Glaze* that the challenge comes as a bit of a shock. Dr. Hsu's depiction of local patterns of sponsorship and worship is a valuable contribution to our knowledge. Likewise her fascinating study of the rise and technical development of the *liuli* (琉璃) glazing of the architectural kilns, and in particular the workshops of the

---

133 Zhang Hongyin, "Yixian Louting Longmensi Shanzidong Diaochaji (Report of the Investigation of Shanzidong and Longmen Temple in Louting Village, Yixian County)", *Wenwu chunqiu*, 2003.2, pp. 56-60.

134 So well-established that it was included in a revised local gazetteer, *Yixian zhigao*, drafted by Shou Pengfei (1873-1961) in 1944. This also picked up the names *Baifowa* and *Bafowa*, 100 Buddha Valley and 8 Buddha Valley, which do not appear in the earlier 1747 gazetteer See Hsu, Op. Cit. p. 33.

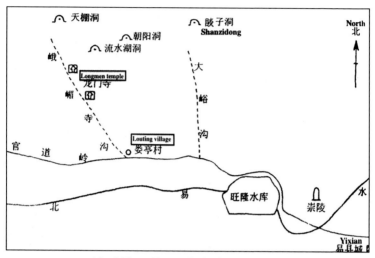

Map 2 Zhang Hongyin's sketch map of Yixian

Qiao (喬) family of Yangcheng (陽城), Shanxi during the late Ming. Regrettably, she seems to have allowed her admiration for the latter to colour her judgment on dating.

On her first visit to Yixian, Dr. Hsu was able to locate both the second and third steles found earlier by Zhang Hongyin, at the Shanzi Grotto and to photograph them. She noted that the third was dated 1667 and identified various donors and sponsors of later restoration work.[135] On her next visit, Hsu also found and photographed Zhang Hongyin's first, 1741, stele in the long-derelict grounds of the Longmen Temple. However, she seems to have had no more luck than Zhang Hongyin in locating the other two steles recorded by Perzynski, with the poetic landscape description linking the Longmen Temple with Shanzi Grotto, and the tantalizing text: "*All these Buddhas came from afar*". Perversely, Dr. Hsu does not admit to not finding either stele. Instead, in speculating about how the Luohans were transported to Yixian

---

135   Note: In the caption to both illustrations in Hsu's *Monks in Glaze* the date is mis-printed
        as 1677.

she suggests, "Its off-site location gave rise to the local lore that 'all these Buddhas' came from afar', and that they had arrived during the Yuan dynasty," and then continues in self-justification, 'Such word-of-mouth accounts were not uncommon in remote places where the majority of the population was illiterate, but these unofficial records are also helpful clues leading to some historical truth."[136] This is fascinating, but whose word and from whose mouth?

Hobson referred to a "local tradition", but Perzynski claimed only to have seen the words on a stele. Hsu suggests that "the Yuan connection…could very likely have come from the lamaist monks assigned to guard the imperial Xiling tombs (清西陵)," noting that Perzynski had stayed at the Yongfu Monastery (永福寺) there. However, the only oral tradition quoted by Perzynski related to Xuanzang (玄奘), the 7th Century itinerant monk. Perhaps, like Hobson–"the natives apparently had a tradition"– her memory played tricks on her.[137] Whatever the reason, she repeats the expression "local lore" two pages further on and, when she finally mentions Perzynski towards the end of the book, it sounds like a confirmation of her theory, "Friedrich Perzynski, the German explorer who introduced the Yixian Luohans to the outside world, identified the phrase (*those Buddhas*) in at least two inscriptions he saw."

Like Richard Smithies and many other scholars before him, Dr. Hsu is a believer. She has fallen under the spell spun by Perzynski's ingenious myth. Unlike Smithies, however, she does not think that the statues came from elsewhere and were placed in the caves for safekeeping. Rather, she believes that they were specifically commissioned to be placed within the cave shrine of Shanzi Grotto. Her faith in this theory is so strong that it is

---

136 Hsu, Op. Cit., pp. 67, 69 and 184.
137 Hobson, Op. Cit., 1925, p. 6.

unshaken either by her failure to find the two inscriptions mentioned above, or by the absence of any shards in the caves that can be dated to earlier than the Ming. It is almost as though she wraps the Luohans in Ming mantles because she cannot find any earlier clothes in the wardrobe.

Dr. Hsu opens her re-appraisal with a legitimate question: why are there no other examples of such *sancai* between the Liao (907-1125) and the Ming (1368-1644)? In doing so, she unwittingly repeats the argument of the Parisian critics which so irritated Hobson in 1914. The latter, while accepting that uniqueness might lead to differences of opinion as to the statues' age, was categoric that, technically, the glazes used were wrong for the later dates they suggested. The fact that Tang-type glazes reappeared in the Ming was, in his view, not sufficient in itself to justify a later date, when stylistically the statues were very different. This author could not agree more and suggests that the rhetorical question affords no support to the rest of Dr. Hsu's theory.[138]

Stripping away all the trimmings, Dr. Hsu's theory that the Luohans must have come from the caves above Yixian, rests on a single shaky leg, and that is her interpretation of an inscription on one of the steles seen by Perzynski, and located again by both Director Zhang and herself. This is the *Record of the Successful Completion of the Images* stele dated 1519, describing the benevolent deeds of Song Jun (宋均), whom Dr. Hsu promotes as a member of the *"wealthy and prestigious"* Maoshan Guard, and detailing the various statues and images that he commissioned over several years, and the different temples to which he donated them.

Dr. Hsu prides herself on her epigraphy and, to her credit, has

---

138   Hobson, Op. Cit., 1915, p. 79.

carefully deciphered almost every character on each of the steles she found, despite their being worn in places. She has also been meticulous in placing square brackets around any characters that, while illegible, can be reasonably adduced from context, and using empty square brackets to designate portions that are indecipherable. She uses the same simple devices to indicate the same in her faithful English translations. The following passage is the relevant portion of the inscription on the stele of 1519, as translated and formatted by Dr. Hsu:

"Beginning in the sixth year of the Zhengde reign-period [1511], his efforts [in this regard] continued uninterruptedly, nor were they limited to a single one place. [In that year, he sponsored the] making [of] a Buddhist image for the Guanyin Hall of the Emo temple on the West Mountain; in the seventh year [1512], [he sponsored the] making [of] an image for the Three Officials (Sanguan) Daoist Temple in this prefecture, a luohan figure for the Xingguo Buddhist temple in this prefecture, and an image of Maitreya for his own family. The following year [1513], he commissioned three large Buddha images for Chuiyun temple in Xiahuanghao village, one image of a Daoist deity Zhenwu [for a temple] in Dongguan (Eastern Gate), in the eastern part of the prefecture, and a large Buddha image for the Wulihe temple. Moreover, [he donated] thirteen [wooden] sculptures consisting of twelve Complete Enlightenment Bodhisattvas and one Buddha, all magnificently gilded with bright and dazzling appearances. [For their installation], workers were ordered to prepare niches, one for each of [the thirteen sculptures]. [The thirteen figures were then] sent to the mountains.

On the Hundred Flowers Mountain about 40 li (20 km) northwest of the Yizhou seat, there is a grotto named Shanzidong. A body of water inside it never dries out; it is cool and tastes fresh all year round. The mountain is high and precipitous and the tall trees grow unevenly. The cliffs are steep ad jagged as if they were cut by a sword and chipped with an axe. This wonderfully strange and stunningly beautiful landscape is difficult to draw by even the most skilful artisans. This is a place where visitors become oblivious of the outside world and forget to return home. Indeed this is the site for ancient recluses and modern pursuers of immortality. The grotto is large enough to accommodate a hundred people.

[I], Monk Daojinshan of the Bajian village, whose lay surname was Wen, practiced in this mountain site for many years, living a frugal and simple life. [I[have endured hardship and loneliness, and given up family life, love and material desires. Together with [my] friend Qi Yuan, we built a three-bay [worship] hall in the grotto, its beams and columns beautifully painted. [In this hall, we] practiced Daoist and Chan meditation and burned incense to pray for the blessing of the people, thus [undertaking] an enterprise for public well-being.

The making of the images [under the sponsorship of] Song Jun, began in the sixth year of the Zhengde reign-period (1511). and was completed in the fourth month of the fourteenth year of the Zhengde reign-period (1519) with the dispatch of the images to the grotto (i.e. the Shanzidong) and their safe installation [therein], thus successfully completing this exalted task."

There follows an extended description of the author's reason for proposing that Song Jun's philanthropy be recorded for posterity, an encomium, the process of budgeting for the work, the drafting of the text and the identities of both the calligrapher and the carvers of the tablet.

The division of this part of the inscription into four "paragraphs" is Dr. Hsu's and it makes both for easier reading and simpler description of how she arrives at her conclusion. She acknowledges that the Chinese characters used to describe the gilt wooden carvings of twelve Bodhisattvas and a Buddha in the first paragraph put the medium beyond doubt. However, she goes on to argue that *"images"* in the last paragraph must refer to a different set, because they are separated from the gilt wooden carvings by what she terms two "prosaic" paragraphs. Further, she argues that these "images" must be the Luohans because they took eight years to produce, even though there is no reference to their being made of clay or glazed in *sancai* (三彩).[139] That is tenuous at best. It is also surprising because Dr. Hsu must be aware from her epigraphic studies that parenthetical passages are commonplace.

Any objective reading accepts the "prosaic" passages as parenthetical because, while the images in the paragraph preceding the landscape description are both numbered and described, but not dated, those in the final one are dated, but neither numbered nor described. Indeed, it is the final paragraph that identifies the dates of commissioning and installation that are missing from the first. The number and medium having been described in the first, there is no need to repeat them in the last. This is best demonstrated by running the first and fourth paragraphs together, and removing Hsu's square brackets for ease of reading:

'Moreover, he donated thirteen wooden sculptures consisting of twelve Complete Enlightenment Bodhisattvas and one Buddha, all magnificently gilded with bright and dazzling appearances. For their installation, workers were ordered to prepare niches, one for each of the thirteen sculptures. The thirteen figures were then sent to the mountains. The making of the images under the sponsorship of Song Jun, began in the sixth year of the Zhengde reign-period (1511).and was completed in the fourth month of

---

139   Hsu, ibid. pp. 26-7.

the fourteenth year of the Zhengde reign-period (1519) with the dispatch of the images to the grotto (i.e. the Shanzidong) and their safe installation therein, thus successfully completing this exalted task.'

Had the reference been to a separate set of terracotta, it is difficult to believe that they would not have been described, and that neither their number, nor the medium of their production would have been recorded on the stele. Set aside that for a donation of this significance, we would have to assume both that a provincial military man had access to imperial workshops and, on his soldier's salary, could afford such sculptures.

Hsu looks to the second stele found by Perzynski at Shanzi Grotto to reinforce her thesis. Dated 1667, it records a later renovation of the grotto and its images, but again there is no reference to Luohans, to terracotta figures or to *sancai* (三彩) glazing. To argue from her reading that "the 'multiple Buddhas' from the east and west caverns" means the *sancai* Luohans is simply disingenuous; doubly so given that she had already provided the dimensions of the grotto and reproduced Perzynski's photograph of the main cave. The cave is big, but not big enough to house thirteen, let alone sixteen life-sized Luohans. The narrow two-level side platforms are not wide enough to hold them, never mind their rocky plinths; nor are the twin "uvular" caverns behind the main altar. Ironically, she admits this, noting, "As the sizes of these caverns are not large enough to accompany (sic) sixteen large luohan sculptures, they may have been used as storage chambers for those needing repair."[140]

The admission glosses over an important detail. The 1519 stele is very precise and relates that workers were tasked to prepare individual "niches" for the gilt-wood Buddha and the

---

140   Hsu, Op. Cit. p.20, where Shanzidong's dimensions are given as 38 m deep, 6.5 m wide with an opening 8 m high and 4 m wide; see also p. 23. See also figs. 1.11, 1.13 and 1.14.

twelve bodhisattvas. No niches are evident in the photographs of the main cave, but Dr. Hsu did find traces of painted aureoles on the walls of the eastern uvular cavern and her photograph of this does show the shallowest of roughly-hewn recesses above a narrow platform that might qualify for the term. Again, they are neither big nor deep enough to accommodate the larger-than-life-size Luohan statues, but slimmer gilt-wood images might have fit.

In her concluding chapter, Dr. Hsu describes the *Record of the Successful Completion of the Images* stele as being "at the heart of my research findings." That is unfortunate; remove the heart, and the body beautiful turns to dust. It is doubly unfortunate because Dr Hsu's study of the Qiao (喬) family workshops at Yangcheng (陽城), Shanxi during the late Ming is a valuable contribution. However, in inviting comparison of several of their statues with the Luohans, she allows admiration to blind her to their obviously different inspiration, artistry, glazing and quality of execution. She quotes Hobson's magisterial verdict, "...there is no parallel in the conventionalized Ming statuary with such works as these..."[141], but dismisses it, "Scholarship on religious art has advanced considerably over the last century, bringing to light some remarkable statues in Ming and Qing temples." She may well be right about the advance of scholarship, but looking at the examples she provides in support of her claim, the author is reminded of Sickman's description, "mannered, dry and uninspired."[142] She faults Gridley's stylistic comparison of the Luohans with the statues excavated at Longquanwu (龍泉務) on the basis that the latter are triangularly slimmer, and yet excuses herself for no lesser differences in decorative scheme and glazing technique between the Yixian Luohans and the Ming

---

141   Hobson, R.L., *A New Chinese Masterpiece etc* Op. Cit., p. 70.
142   Sickman and Soper, Op. Cit., p. 102.

dynasty Nanyang (南陽) group "as most likely due to different visual sources".[143]

Dr Hsu devotes two whole chapters to iconography, with an extended excursus tracing the evolution of Luohan representation via Guanxiu's (貫休) caricatures, rock carvings in *Yanxiadong* (煙霞洞) and *Feilafeng* (飛來峰), the Misty Twilight and Flying-In Peak grottoes near Hangzhou (杭州), through Dunhuang (敦煌) murals, painted clay temple sets in Shanxi (山西) and Shandong (山東), and Yuan dynasty paintings to the copy books of the Tibetan Jivarama. (**Fig.66**) It is a fascinating, highly erudite and wide-ranging disquisition. She leads us through the garden, not omitting the maze, and pauses for breath at end of the first chapter with, "As large, low-fired, glazed ceramic sculptures, the Yixian Luohans retain the essential formal characteristics of the Guanxiu tradition with necessary modifications. Through sophisticated facial modelling inspired by the post-Yuan development of luohan imagery and Tibetan

Fig.66 Rock carvings at Feilaifeng near Hangzhou. Author's photograph

143   Hsu, Op.Cit., chapter 3 *The Efflorescence of Ming Sancai Sculpture,* p.89.

hierarch portraiture, the kiln artisans successfully manifest the luohan's (sic) transcendental spiritual quality and power of deep concentration."

In the second chapter, she continues the journey through Yuan dynasty court paintings and portraiture and finally attempts, with some success, to match each of the terracotta Luohans with a counterpart image from Guanxiu (貫休).[144] She concludes that "the luohan figures from Yixian...are evidence that the imperial artisans drew on models that featured both the Guanxiu luohan and Tibetan Buddhist images....they created an assembly of ceramic sculptures that embody post-Yuan cultural transformation and iconographic synthesis."

The non-specialist reader can be excused for feeling a little confused, but what the author finds more puzzling than the winding path to this destination is the one broad evidentiary avenue that she declines to explore. The life-like Luohans in the gloom of the grottoes at *Yanxiadong* (煙霞洞) are contemporaries of the equally life-like lacquer heads of the Liao dynasty (907-1125), and the stoneware statues of Inner Mongolia. They are only a generation away from Guanxiu's iconic portraits, yet they share none of that artist's grotesque exaggeration. Where he steered towards caricature, they aim for realism and the spark of inner life. With all due respect to Dr Hsu, the sculptors who created the Luohans belong to this latter family; they are neither descendants nor even close relatives of Guanxiu.

It remains only to note that Dr. Hsu mentions, but deals somewhat cavalierly with the scientific evidence enumerated in the previous chapter. She describes the results of the 1987 thermo-luminescence testing of the MFA Boston's Luohan as

---

144   Hsu, ibid., pp. 159-82. Hobson, Op. Cit., 1925, p. 4, had been the first to attempt a match: *"Our statue, to judge from its attitude, appears to be that of Sohinda Sonja (in Chinese Su Pin t'o) seated in contemplation with folded hands..."*

"inconclusive". (A footnote explains that a sample from the body "appears to have been last fired during the Ming dynasty rather than the Liao," while that from the head was different in composition but "appears to have last been fired in antiquity.") However, she dismisses the later results from tests on the Luohans in the Penn museum and the Met, citing variations arising from environmental factors. That nothing can come between her and her Ming *idée fixe* is testimony to the enduring power of myth, a myth originating in the colourful account of a German Sinologist-salesman.

Nevertheless, we should be grateful to both Director Zhang Hongyi and Dr. Hsu. While the findings of their field work go some way to corroborate and clarify Perzynski's account of his visit to Yixian, they add absolutely no evidence to support his story that the statues came from, or were temporarily housed in the caves there. Rather their testing of the fragments and reading of the steles add more weight to the notion that the caves never contained any pottery or ceramic figures from earlier than the Ming. Which begs the question: if the Luohans were never there, where did they come from?

In his 2011 lecture at the Penn Museum, Derek Gillman, at that time President and Executive Director of the Barnes Foundation, offered a very different solution to this riddle.[145] Ignoring all other arguments, but accepting a proximate 11th-12th Century dating, and coyly tiptoeing around Perzynski's account, Gillman focused his enquiry on from whence the Luohans originally came and pulled a ruined Buddhist temple out of his hat. Superficially, Changle Temple (昌樂寺) is not a bad choice. It sits at the entrance to Xiangtangshan Grotto (響堂山) at Drum Mountain, 260 kilometers south of Beijing, and would have provided a

---

145 Gillman, Derek, *The Penn's Glazed Luohan in Context–Chinese Buddhist Art During the 10th–13th Centuries*, a lecture given at the Penn Museum, 8 August 2011.

convenient resting place for pilgrims visiting grottoes. Gillman ingeniously implies that the statues in the temple were thus hidden in plain sight, their beauty overshadowed by the greater wonders within the mountain. He was also doubtless aware that neither the French sinologist Edouard Chavannes nor the German architect Ernst Boerschmann (**Fig.67**) had included Xiangtangshan in their respective surveys, and the existence of the Luohans could therefore have gone unnoticed by Western scholars.

Fig.67 German architect Ernst Boerschmann (1873-1949), who surveyed much of China's built heritage in the early part of the 20th Century. Public Domain

In support of this theory, Gillman noted that Changle Temple was originally built in the Tang, but renovated in 1159 during the Jin (金), which roughly fits within the parameters of both sets of thermo-luminescence dating. The temple also had a Luohan hall, although this was destroyed by fire in the 1950s. Its 12th Century renovation coincided with the Jin Emperor's urgent need to raise money for a naval war against the Song, and Gillman notes that temples were a popular franchise. It is a little unclear to this author how he reconciles the Jin Emperor's shortage of funds with the donation of a set of expensive life-size *sancai* (三彩) glazed terracotta Luohans, but we will let it pass *pro tem*. While little remains of the temple today save for the ruins of a pagoda (**Fig.68**), the latter quite coincidentally was faced with *sancai* tiles, and a kiln capable of producing ornate and technically difficult *sancai* pieces has been excavated at Guantai, Handanxian (觀台,邯鄲縣) only 24 kilometres south of Xiantangshan. (**Fig.69**) Chinese archaeologists have demonstrated that the kiln flourished during the years 1150 to 1220, which again fits roughly within the dates

*Fig.69 Architectural finial, Jin dynasty
(1115-1234) stoneware with sancai glaze;
excavated from Guantai kilns, Hebei. After
Beijing daxue kaoguxi, 1997, plate 32*

*Fig.68 A pagoda, all that remains of Tang
dynasty (618-907) Changle Temple, near
Xiangtangshan Grotto, Shanxi. Public
Domain*

derived by thermo-luminescence testing.

Xiangtangshan Grotto itself has a still longer history, dating to the Northern Qi (北齊) of the 6th Century. Its decorations were sponsored by that dynasty and benefited over the centuries from numerous other donations. Western interest in Chinese sculpture from the end of the 19th Century led to Chinese dealers searching far and wide for saleable examples and, as Gillman was happy to tell his Philadelphian audience, the beautiful statues sold by C.T. Loo to the Penn Museum in 1909-10, were taken from Xiangtangshan. Although he did not mention them, so also were several others sold by C.T. Loo and Charles Vignier to the Freer and elsewhere.

Gillman's thesis has some logic on its side. It is also quite a clever one because it is relatively easy to reconcile with both the known and provable facts and those that are only reported in Perznski's account and thus less easily verifiable. It is almost as if Gillman was reluctant to throw away the safety net provided by the German's tale. Although he did not try to demonstrate this on the night, he could, for instance, have argued that the removal of the Penn's huge statues from Xiangtangshan and their transportation to Beijing convincingly illustrate that there was no logistical barrier to moving the large and heavy Luohans over such long distances, and that a network of agents, carriers and conniving officials was already in place before 1913. It is surely no coincidence that the first statues from Xiangtangshan appeared on the market so soon after the railway line connecting Beijing and Hankou was completed. It runs only 30 kilometres east of the grottoes and, as we know from Perzynski, it had a spur line into Yixian and Lianggezhuang (梁各庄), the village nearest to the Western Tombs. The Commandant responsible for the protection of the tombs could well have been a key link in the chain, because Yizhou is the last major town on the road north to Beijing. You will recall from Perzynski's account that the Commandant was aware of looting, but apparently willing to remove the Luohan from the Yamen to a temple and then turn a blind eye should Perzynski have subsequently purchased it. The Yamen with its multiple discreet courtyards would have provided the perfect staging post for pieces en route to the capital, reducing the risk of dealers having too many pieces on their premises at one time.

Similarly, the suggestion that the Luohans were actually from Xiangtangshan does not conflict with Perzynski's observations in Yixian. There can be little doubt that independent enterprising villains at Luoting Village (娄亭村) and elsewhere, made redundant when shortage of funds halted work on the emperor Guangxu's mausoleum, and knowing of the new demand for antiquities, went foraging on their own account–"*Frost und Hunger zerreiben alle Ehrfrucht*" ("Cold and hunger erase all reverence").[146] Hence the Commandant's complaints and the trail of debris noted by Perzynski in the caves and on the paths leading from the caves he visited. While he wanted to believe that the fragments came from damaged Luohans, they more likely came from other lesser sculptures looted by villagers from these local shrines. Similarly, the fragments in the Yamen, if in fact Perzynski saw any there, could have come from those Luohans that did not survive their long journey from Xiangtangshan intact. Finally, the fact that two of the Luohans were originally displayed without a base, but that C.T. Loo was later able to supply them, suggest that, while there may have been problems of coordination, there was a single organized chain of transmission. Perzynski may have been an accurate witness to only a small part of the process and may have drawn false conclusions. However, those who actually controlled it would have had no interest in contradicting him. So, Gillman's speculative theory is plausible and opens up new possibilities. Unfortunately, it founders on dating.

While Changle Temple (昌樂寺) was built in the Tang dynasty and had a Luohan hall before that burned down in the 1950s, its major renovation was carried out under the Jin, not the Liao, i.e. it post-dates the Liao. The finds excavated from the kiln site at nearby Guantai (觀台) that Gillman refers to do demonstrate that it was capable of producing technically difficult, decorative *sancai* architectural elements. The only fly in this ointment, once again, is dating. Chinese archaeologists have demonstrated that this kiln flourished between 1150 and 1220, i.e. during the Jin dynasty. Thus, while the logistics might be plausible, and the

---

146 Perzynski, Op. Cit., p.144.

coincidence of other major statues being sourced by C.T. Loo from Xiangtangshan might sound attractive, in order to accept Gillman's thesis we would have to reject the near consensus that has emerged on the Luohans' Liao dynasty origins. As we shall see shortly, recent research on the clay used in the Guantai kilns has further undermined his theory.

Gillman delivered a revised version of his theory in a lecture to the Oriental Ceramic Society two years later in London. By that time, his preference for the statues' original location had shifted northwards from Xiangtangshan to Daqingshou Temple (大慶壽寺), the Temple of Celebrating Longevity founded by the Jin emperor Shizong (世宗; r. 1161-89) in 1186 during the building of the Jin's new southern capital, Zhongdu (中都), in present day Beijing.

He paints a convincing picture of time and place, coupling imperial extravagance on the construction of the new city with the vigorous reassertion of Chan Buddhism in northern China in this period. While copper was in short supply, this was a time of lavish sponsorship, when no expense would be spared on sculpting sacred images to adorn temples and monasteries. He continues to promote Guantai (觀台) as the source of the fine glazed architectural components favoured by the court, but is prepared to concede that the statues might have been made at Longquanwu (龍泉務) with the assistance of skilled sculptors brought in especially for the task, noting that, "The latter possibility geographically aligns temple, sculpture and kilns." He reinforces his Jin dating, relying on the expertise of Nigel Wood. Pointing to the Luohans' pale red lips, he notes that "iron-red and manganese-iron-black lead glazes were first employed in China in the second half of the 12th Century, appearing in Cizhou wares, predictably at Guantai during its third period, 1149-1219," and concludes categorically, "The luohans can, therefore be no earlier than the mid-12th Century."[147]

Unfortunately, Daqingshou Temple (大慶壽寺) no longer exists, which radically reduces the scope for testing Gillman's thesis. The main halls were destroyed by fire in 1538, leaving only the two reliquary pagodas standing, a nine-storey one for the great Abbot Hai Yun (海雲; 1203-57), spiritual adviser to Khublai Khan, and its seven-storey companion for his disciple Ke'an (可庵). (**Fig.70**) As a mark of respect, the Great Khan had ordered that the new walls of Khanbaliq be built thirty paces away from the pagodas. No such niceties clouded the judgment of socialist town planners and, in 1955, the familiar landmarks were demolished over the strenuous objections of Liang Sicheng (梁思成) to make way for the westward extension of Chang'an Avenue. A statue of the Abbot discovered within is now in the Capital Museum. (**Fig.71**)

Fig.70 The twin reliquary pagodas of Daqingshou Temple, Beijing, before they were demolished in 1955. Public domain

147 Gillman, Derek, "The Imperial Luohans of Zhongdu and the Reassertion of Chan (Zen) Buddhist Influence in North China", a lecture given on 3 November 2013, *Transactions of the Oriental Ceramic Society*, London, pp. 41-52.

With apologies for this digression, Gillman's choice of Daqingshou Temple (大慶壽寺) is nevertheless an attractive one and should not be casually discounted. However, while he has demonstrated a willingness to shift the location of the Luohans' original home, he cannot quite bring himself to relinquish the romance of removal to the caves for protection against pillage. Rather he suggests that they were moved to Longmen Temple (龍門寺) by river after the Mongols forced the Juyong pass (居庸關) in 1213, arguing

Fig.71 The statue of Hai Yun, Abbot of Daqingshousi (1203-57), found beneath the reliquary pagoda there in 1955. Courtesy of the Capital Museum, Beijing

that they would have been safer there than in any larger garrison town that would have been targeted by the invading army. Ironically, like Dr. Hsu, he refers to the "local tradition" that the Luohans were brought to Yixian during the Yuan, citing Hobson who, as we have pointed out earlier, somehow absorbed this idea from Perzynski's speculations rather than any other source.

Amongst recent writers about the Luohans, Gillman is not alone in suggesting that researchers should look further afield than Yixian, and there may be many other candidates than the Changle and Daqingshou temples with some link to the Liao or Jin dynasties. Once we remove Perzynski's blinkers, all sorts of other possibilities present themselves, one of which was revived when a tenth Luohan surfaced unexpectedly in France in 1998 (**Fig.72 and Plate IX**).

Imagine the mixture of surprise, delight and awe experienced

Fig.72 The Luohan Tamrabhadra; Liao dynasty (907-1125); H 105 cm excluding base. Courtesy of Musée Guimet; Photo © PMN-Grand Palais (MNAAG, Paris) / Thierry Olivier

by Christie's specialist team on their first encounter with the missing monk. In Colin Sheaf's words, "When it emerged from an old crate, its overwhelming sense of calm made an immediate impression, for it represents a rare brief moment when the modeling of Chinese ceramic sculpture reached the peaks achieved by Buddhist sculpture in other media, notably stone and bronze."[148]

As to its own history, in Richard Smithies' words, "The only information forthcoming was that it has been in a private collection since the early part of the century."[149] A private sale was negotiated with a Hong Kong collector, T.T. Tsui, who magnanimously agreed to gift it to the Musée Guimet when, anecdotally, administrative difficulties were encountered in securing an export license. While similar in size, posture, life-like expression and many other respects to the other statues, the colouring and pattern of its garments do not match theirs, and this has led some to suggest that it may have been an early replacement for a damaged original, but there is no doubt as to dating, nor that he belongs to the brethren. Comparison by the Conservateur Général, Jean-François Jarrige, with Song etchings of the eighteen Arhats has also given us his name, Danmoluobatuo (Sanskrit: *Tamrabhadra*), which derives from Sri Lanka where his cousin, the Buddha, sent him at the

148 Sheaf, Colin, *A Gift for the Guimet*, in Christie's Magazine, Jan/Feb 1998, p.20.
149 Smithies, Op. Cit., 2001, p.33.

head of a large number of other monks.

Three years later, a very similar mixture of surprise, delight and awe must have been felt by Maria Menshikova, the newly-appointed curator of Chinese decorative arts at the State Hermitage Museum in St. Petersburg, when she opened the door of a storeroom that had remained locked for many years, and found a sackcloth bundle with no label. Perzynski's "Priest" had been waiting for her for half-a-century. (**Fig.73 and Plate X**) (The American art historian Stanley Abe confirmed the sighting in 2007.)[150] Lovingly

Fig.73 Perzynski's "Priest" following restoration - bust of Liao Dynasty sancai Luohan from Yixian; H 54 cm. The State Hermitage Museum, St. Petersburg, Inv. No. VF-3930; Photograph © The State Hermitage Museum, St. Petersburg. Photo by Alexander Lavrentyev

restored–a "nerve-wracking experience" as she recalls it–the long-lost bust believed to have been destroyed in the bombing of Berlin, is now on public display.[151]

In an exemplary instance of international cooperation, material from both newly-emerged statues was brought together for scientific examination by specialists from China, France, Russia

150 Abe, Stanley, in Rujivacharakul Vimalin edit., *Collecting China: The World, China and a Short History of Collecting,* University of Delaware Press, 2011, p. 110, footnote 88.

151 Menshikova, Maria, "The Arhat from I-chou", *Transactions of the State Hermitage,* 39 (2008), pp. 114-118. Menshikova, then Senior Research Fellow and curator of Chinese decorative arts at the Oriental Department had been scheduled to give a talk entitled *Date, History and Restoration of a Ceramic Lohan Sculpture from Yizhou* at the School of Oriental and African Studies, London on 1 November 2013, but it was cancelled "*due to visa issues*". When she eventually delivered it in March the following year, she said that there were no records of how the Luohan reached the Hermitage, but conceded that it probably arrived in 1945 or 1946.

and the United Kingdom. The result of this joint investigation threw new light on both the age and location of the production of the Luohans. The technical analysis, while complex, can be summed up fairly simply. It showed beyond all reasonable doubt that the clay in samples from the Guantai (觀台) kilns was totally unlike that used in the Guimet and Hermitage Luohans. Both of the latter had been produced using quite a rare clay that is found in a relatively small deposit just to the west of Beijing, i.e. close to both the kiln site excavated at Longquanwu (龍泉務), and Liuliqu (琉璃渠), where glazed tiles are produced to this day.[152] It would seem that Derek Gillman had had early warning of these findings, when he came to revise his Guantai theory.

To return to the Guimet's new prize, in announcing its acquisition in *Arts Asiatique,* Jacques Giés made passing reference to a doubt raised by Dr. Otto Kummel in an illustrated essay he wrote to accompany Perzynski's Berlin exhibition of 1913-14.[153] In that article, Dr. Kummel suggested that the statues possibly came from either Yixian in Hebei, which Perzynski had visited, or another Yixian county–similar in sound, but a different Chinese character, (義縣 vs 易縣)–in Liaoning province (遼寧) some 450 kilometres east-northeast of Beijing.[154] Liaoning's Yixian is home to the Wanfotang (萬佛堂) Grottoes and a number of Liao dynasty temples, but the coincidence of a similar sounding place name aside, it is not clear what drove Dr. Kummel to make this connection. The tonal coincidence could have confused Perzynski's Japanese acquaintance, or Perzynski himself, and perhaps Dr. Kummel wished to do no more than raise a small doubt about his countryman's story, or cover his academic bets. It is likely that two years before Perzynski's exhibition,

---

152   Wood et al, Op. Cit., 2015, pp. 35-36.
153   *Arts Asiatique*, tome 53-1998, pp. 71-2.
154   Kummel, Op. Cit., 1914, p. 458.

Dr. Kummel would have seen another exhibition, that of Ernst Boerschman's drawings and photographs, in the same hall at the *Kunstgewerbemuseum*. So he could well have seen Boerschman's photographs of Linyang Temple (靈巖寺) in Shandong, and its lively Luohan hall, and possibly this triggered the thought. Be that as it may, the suggestion was repeated by Jacques Giès in the more recently published Musée Guimet catalogue, without either attribution or further elaboration.[155]

Could it be that Perzynski went to the wrong place? That is an intriguing thought but if, as the next chapter will discuss, the aim of his informant was either to get him out of the way or to divert attention from the real source, it would not really matter to which Yixian he went because both trails were equally false. The problem with even the more recent research summarized in this chapter, as suggested in its opening quotation, is that the authors may be using different analytical nets, but they are all still fishing in Perzynski's pond.

---

155   Giés, Op. Cit. 1998, pp. 13-14.

6

RESCUED FROM THE RUBBLE

"I have wound my way through a jungle of lies and am on the track of only half the truth. In China, nobody gets to know the whole truth"

Friedrich Perzynski[156]

AS EVERY spy-master, spook and espionage author understands, all good cover stories, or what the late John le Carré called "legends", rely on verifiable circumstantial facts to camouflage a significant fiction. Perzynski based his legend on a real but fruitless visit to Yixian. The circumstantial details have stood the test of time and, even more recently, have been in large part corroborated by investigations in the field. He did visit Yixian. He did scramble up the steep slopes of the range of hills surrounding the Western Tombs. He did reach a number of almost inaccessible caves. He did find some ancient steles. He did find a few fragments of broken sculpture of uncertain date. He did meet the extraordinary cast of characters he describes. The significant fiction at the core of his tale is his claim that, while in Yixian, he saw some of the *sancai* (三彩) glazed terracotta Luohans. He did not, nor did he find any tangible evidence of

---

156 Perzynski, Op. Cit., p.151: *Ich habe mich durch ein Dschungel von Lugen hindurchgewunden, bin der halben Wahrheit auf der Spur. Die ganze Wahrheit erfahrt niemand in China.*

their ever having been there.

There have always been some who doubted parts of his tale, but they have been far outnumbered by believers. The inconsistencies, sleights of hand, the give-aways have always been there, and they have been reinforced by Director Zhang Hongyin (張洪印) and Dr. Hsu's failure to find key inscriptions and any *sancai* shards or fragments dating from the Liao dynasty. While the absence of proof is not proof of absence, it is past time that we revisit the riddle of the statues' origins, ignoring Perzynski's tall tale, and attempt to reconstruct what actually happened in Beijing when the Luohans were rescued from the past. A quick review of his and more recent attempts to explain away different aspects of the mystery will help focus minds on the key components.

Whatever his motives, the theory advanced by Perzynski was ingenious: the Luohans were very old, possibly from the Tang dynasty (618-907); nobody had seen them because they had been hidden in the caves; they had been taken there from an unspecified temple, possibly since destroyed, to save them from destruction; but only eight survived the journey and some of those were broken when bandits tried to take them back down the mountain.

This idea of sacred images being saved from the clutches of barbarian invaders was a romantic notion that would be very acceptable to lovers of art and historians alike, not least because it left their real origins shrouded in mystery. Perzynski did not provide answers to all parts of the riddle, but those that he offered were plausible.

Among contemporary scholars, Richard Smithies is the most closely aligned to Perzynski, believing implicitly that the Luohans were transported to the caves at Yixian to keep them out of harm's way. Until relatively recently, he was also an adherent of the early 10th Century Tang school of dating and suggested the kilns at either Taiyuan or Xi'an as the most likely place of manufacture. He has since conceded that the statues date from the Liao dynasty (907-1125), but has not foresworn his theory that they were an imperial gift to one of the monasteries on Mount Wutai despite the nearly impossible logistics that would have been involved in getting them from thence to Yixian.

Dr. Hsu bravely attempted what she termed a "bold re-appraisal", but she was neither brave nor radical enough to debunk Perzynski's myth. Like Laurence Sickman, she convinced herself that the caves at Yixian were a pilgrimage site in their own right, and that they had benefited over the centuries from the repeated generosity of local believers and other wealthier patrons, including a Manchu military officer. Discounting both the stylistic and scientific evidence already available, and influenced by the absence of pre-Ming material on site, she argued that the statues must have been made at one of the specialist *liuli* (琉璃) kilns at Yangcheng, Shanxi, nearly 500 kilometres away on the other side of the mountains, and is very reluctant to consider Longquanwu (龍泉務) as an alternative candidate.[157] She explained away the logistics of distance with some careful analysis of possible riverine and canal transportation in the early Ming and, despite having personal experience of the climb to the caves, was unfazed by the near inaccessibility of the site for porters bearing large and very heavy loads. She also offered no explanation of how a comparatively minor military official could have afforded work of imperial quality, or why he would have commissioned the statues for an off-the-beaten-track place like Yixian rather than a better-known and more accessible pilgrim destination.

---

157   Hsu, Op. Cit., p.185.

Derek Gillman's first theory, while relatively easy to reconcile with Perzynski's account, looks beyond it to where the statues might originally have resided. He tacitly accepts Perzynski's explanation for damage and wastage over time and ingeniously suggests that the Luohans may have gone unremarked because they were hidden in plain sight, their beauty overshadowed by the greater wonders of a famous nearby grotto, which at that time had not yet been surveyed by foreign archaeologists. He explains away the logistical difficulties by referencing C.T. Loo's proven ability to move large and heavy statues from Xiangtangshan (響堂山) to Beijing and beyond. Unfortunately for Gillman, his theory hangs or falls on a combination of dating and clay. Both the Changle (昌樂) and Daqingshou (大慶壽) temples date from the Jin dynasty rather than the earlier Liao, as does the Guantai (觀台) kiln, where the clay used has a very different composition from that from which the Luohans were formed.

And that is a problem because, just like a complex mathematical equation, the riddle of the terracotta Luohans must be solved for all of its five parts at the same time. One hundred years after they sprang their beautiful surprise, the five questions remain the same: when were they made; where were they made; where were they found; why had nobody noticed them before; and why is the set incomplete? Some parts of the riddle have been solved or at least seem closer to solution, but one out of five, or two out of five is not good enough. Any theory must satisfy all five queries. Friedrich Perzynski's caves cleverly seemed to provide a satisfactory explanation, but only by conveniently avoiding parts of the riddle. His tall tale does not stand up to close inspection, despite which scholars seem reluctant to throw away this crutch. This is puzzling. Surely it would be better to attempt to build an explanation purely on the foundation of the limited objective evidence available, rather than rely on the highly suspect reported facts in a sales brochure. So, let us clear our minds of Perzynski's mythical "*Eight Luohan Mountain*" and examine the five parts of the riddle one by one.

As to when they were made, scholars have overcome an earlier prejudice that had blinded them to the artistic sensibilities of the pastoral and nomadic tribes that nibbled at the northern fringes of Tang territory and, notwithstanding Dr. Hsu's more recent *idée fixe*, have determined through both stylistic and scientific analysis that the statues date from the Liao–Jin dynasties, with a majority in favour of the former.

As to where they were made, the excavations of the kiln at Longquanwu (龍泉務) have demonstrated that the Liao had the necessary technical skills–having forcibly relocated the best of the Ding potters there–and an industrial facility capable of undertaking such complex work conveniently close to their southern capital, today's Beijing. Nigel Wood and colleagues have most recently further shown that two of the Luohans were fashioned from clay which shares the same distinctive characteristics as clay from the relatively small deposit on which Longquanwu relied. There is as yet no proof that the statues were fired there, but these facts provide us at least a plausible working hypothesis, and so far no shards or other evidence of the production of *sancai* Buddhist statuary have been found at any other more northerly kiln site.[158]

As to from whence they came, it seems safe to assume, given their quality, that they were imperial commissions and gifted to an important temple somewhere in lands under Liao rule. Given their weight and fragility, even allowing for waterborne transportation, they were not ideally suited for lugging long distances or over difficult terrain. Thus there seems no good

---

158   Gridley, Op. Cit., 1995, p. 28.

reason to look in remote or inaccessible locations and every reason to search for potential candidates in or around the Liao's southern capital, i.e. Beijing.

The last two parts of the riddle are more difficult, but the pattern of appearance and sale, the missing members and their damaged condition all offer important clues, as do some of the inadvertent admissions and emotional outbursts in Perzynski's account. Let us use these to reconstruct what happened in Beijing the year that he arrived there, and let us start by re-examining how the Luohans came to market.

The pattern of purchases indicates that seven statues and a bust were all in Beijing and available for inspection by dealers in the summer of 1912, and that their sale lasted barely six months. The old hands, Worch's agent and George Crofts, secured the first four, destined eventually for Philadelphia, Boston, London and Toronto, ahead of new-kid-on-the-block Perzynski's one-and-a-half–for New York and Berlin–and Terasawa Shikanosuke's for Japan. We know that Perzynski saw both the bearded, gap-toothed Luohan that ended up in Boston and the "Older Monk" holding a scroll that landed later in New York because he mentions them in his account, but he saw them in Beijing, not Yixian. He let slip as much when recalling the dealers removing the wrappings from "*statues*" plural, not just the bust, as we will see below. By the end of the year, the "Older Monk" had been shipped to New York for eventual placing with the Met (see below), and the sale was effectively over. Except that when the Penn and the MFA realized that they had bought their Luohans *sans* base, it was C.T. Loo, whose name has not so far appeared in the credits, who in 1916, rescued them from embarrassment by providing the rocky stands on which they now sit. Then, some twenty years after the appearance of the first Luohan, the same gentleman sold the ninth Luohan to the Nelson-Atkins Museum in Kansas City.

The slender evidentiary thread linking the Luohans to C.T. Loo becomes thicker and stronger the deeper one delves into the archives. From the MFA Boston's correspondence with Yamanaka & Co. and C.T. Loo, it would appear that Edgar Worch's "agent" in Beijing was in fact C.T. Loo, and that the precocious young man cannily used his relationship with the older and very reputable Worch to pull in potential purchasers when the statues made their first appearance in the West.[159] We know that he was in Beijing at the time, having traveled Trans-Siberian from Paris that summer looking, amongst other things, for archaic jades for Dr. G. Giesler, Chairman of France's Northern Railways Company. Jean-Henri d'Ardenne de Tizac, the Conservateur of the Musée Cernuschi, had called on him in the spring of the same year ostensibly to discuss a proposed exhibition of just such jades.[160] Could it be that C.T Loo had already got wind of the Luohans, knew where the statues were stored and had begun to orchestrate their retrieval, repair and sale?

We earlier saw that Perzynski felt that his Japanese colleague had deliberately sent him on a wild goose chase, and this author has suggested that this might have been to get him out of the way while deals were done in Beijing. Perzynski probably resented the fact that Terasawa Shikanosuke was able to purchase one of the Luohans for his client Kojiro Matsukata.[161] However, there might have been a bit more to it than that. Recall that it

---

159 Wang Yiyou, Op. Cit., pp. 88 and 112 and related footnotes refer.

160 C.T. Loo in his Preface to *An Exhibition of Archaic Chinese Jades, Arranged for the Norton Gallery of Art, Palm Beach, Florida, Jan 20 to March 1, 1950.* (C.T. Loo Inc.,NY, 1950), quoted in Michael St. Clair, *The Great Chinese Art Transfer: How So Much of China's Art Came to America* p. 108.

161 As noted by Bosch Reitz and confirmed by Harada Yoshito, Op. Cit., 1940, pp. 299-305. The Luohan later passed from Matsukata to Tsutsumi Yasujiro, Chairman of Seibu Railway Company. He displayed it in the *Takanawa Bijutsukan* in Tokyo, built in 1960 to house his collection, but it is now in the Sezon Museum of Modern Art, founded by his son Seiji, in Karuizawa, Nagano Prefecture.

was other unidentified art dealers who showed him his first statue in Beijing. Perzynski describes them first as "owners" (plural), and five paragraphs later as "art dealers" (plural again), carefully distinguishing them from "Beijing curio dealers". So, though he does not name them, it is safe to assume that it was international dealers such as George Crofts, C.T. Loo and Terasawa Shikanosuke, who were whetting his appetite with a first look at the dramatic bust.

More than that, the eventual pattern of sales suggests an unusual degree of orchestration, and that reflects the unique commercial challenge faced by the dealer, or dealers, who discovered the damaged statues and persuaded the temple to relinquish them for sale. Nothing like them had been seen before in the West. The statues were obviously rare and, but for the damage, would immediately have qualified as museum quality. That would have limited the market. C.T. Loo had learned the hard way about merchandise that would not move. He had yet to find buyers for several of the eight 6th Century Bodhisattvas from Xiangtangshan (響堂山) that he had acquired in 1910, and had been obliged to sell a half-share to the French dealer Paul Vignier.[162] Would there be a market for *sancai* (三彩) sculpture? Certainly not in China; save possibly a wealthy expatriate. What about Europe?

Bear in mind that before 1900 nobody there had ever seen Tang *sancai* ware, never mind a monumental statue. The Luohans might well have been regarded with suspicion. Would there be a market for so many at the same time? The dealer(s) had to de-risk the transaction by working closely with competitors to exploit their collective international connections. It helped that most of

---

162 Loo, C.T., "An Exhibition of Chinese Sculptures: C.T. Loo & Co. New York City", New York: Loo, 1940, preface. See also Steinhardt, Nancy, The Chinese Rotunda, *Arts of Asia*, 38 (5), September-October 2008, p.87. Working with Vigniers, it would be six years before C.T. Loo disposed of the last one.

them knew one another. George Crofts was used to working with S.M. Franck & Sons in London and that company operated as a wholesaler for museums and others in both England and North America. C.T. Loo had a close connection with Edgar Worch in Paris. Terasawa Shikanosuke knew the Japanese market and had links to the United States through Yamanaka & Co. The latter's reputation was high, having just secured rights to the sale of the Prince Gong's collection. Together they could cover all the major museums, but they would have to move quickly and market the Luohans cleverly. A decade later and C.T. Loo's reputation would have been sufficient to secure sales single-handedly, but in 1912-13 he did not yet command such respect, had only his Paris gallery and a newly-opened Beijing branch, and would have had to work with others to manage the distribution outside Europe.[163]

They apparently tried to recruit Friedrich Perzynski to assist with sales in Germany, but concluded that he was too new to be trusted to play by their rules. The others knew that he was eager to buy, perhaps too eager–"Its owners feasted their eyes upon my profound amazement as they showed it to me,"–and might have been tempted to pre-empt their carefully laid plans. Perzynski thought he had been accepted as one of them because he used the first person plural, "At the time **we** called him the Priest," but he was not absolutely sure because he commented later "The owners of the disciples of the Buddha were art dealers....Did **they** suspect what torches of envy they had lit in me when they removed the wrappings from the sculptures." (Note the plurals "disciples" and "sculptures".) He was right, they did not trust him. They had to find some way to slow him down a bit, to get him out of the way. And so they did, and so their sales strategy

---

163   Wang Yiyou, Op. Cit., has some fascinating insights into the way dealers *"both cooperated with and competed against one another"*.

largely succeeded.

In an early hint of his genius, C.T. Loo prevailed on Edgar Worch to use his connections to secure the Musée Cernuschi for the exhibition that would launch the Luohans on the Western art world. Whether or not Worch underwrote the sale is unclear. Judging by their speed of response, it appears that either Worch or Yamanaka had tipped off the Penn Museum and Boston's MFA in advance that there would be something special on display and the Penn Museum took delivery of the first statue in May–June 1914. It is not clear whether the museums concluded arrangements directly with Worch, whose stock and shop in Paris were confiscated by the French government at the outbreak of World War I, or via a third party, such as Yamanaka. Today the label in the Penn lists the Luohan as a *"Gift of A.G. Worch"*, i.e. Edgar Worch's Uncle Adolphe.[164] However, there is every indication in later correspondence between Boston's MFA and Yamanaka in New York, from whom it took delivery of the second Luohan, that C.T. Loo had sheltered behind Worch's reputation and had acted at least as shipping agent or intermediary between Worch and Yamanaka. George Crofts was also successful in placing two of the Luohans with S.M. Franck & Sons in London.

The first of these, as we have seen, was quickly snapped up by R.L. Hobson at the British Museum in the summer of 1913, although it was not unveiled to the public until May the following year. Charles Trick Currelly, clergyman, archaeologist, curator and first director of the Royal Ontario Museum, had learned of it and let it be known that he wanted one too for

---

164 In an exchange of e-mails with the author, Evan Peugh, the Penn's Archivist, noted that the museum purchased several pieces from Worch, some of which are listed as gifts and others as purchases, but *"I believe they were all purchased. There was a bit of a controversy regarding the sales since Worch was a German living in Paris, when the first world war broke out. The French government appears to have seized his property, considering him an enemy of the state, and tried to nullify some of his transactions. The matter appears to have been resolved around the mid-1920s."*

Fig.74 Charles "Trick" Currelly, clergyman, archaeologist, curator and first director of the ROM in Toronto. Public Domain

Fig.75 Sarah Warren "took one look and reached for her cheque book." Courtesy of the Royal Ontario Museum, Toronto

Toronto. **(Fig.74)** Julius Spier, who had taken over management of the company from its founder Solomon Mark Franck's in 1909, doubtless told his prospective client that he would try his very best, smiled secretly to himself, moved Crofts' second statue, still in its original wrapping, from the corner of the warehouse and waited for Currelly to appear in London. And appear he duly did.

In the summer of 1914, on the eve of the Great War, he arrived in London accompanied by a group of the museum's patrons, amongst them Mrs. H.D. "Sarah" Warren. **(Fig.75)** This formidable woman, who had first met Currelly in Egypt at a dig he was doing at *Deir al-Bahri* in Egypt five years earlier, had taken over the running of Dominion Tire and Rubber on the death of her husband and become a member of the ROM's first Board of Trustees. She was invited to visit by Spier to view Croft's second statue and she had no hesitation. She took one look at the Luohan and reached for her cheque book.[165] Never was an impulse purchase so welcome, or so propitious. A photograph of the Luohan taken before it left London for Toronto was turned into a postcard, and it was this postcard that drew George Crofts to the museum four years later, sparked a friendship with Currelly and opened the floodgates for Chinese antiquities sourced by Crofts entering the ROM's collections. With its little cloak or cowl slung casually over shoulders like a cricketer's jersey, the ROM Luohan's near-talismanic status is reflected in its appearance together with

Fig.76 *"...slung stylishly over shoulder like a cricketer's jersey."* Detail of 914.4.: Figure of a luohan, moulded earthenware with glaze, Liao-Jin Dynasty, 11th century, reportedly from Yixian, Hebei Province, China; ROM2016_15019_11. Courtesy of the Royal Ontario Museum © ROM.

the popular Parasaurolophus skeleton on a stamp issued to celebrate the ROM's centenary. **(Fig.76 and Plate XI; Fig.77)**

Ironically, it was C.T. Loo who was left holding the baby, so to speak. He had reserved the "Older Monk", the one holding a scroll in its hand, for himself. It was arguably the best-preserved of the set and, since the Penn and Boston had already been provided for, he probably planned to sell it to the Met in New York. However, Perzynski managed his own marketing very well. Publishing the romanticized tale of their "discovery" just ahead

---

165   Chen Shen, "Objectives and Challenges: Past, Present and Future of Collecting Chinese Antiquities in the ROM", in Jason Steuber and Guolong Lai ed. Collectors, *Collections & Collecting the Arts of China: Histories & Challenges*, University Press of Florida, 2014, pp. 249-50.

Fig.77 On the ROM Centenary stamp its luohan shared the stage with the equally popular Parasaurolphus skeleton. Public domain

of his exhibition in Berlin, he successfully sold the dramatic bust to the private German collector, Harry Fuld, possibly with a little help from Edgar Worch[166], and, something of a coup, contracted with the Met for the sale of the "Younger Monk" before C.T. Loo could get its elder brother to New York. In the event, because war intervened, Perzynski was not able to deliver his statue until six years later, which must have irked C.T. Loo something awful. He had managed to ship the "Older Monk" clutching its scroll to New York quickly, but not quickly enough, for by then the Met was not interested. (**Fig.78 and Plate VI)** Perzynski had beaten him to the punch, and the Met's curator was anxiously awaiting the arrival of the one purchased in Berlin.

Thus, in 1916, we find the frustrated C.T. Loo writing a personal invitation to John D. Rockefeller, Jr. to view his pottery Luohan "…so I may better explain its full history to you. It is certainly the most unique piece that we can imagine from the pottery world. The photo is not a good one and does not show the real beauty of expression or color of the figure."[167]

The story does, however, have a happy ending. European hostilities being over, Perzynski eventually delivered on his

---

166 One writer has claimed that Fuld bought the statue from Worch, who presumably either bought it from Perzynski or acted as intermediary, but offered only indirect evidence. See Jirka-Schmitz, Patrizia, "The Trade in Far Eastern Art in Berlin during the Weimar Republic (1918-1933)", *Journal for Art Market Studies*, vol. 2, no. 3, 2018, p. 4.

167 C.T. Loo's letter to John D. Rockefeller Jr., dated 27 April 1916; see Daisy Wang Yiyou, Op. Cit., 2007, pp. 68-9, footnote 103.

contract, and in 1921 the Met decided that two would be better than one. As a result, visitors to the museum today enjoy the double pleasure of viewing younger and older brothers contemplating the infinite in their different ways, seated either side of the entrance to Gallery 208.

Mr. Ushikubo aside, nobody has so far offered a satisfactory explanation for the fact that the first two Luohans were exhibited at the Musée Cernuschi *sans* base. One possibility is that restoration

Fig.78 The Met's "Older Monk"; luohan, Liao dynasty (907-1125), ca. 1000. Stoneware with three-color glaze; H 104.8 cm. excluding base. Metropolitan Museum of Art, New York, Frederick, C. Hewitt Fund 1921, Acc. No. 21.76

of the bases took longer than expected so that there were only sufficient for the two that Crofts shipped to London. Two years later, however, C.T. Loo was happy to supply the missing stands to Boston's MFA and the Penn without charge. The fact that he was able to do so once again points to the centrality of his part in the drama, as does the final act. On close inspection, it is plain for all to see that the last of the Luohans to reach North America is the most heavily restored. Indeed, it looks as though it was quite literally a "basket case", possibly the baskets of fragments that Perzynski claimed that he saw in the Yamen. No matter, C.T. Loo had plenty of time to complete its reconstruction. For it was not until 1933 that Lawrence Sickman walked through the doors of his shop in Beijing and bought both the Luohan and the astonishingly beautiful Liao dynasty carved wooden Guanyin for the Nelson-Atkins Museum, which opened its doors to the public on December 11 the same year.

Another irony is that what started as a ruse to sideline Friedrich Perzynski rebounded to the advantage of the other dealers. The legend he concocted furnished the perfect cover story for what may well have been a less than legitimate process of discovery and acquisition. The Republican Government had just introduced a new law banning the removal of "ancient objects", and awkward questions of provenance could all be redirected to Perzynski's account.

Again, the exchange between J.E. Lodge, the curator of Boston's MFA, and Yamanaka & Co. in New York is instructive. As we saw earlier, Lodge had come to the conclusion that the Luohan's head and body might not have been the work of a single artist, or even of the same date. When he called Mr. Ushikubo, manager of Yamanaka's New York branch, from whom the museum had acquired the statue, the latter's first reaction was to try and distance the firm from any suspicious activity. "I enclose herewithin," wrote Ushikubo, "a letter from Loo & Cie, Paris, from which you will kindly understand that the figure was shipped to us direct from Paris."[168] However, he undertook to check its provenance very carefully on his next visit to Beijing.

At this point, the author must confess to the redaction of a couple of key words from the text of Ushikubo's letter quoted in Chapter Three. Quoted in full, with the author's emphasis added, the relevant paragraph of his report read: "I tried to secure full information in regard to the Lohan figure of the Boston Museum. Fortunately, I have had an interview with Mr. Terazawa (sic) who brought the figure with a few Chinese partners **from the temple**. The number of figures he brought out are three: one figure perfect, after a hard task; and the other two by breaking on account of their packing, etc. It was almost impossible to

---

168   Wang Yiyou, Op. Cit. 2007, p. 88, footnote 167.

carry life-size figure in perfect condition such a long journey and obliged to break the heads, bodys (sic.) and stands and carry back only the heads and bodys (sic.), leaving behind stands at that time."[169]

We must assume that Lodge was familiar with Perzynski's version of the statues' provenance, so the reference to a "temple" would have puzzled him. It was certainly enough of a surprise for him to immediately contact C.T. Loo. The MFA's archive does not contain a record of what exactly was said, but the inadvertent reference to temple rather than grotto was probably brushed aside as a slip of the pen and for the rest it is clear that C.T. Loo sang from the same hymn sheet as his Japanese colleague since shortly thereafter Francis Stewart Kershaw, writing on behalf of the MFA, thanked Loo "…for the details concerning the original situation of the pottery Lo-han. It confirms the information in Perzynski's account."[170]

In the meantime, Loo had delivered the Luohan's missing rocky base to the museum without any additional charge. Significantly, there is no record of any correspondence with Edgar Worch, in whose name the Luohan had been exhibited in Paris, on the subject of either the head or the base.

With the wisdom of hindsight, it would be more accurate to say that this exchange confirms that Yamanaka and C.T. Loo were in cahoots. It also supplies one more piece of the jig-saw puzzle. It was obviously convenient to point the finger at the distant Terasawa and to say that it was he who had been responsible for the transport of the Luohans from wherever they originally came from to Beijing, because he had already been

---

169 Letter to Lodge dated September 6, 1916, folder and box unknown, AAOA-MFA; see Daisy Wang Yiyou, Op. Cit., 2007, p. 112, footnote 245..

170 Kershaw, F.S. to C.T. Loo, January 18, 1917, folder: Lai-Yuan Co., box: Unofficial Correspondence L, 1910-1922, AAOA-MFA; see Daisy Wang Yiyou, Op. Cit., 2007, p. 113, footnote 245.

referenced and cursed in Perzynski's account. Ushikubo also spread responsibility for the damaged condition of the statues a little wider by reporting that Terasawa had been working with "a few Chinese partners." However, in reporting his conversation with Terasawa, he innocently let slip the latter's equally innocent reference to a temple. Terasawa probably had not read Perzynski's account and neither he nor Ushikubo would have been as sensitive as C.T. Loo to the importance of sticking to this part of the narrative.

Theirs was a conspiracy of silence that held because none of the conspirators had any interest in disavowing Perzynski's audacious claims. The author has not been able to establish the date of Terasawa's death, but Crofts died in 1925, Yamanaka in 1936 and C.T. Loo in 1957. Perzynski passed away in Brazil in 1965 and Worch seven years later in New York. One younger man, who might have heard his elders trading "war stories" over a drink, is the latter's nephew-in-law Henry Trubner. His father, who had sourced for Worch in Beijing in the 1920s, died there of black measles and Edgar and his wife took care of young "Heinz", having him schooled in Montreux, and Cranleigh, UK. His mother settled in New York and Edgar, her sister and Heinz followed her shortly before the war. There he met and mixed with all the dealers, including C.T. Loo before heading for Harvard, where he studied under Langdon Warner. His subsequent curatorial career took him to Los Angeles County Museum, arriving just in time to deal with the controversy over the Munthe Collection; the ROM, where he met one of the Luohan; and finally Seattle with its lovely lacquered head. If he knew anything, he whispered not a word; if he suspected, he saw no evil and opted to lift no stone.

Which brings us to the most remarkable feature of the various stories surrounding the Luohans, one of those dogs that definitely did not bark, and that is the very curious fact that nobody seems to have seen them before they came to the attention of foreign dealers in Beijing in 1912. There are no records or photographs of them either as a group, or individually. None of them appears in any paintings, or etchings, or gazetteers, or travelers' tales. Scholar officials, who routinely commented on things of beauty–witness Su Shi's (蘇軾) poems in praise of the Eighteen Arhats paintings by both Guanxiu (貫休) and Zhang Xuan (張玄)[171]–seem to have either ignored them, or been ignorant of their existence. How can this be? Things of beauty inevitably attract attention, whether coveted by crooks, or connoisseurs, or the merely curious traveler. If the statues had been tomb furnishings, that might be understandable; likewise if they had been hidden away and the hiders had perished before being able to pass on their secret, as Perzynski suggested. Barring the deliberate slaughter of all workers involved in such an operation, however, after the manner of royal tombs, it is highly unlikely that there would be no human memory of their hiding.

Lawrence Sickman, then Director Emeritus of the Nelson-Atkins Gallery in Kansas City, was only the latest to be seduced by Perzynski's suggestion: "No, rather than having been moved a great distance, I prefer to embrace the idea that the whole ensemble was a marvelous, creative and deeply pious concept–that of placing the disciples in these remote, hard of access caves (which were already there), and thus making a place of pilgrimage on the well-traveled east-west trade route."[172]

However, pilgrim trails leave indelible marks on the landscape over hundreds of years and there is no evidence to suggest that the caves at Yixian ever attracted pilgrim feet from

---

171   Jin Shen, Op. Cit., p. 64, and Hsu, Op. Cit., p.p. 116-7.
172   Laurence Sickman, private correspondence quoted by Richard Smithies, Op. Cit., 1984, p. 269.

afar. Rather, the recent work by Zhang and Hsu suggests only very local interest, which is hardly surprising as there are several far larger grottoes and caves all over China to which faithful pilgrims have flocked generation after generation. Perzynski's caves were much less grand than these grottoes and, while no more remote, were much less accessible.

Perhaps, as Gillman suggests, the statues were simply hidden in plain sight. For example, they could have been in a place to which access was restricted, such as an imperial estate. The Western Tombs are just next door to Yixian, and Perzynski's reference to peasants being apprehended by soldiers, and the Commandant's complaints indicate that there may have been some pilfering there. But the Tombs were relatively recent constructions and seem an unlikely site for a hall of Liao dynasty Luohans. Alternatively, the Luohans might have been open to view, but in a place where, as Derek Gillman speculated, other more remarkable, more ancient or more costly pieces put humble glazed pottery in the shade. However, neither hypothesis explains their damaged condition and missing members. No, the incompleteness of the set, the heavy restorations evident on the survivors and the fact that nobody had seen them before all point to either a derelict temple or the discarded remnants of a set damaged beyond repair. They had disappeared from human memory not because they had been hidden in distant mountains, but because they were no longer in use.

There is no shortage of temples in and around Beijing dating from the Liao dynasty or earlier. Nancy Steinhardt's survey identified only one near Yixian, but the Kaiyuan Temple (開元寺) is manifestly too small to have accommodated the Luohans.[173] As a working hypothesis then, it should be possible to narrow

---

173   Nancy, Steinhardt, *Liao Architecture*, Honolulu, 1997.

the scope of search using the rational criteria suggested by investigations so far. Thus, on logistical grounds, we should confine our search to an area with relatively easy water-borne access to the kilns at Longquanwu (龍泉務) or, in other words, Beijing and its immediate surrounds. Like Gillman, we should be looking for a royal temple, a temple of sufficient stature to merit imperial endowments. Obviously, the temple must have an historical association with the cult of the luohan. That is, it must have, or have had a Luohan Hall sufficiently large to have accommodated the statues. Perhaps less obviously, it must be of a scale sufficiently grand to allow abandoned statuary to lie forgotten in storage. Even allowing for all these criteria, there is no shortage of candidates.

In the modified 2013 version of his thesis, Derek Gillman postulated the Jin dynasty Daqingshou Temple (大慶壽寺) as the most likely recipient of imperial largesse. It is in many ways an excellent candidate, but there is a long gap between the destruction of the main body of the temple by fire in 1538 and the rediscovery of the Luohans in 1912. Gillman avoids this trap by accepting Perzynski's tale of their having being removed in 1213 ahead of an invading army, but Eileen Hsu poured cold water on that idea, pointing to the absence of any archaeological or textual evidence, noting the Mongols' well-documented religious tolerance and citing the respect later shown this temple by Khublai Khan, when building the walls of Khanbaliq. Nor is Daqingshousi the only potential candidate in Beijing.

For the sake of argument, but not quite at random, Fayuan Temple (法源寺), the Temple of the Origin of the Dharmas, is one which has at least an equal claim. It is Beijing's oldest temple and also its largest, sprawling across some 6,700 square metres. Situated to the south and west of the Forbidden City and roughly equidistant from the Temple of Heaven, it lies only an easy 25 kilometres from the Longquanwu kilns by river and canal. Sometimes known as the Martyrs' Shrine, it has seen much history. It housed the Song emperor Qinzong (欽宗; r.1126-27), when he was captured by the Jin, and Xie Fangde (謝枋得; 1226-1289), the Southern Song rebel leader, starved himself to death in captivity there, long before it was used to store the coffins of late Qing reformers. The temple was founded by the second Tang emperor, Taizong (太宗; r. 626-49), following a disastrous war against the Goguryeo kingdom in what today is Korea, and it was named the *Minzhong Si*, (憫忠寺) in honour of all the soldiers who had died in that campaign. During the iconoclasm and violent anti-Buddhist persecutions of emperor Wuzong (武宗; r. 840-46), the temple was all but destroyed and a stele excavated at the temple records its subsequent restoration by the emperor Xuanzong (宣宗; r. 846-859).[174] In 1057, the temple was leveled by an earthquake, but it was rebuilt *in situ* by the Liao.

Just under seven centuries later, on November 30, 1731, Beijing was struck by a still more powerful earthquake that killed 100,000 of its inhabitants and devastated much of the capital. It took another four years before work could begin on reconstruction of the temple, but, in the twelfth year of the Yongzheng (雍正) emperor's reign (1735), a major refurbishment was undertaken, as part of which eighteen life-size wooden Luohans, were installed in the wings of its main hall, where they can still be seen today. It is not unreasonable to suppose that they replaced an earlier set. The carved wooden Luohans are included, along with the temple's other relics, paintings and treasures, in the two inventory rolls that survive of a six scroll history of the temple compiled by an official, Huang Weihan (黃維翰; 1851-1936; *jusi* Guangxu year 21, or 1896),

---

174   "Record of Restoring the Buddha Relic at Minzhong temple, c. 713-756", in "A Promise to the Buddha – Devotion and Praxis in Buddhist Stele Inscriptions", *Academica Sinica*, 2014-15.

in the closing years of the Qing.[175] The two inventory scrolls make no mention of any *sancai* statuary and, very unfortunately, the other four scrolls have been lost. Today, Fayuan Temple is home to the China Buddhist Institute and houses the China Buddhist Literature and Cultural Relics Museum. It is a good potential candidate; to be sure, not the only one, but its history is instructive.

Earthquake damage would go a long way to explaining why only nine-and-half Luohans have survived, and why almost all are heavily restored. It would also explain the collective amnesia. The destruction having natural causes, and the damage being widespread, the statues' existence would have been more easily forgotten and forgiven in a way that desecration by foreign troops could not be. Following a quake such as those that shook the region in 1337, 1679 and 1731, the battered survivors would have been moved to a temple workshop for restoration, together with the fragments, the latter being sorted by baskets to see if any of the others could be salvaged. When repair of more than half a set proved impossible, the decision would have been taken to replace them. No one having the heart to dispose of the remnants, it is possible that they were simply left to gather dust in a workshop or store, until an enterprising abbot realized, or was persuaded, that sale of these damaged goods to foreigners might help with fund-raising. Such transactions were not unknown. Thus the monks of Guangsheng Temple (廣胜寺) in Shanxi Province were not embarrassed to carve in stone a record of their sale of Yuan dynasty murals to raise funds for refurbishment of roofs at risk of collapse.[176] Fayuan Temple with its extensive grounds and beautiful flowering trees is not the only potential candidate, but this sort of scenario, while speculative, is arguably

---

175 Wang Shuyan & Huang Weihan, *Fayuansi Zhigao*, Yangzhou, Jiangsu Guangling Guji Keyanse, 1996.
176 Chiang, Renee, "C.T. Loo: Gentleman-Scholar, Businessman or Traitor", *Bulletin of the Oriental Ceramic Society of Hong Kong*, Number 16, 2013-16, p.49.

more plausible than the other theories advanced so far. It also fits with the stories that still circulated amongst the dealers in Beijing in the 1980s of a young C.T. Loo disguising himself as a monk to gain entry to a temple where he found the statues, and the subsequent, possibly dubious arrangement that allowed him to remove them to his own workshops for repair.[177]

However, once we debunk Perzynski's myth, the real problem with both Gillman's choice of Daqingshou Temple and, hypothetically, Fayuan Temple, is that they are too close to the city centre. Ushikubo's report of his conversation with Terasawa might have been a bit garbled, but the reference to "such a long journey" is clear enough. The temple was not inside the city walls; it had to be somewhere outside them, close enough to be accessible, but still far enough away to present a logistical challenge for the carriage of large, heavy objects. The obvious place to look is towards the West where a broad arc of hills shelters the Zhili (直隸) plain with a protective bulwark that has been the northern capital's first line of defense down the ages. The Xishan (西山), or "Western Hills" as they are called, also provide the city with water via the Yongding River (永定河) that wriggles through the narrows near the Longquanwu kiln site before spilling into flat and open land at Mentougou (門頭溝). Now a suburb of modern Beijing, this edge of the plain is caught in the crab-like pincers of foothills protruding on either side of the valley, whose slopes were populated with any number of shrines and temples.

These Western Hills were hardly unexplored territory. Guidebooks to temples and places of natural or historic interest in and around the capital city had been in circulation since the late Ming dynasty.[178] Beijing's well-to-do sought refuge there

---

177   The author is indebted to Anthony Lin Hua Tien for this anecdotal evidence.
178   Liu Tong and Yu Yizheng, *Di jing jing wu lue* (Notes on the Sights of the Imperial Capital), 1635; see Naquin, Susan, "Sites, Saints and Sights at the Tanzhe Monastery", in *Cahiers d'Extrême-Asie*, 1998, 10, pp. 189.

from the heat of summer. Scholar candidates, when not swotting for imperial examinations, swanned around them as tourists. Eminent eunuchs and senior officials looked to the hills for their retirement homes. Foreigners later followed suit. The Russians were the first non-religious foreign delegation allowed to reside in the Chinese capital, and in the early years of the 19th Century, they were also the first to appreciate the advantage of spending the hot summer months in the comparative cool of the hills. From 1860, when he arrived in Beijing to take up the appointment as the first British Minister, Sir Frederick Bruce, Lord Elgin's brother, followed their example, notwithstanding the damage so recently done by marauding French and British troops. By the late 19th Century, the Western Hills had become a popular resort for Beijing's foreign community, many of whom rented temples for outings, picnics, more or less decadent parties, or, in the case of St. John Perse, for more meditative literary purposes.[179] This would continue even after a new railway line brought the coastal resort at Beidaihe (北戴河) closer.

The temples on the hills on the northern side of the river were the most popular because they were the most convenient. They included the so-called Badachu (八大處), the "Eight Great Sites", which were a relatively easy day-trip from the city. In a general sense, this popularity counts against them in our search for the original home of the Luohans. They were no longer places of pilgrimage to be approached with reverence if not awe, so much as summer resorts to be idly exploited and explored. The chances of statues of such beauty going unobserved diminished accordingly. Nevertheless, keeping our minds open, let us take our own tour to examine the possibilities on this side of the Yongding River (永定河).

---

179 The poet-diplomat Alexis Leger, pen-name St. John Perse (1887-1975) wrote his epic *Anabasis* while staying in a house behind the village of Guanjialing in the Western Hills.

By the early years of the 20th Century, a motorable road allowed cars to get close to the edge of the plain near Badachu, or you could take a train from Xizhimen (西直門) in northwest Beijing–today the site of Beijing North Railway Terminus–to Huangcun (黃村), where donkeys could be hired for an hour's ride to Chang'an Temple (長安寺), the Temple of Eternal Peace. **(Map 3)** Built at the foot of Cuiwei hill (翠微山) during the Ming dynasty, this one need not detain us. The next in ascending order is Lingguang Temple (靈光寺), the Temple of Divine Light, which dates from the Tang, but was burned to the ground by the Eight-Power Allied Forces. Badachu had been one of the Boxers' strongholds during their uprising in 1900 and the priest here had actively assisted them. As part of the reprisals, the temple's ten-storey, brick-built octagonal pagoda was destroyed. The Zhaoxian Pagoda (招仙塔), as it was known,

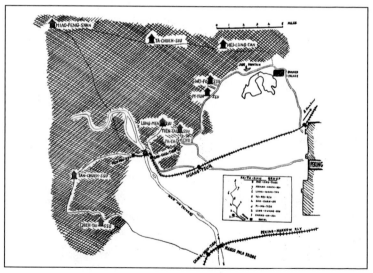

Map 3 Map of the Temples of the Western Hills reproduced from G.E. Hubbard's
The Temples of the Western Hills, 1923

had been erected during the Liao dynasty at the behest of Lady Zheng (鄭), the mother of the then prime minister Yelü Renxian (耶律仁先), to house a tooth relic of the Buddha. Chinese accounts of the desecration focus on the discovery in the ruins of a stone chest, with a wooden box within containing the relic, but make no mention of the loss of any treasured terracotta statues.[180]

Continuing our climb, a path to the right leads via the Zhengguo Temple (鎮國寺), the Temple of Pacifying the Nation, to the Mimoyan (秘魔崖), the Mysterious Devil's Cliff. A covered way, punctuated with little pavilions, runs several hundred feet along the edge of a ravine to a rock cave, where, in the 7th Century lived the monk Lu Shi (盧師). Hence the name of the hill on which the temple stands. The temple, which is sometimes referred to as the Temple of Buddhahood, is reputed to be the oldest of the Badachu sites with origins in the Sui or Tang dynasties, but it does not appear to have attracted imperial attention.

Retracing our steps to the main trail, we continue on to the beautiful little 1151 nunnery known as Sanshan'an (三山庵), Three Hill Temple, after the Cuiwei (翠微), Pingpo (平坡) and Lushi (盧師) Hills that surround it. A little further on can be found Dabei Temple (大悲寺), the Temple of Great Mercy, which was founded in the Song and whose Ming dynasty Luohan Hall is graced by a famous set of eighteen sandalwood statues that are believed to have been carved by the Yuan dynasty sculptor, Liu Yuan (劉元). Barring some dreadful accident, it seems improbable that a beautiful set of *sancai* terracotta Luohans would have been replaced by wooden ones at such an early date, or that their fragments would have survived so long; and so, no luck so far.

The sixth temple, the Longwangtang (龍王堂), or Temple of the Dragon King was built during the Kangxi reign of the Qing.

---

180 Reconstruction of the Zhaoxian Pagoda was completed in 1964.

Known to foreigners as "Sir John's Place", it was originally another small nunnery, but for many years provided rooms for Sir John Jordan (1852-1925), who served as British Minister in China from 1906 to 1920. Compare and contrast Xiangjie Temple (香界寺), the Temple of the Fragrant World, higher up the hill, which served as a Summer Villa for both the Kangxi (r. 1661-72) and Qianlong (r. 1735-96) emperors. Dating from the Tang, and sometimes regarded as the most important of the Badachu group of temples, its central feature is the Scripture Repository, within which reside statues of Kasyapa, Sakyamuni and Maitreya–the Past, Present and Future Buddha–flanked by eighteen polychrome Luohans. Given the long periods of residence of successive emperors and their staff, it is improbable that the existence of an earlier set, however damaged, would have escaped imperial curiosity. Finally, perched on the summit of Pingpo Hill, is the Baozhudong (寶珠洞), or Cave of Precious Pearls, which dates only from the Qianlong reign (1735-96) and whose chief point of interest was the mummy of a former priest in a cave behind the temple.

In short, of the eight "temples" that make up the Badachu, only four date from early enough to qualify, and only two of these, the Xiangjie Temple (香界寺) and the Dabei Temple (大悲寺), merit any consideration, and even they do not stand up well to closer scrutiny. There are, however, a few other possibilities on the northern side of the river and, in the interests of completeness, we should stretch our legs a little further.

From the Baozhudong (寶珠洞), it is only a half-hour stroll over the hill to Tiantai Temple (天台寺), which housed an imperial mummy dating from the Shunzhi–Kangxi reigns (1644-1743). Beyond that, the Longmen Temple (龍門寺), or Dragon Gate Temple, known to foreigners as "White Pine Temple" because of its distinctive avenue of white pines, is in fact a mausoleum.

Built by one of the last Ming emperors, it was eventually taken over by a member of the successor dynasty, the Qing. For hikers in the early years of the 20th Century, another three-quarters-of-an-hour was sufficient to take them back down to the river and the road, or the railway station at Sanjiadian (三家店).

Further north, and not too far from the road that circled back from Badachu to Beijing via the Summer Palace, are Biyun Temple (碧雲寺), the Jade Cloud Temple, and Wofu Temple (臥佛寺), the Sleeping Buddha Temple. The former sports an Indian style *dagoba*, and Tiger Balm Gardens-like dioramas of Heaven and Hell, including Arhats perched on miniature mountain tops. It also boasts two halls, each housing 500 life-size Buddhas in red-gold lacquer. However, it is disqualified by age, having been founded by Mongols during the Yuan. The Wofu Temple, on the other hand, dates from the Tang dynasty and has a Luohan Hall, one of whose occupants, dressed in civilian clothes, stands out from the crowd and is supposed to be the Qianlong emperor. However, its accessibility is at odds with Terasawa's description. Even then, cars could drive directly up to the gates of both temples.

For the more adventurous, or for those with more time on their hands, a circuit to the north of Badachu, taking in the pilgrimage temple perched on the peak at Miaofengshan (妙峰山), Dajue Temple (大覺寺), the Temple of Enlightenment, and Heilongtan (黑龍潭), the Black Dragon Pool, returning via the Summer Palace, was rated a two to three-day excursion by contemporary guides. The temple at Miaofengshan was famous for its roses, which were harvested and dried before being donkeyed down to the city for inclusion in scented teas. For our purposes and from a historical point of view, Dajue Temple at the foot of Yangtai Hill (陽台山) is more interesting. A stele within the temple records its founding as the Qingshuiyan (清水巖), Clear Stream Crag, in

1068, the fourth year of the Xianyong (咸雍) period of the Liao dynasty. It was, however, completely re-built during the Ming in contemporary style, and there is no indication of any former association with the cult of the luohan.

That completes our survey of shrines and temples on the northern side of the river and it is fair to say that there are no convincing candidates amongst them.

On the southern side of the valley on Ma'an Shan (馬鞍山), less than twenty-five kilometres by river and pony trail from the kilns at Longquanwu, there are two ancient temples of a very different character: Tanzhe Monastery (潭柘寺) , the Temple of the Pool and the Mulberry, and Jietai Temple (戒台寺), the Ordination Temple; the first famous for its springs, the second for its pines. **(Fig.79)** Not in any sense remote, they nevertheless required, and merited a bit more time. A 1758 guide to Beijing, noted that pilgrims going to the larger Tanzhe Monastery would usually break the journey and stay overnight at Jietai Temple.[181] By the early 20th Century, the nearest railway station at Changxindian

Fig.79 Jietaisi, Temple of the Ordination, was famous for its pines. Public Domain

181   Naquin, Op. Cit., p. 196.

(長辛店) was only 35 minutes, or four stations by rail down the Peking-Hankow line, which crossed the river just to the north of the Marco Polo Bridge. From there, Jietai Temple was fifteen kilometres by donkey; eleven across the plain and three uphill. For the latter climb, which is quite steep in places, sedan chairs were available for hire by those too lazy to use Shanks' Pony, but contemporary guides still suggested an overnight stay for those intending to go on to the Tanzhe Monastery. The latter was another three-hour hike away. Again an overnight stay was the norm before tackling the equally long climb up over the pass, which rewarded walkers with very scenic views, and down to Mentougou (門頭溝), whence hikers could catch another train back to Beijing.

Three days were considered a minimum for this sort of outing. In making this circuit, foreigners were following a well-beaten path, as the two temples were already popular places of pilgrimage in the early Qing. The path was also well-beaten by the hooves of donkeys carrying coal down to the plain from the numerous small pits dotting the hills between the temples.

Tanzhe Monastery's ancient origins, well-captured in the local dictum "First came Tanzhe Temple, then Youzhou (幽州; now Beijing)", can be traced to 307 CE during the Western Jin dynasty (265-316). It is beautifully sited. The forest of funeral stupa, some dating from the Jin, through which one approaches underline its age. A mid-19th Century wood cut, shows the temple, beyond its entrance arch, ascending the steep mountain slope in a series of terraced courtyards, each towering over the one below. **(Fig.80)** At its highest point, the Vairocana Hall is roofed in yellow tiles, a mark of the special imperial favour that it enjoyed under Khublai Khan, one of whose daughters became a nun and is buried here. The Qianlong emperor had a traveling palace built for his use at the temple and bestowed an imperial title on an enormous

秋尋柘潭

Fig.80 Woodcut of Tanzhe Temple from the travel journal of Manchu nobleman,
Wanyan Lingqing (1791-1846)

Ginko tree beside the main hall. Another on the opposite side of the hall is known as the *"Emperor's wife"* and supposedly put out a new branch on the birth of every heir to the throne. Visitors cannot fail to notice the subtle sound of water rippling through the air throughout the year. The Floating Cups Pavilion, with its dragon's head patterned runnel (**Fig.81**), recalls the leisurely games of cultivated courtiers, the sort of game made popular by the renowned calligrapher Wang Xizhi (王羲之) and his friends at the Orchid Pavilion (蘭亭), composing verses as their cups of wine bobbed downstream. A small ordination altar is sited on the temple's western side, but this and its links to the cult of the luohan pale in comparison with those of its neighbour.

And so we come to Jietai Temple (戒台寺), the Ordination Temple, with its famous triple-tiered altar and long ordination

Fig.81 Tanzhesi, Temple of the Pool and the Mulberry, was famous for its springs and its Dragon Head runnel. Author's photograph

Fig.82 Jietai Temple's long broad ordination terrace. Public Domain

Fig.83 "First Under Heaven", the triple-tiered Ordination Altar at Jietai Temple.
Public Domain

terrace, on which myriad statues of the Buddha oversaw the initiation of generations of young monks. **(Fig.82)** One of the oldest royal Buddhist temples in Beijing, some believe that its foundations date from the reign of Emperor Wen (文; r. 581-604), first emperor of the Sui (隋) dynasty, when it was called Huiju Temple (慧聚寺) or Temple of the Accumulation of Wisdom. Certainly, it was founded no later than the fifth year of the Wude (武德) period (622) of the Tang Dynasty, i.e. during the reign of emperor Gaozu (高祖; r. 618-26). Its present name was acquired when it was substantially rebuilt in the fifth year of the Xianyong (咸雍) period of the Liao (1069). Subsequent restorations in the Jin, Yuan and Ming dynasties basically followed the same layout, as did those in 1760 during the Qing, after all its buildings were destroyed, presumably by the 1731 earthquake. It is a very special place historically, for it was a focal point of the resurgence of Buddhism during the Liao restoration, led by Abbot Fajun

(法均; ca 1036-91) an eminent monk of the Lu (律), or Law sect. Known in Sanskrit as Vinaya, this school was dedicated to the study and maintenance of the rules and code of discipline. In recognition of Fajun's endeavours, the emperor Daozong (道宗; r. 1055-1101), a devout Buddhist, granted him the *Yuzhi jieben* (御製戒本), a sutra copied in his own hand. This was subsequently taken to confer leadership of the sect and became the monastery's most treasured possession. Thus, the extraordinary three-and-a-half metre marble ordination altar built by Abbot Fajun was acknowledged as *primus inter pares*–"First Under Heaven"–with China's other two, at the Zhaoqing Temple (昭慶寺) in Hangzhou (杭州) and the Kaiyuan Temple (開元寺) in Quanzhou (泉州) respectively. (**Fig.83**)

We know what Jietai Temple looked like in the early 20th Century thanks to Lieutnant Fritz Jobst, a young German *Dolmetscher* (interpreter) with the East Asian Occupation Brigade in Zhili (直隸). While the better-known German architect, Ernst Boerschman, was still settling the terms of his second assignment in China with the Foreign Office in Berlin, the inquisitive Jobst helped survey

Fig.84 Jietai Temple as photographed by Lieutenant Fritz Jobst

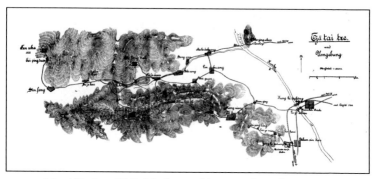

Map 4 Lieutenant Fritz Jobst's map of the approaches to Jietai Temple

and photograph the site, translate some of the steles and produce a small illustrated booklet about Jietai Temple as a souvenir for members of his brigade.[182] **(Fig.84)** At that time, the Temple was the residence of *Puwei* (溥偉), the Manchu Prince Gong, grandson of the late great Qing statesman Prince Kung, who had allowed the soldiers to spend the hot summer months there. Published by the brigade's newspaper in Tianjin in 1905, the booklet comprises sixteen pages of text and sixteen photographs, plus a map of the approaches to and a plan of the temple. **(Map 4)**

Jobst was an amateur scholar as well as an interpreter. He took time to talk to the monks–he reported some thirty in residence–and he took considerable care in describing the temple and its history. He recorded inscriptions by both the Kangxi and Qianlong emperors and the fact that Abbot Fajun's ashes were kept as a relic in a pagoda built in 1091. **(Fig.85)** According to Jobst, in 1905, the upper floor of the two-storey Main Hall housed statues of the Past, Present and Future Buddha, the main image stippled with a "thousand" smaller Buddha figures, while a "thousand" more lined the walls. **(Fig.86)** The lower chamber, where the Abbot instructed his disciples, was a shrine to what

---

182 Jobst, Fritz, *Geschichte des Tempels Tja Tai Tze*, 1905, Tientsin, of which a copy can be found in the *Universitats und Stadtbibliotek Koln*.

Fig.85 The reliquary Pagoda housing Abbot Fajun's ashes. Public Domain

Fig.86 The Main Hall at Jietai Temple; the central Buddha's base stippled with ten thousand smaller Buddhas. Public Domain

Jobst described as the "*God of Healing Diseases*", presumably the *Baisajyaguru*, whose standing statue was flanked by two rows of nine Luohans each. He makes no mention of material, but that is less important for our purposes than the fact of the existence of a Luohan hall. Similarly, the existence of another hall reported by Jobst that contained an image of *Upali*, one of the Buddha's ten great disciples, reinforces the importance of Jietai Temple as a seminary dedicated to nurturing monks who would defend the monastic code, the *Vinaya*.

The main hall had collapsed in the 1880s, but had been rebuilt, and can be seen in photographs taken both by Jobst and later Boerschman, who spent June and July of 1907 in the Western Hills. We also know that when *Puwei*'s grandfather, the statesman *Yixin* (奕诉) the Prince Kung (1833-1898), fell out of favour with the Dowager Empress and was "retired" in 1888, he had to leave his mansion in Beijing and took up residence at the temple. Thereafter he devoted a considerable sum of money to its restoration. Jobst puts the figure at 122,000 taels of silver, by the time the Prince died a decade later. His presence there would probably have put the temple off-limits to most picnicking foreigners and meant that visits were by invitation only, which brings us back, unexpectedly, to Terasawa Shikanosuke.

Recall that Mr. Ushikubo's somewhat confused report to J.E. Lodge, curator at Boston's MFA, indicated that Yamanaka & Co. had a working relationship with Terasawa. Recall also that Yamanaka & Co. had just secured rights to the sale of the collection of Prince Kung. Two thoughts flow from this. The first is that Terasawa would have been pretty busy at this time with all the leg-work required to bring that deal to fruition: inspecting, inventorying, overseeing the packing and crating. The scale of the operation is well captured in a report in the *New York Times* on the sale, which noted "The palace which Prince Kung was obliged to leave with the fall of his family, covered a space the size of twenty New York city lots, and was cared for by 8,000 servants. The art treasures of the palace were neglected and covered with dust and dirt when the arrangement was made for bringing them to this country."[183] The second thought is that since *Puwei* (溥偉), the Prince Gong who had volunteered the sale of his grandfather's collection, resided like his grandfather in the Jietai Temple, Terasawa would probably have had to call on him or his staff there.[184]

He might also have been curious about the place as a two-part article offering guidance for visitors venturing out to Tanzhe and Jietai Temples had appeared only recently in the locally published Japanese journal, *Enjin* (燕塵), penned by someone who styled

183 Davids, Roy and Jellinek, Dominic, *Provenance-Collectors, Dealers & Scholars in the Field of Chinese Ceramics in Britain & America*, Great Britain, 2011, p. 454.
184 *Puwei* needed funds having thrown in his lot with the Imperial Clan Party in the succession struggle. When its leader, Liang Pi was assassinated on 26 January 1912, he fled to Tsingtao, leaving his family at Jietai Temple.

himself Ying Fa Shi (影法帥)[185] Apparently a pseudonym, this monkish moniker translates roughly as "Master of the Law's Shadow", but whoever hid behind it, the article is militarily precise in its detailed description of the routes up and down Ma'an Hill (馬鞍山) and the various shrines, rock-carvings and other sights to be seen along the way. It also incorporates several pages gleaned from two Chinese scholars of the late 18th–early 19th Centuries, namely Li Zongfang (李宗昉) and Wu Xiqi (吳錫麒). Among the local attractions they mentioned were caverns, some of which extended a long way underground, and Li Zongfang (李宗昉) described nervously venturing at night a full *li* (roughly five hundred metres) into an "Ancient Fossil Cave" (太古化陽河). Brandishing a flaming torch that cast disturbing shadows amongst the stalactites and stalagmites, he encountered all manner of "leaping dragons", "swimming fishes", a "seated lion" and even a "Buddha" sitting precariously on a ledge. Bats, a seemingly bottomless shaft and the loud gurgling of a subterranean river combined to send him scurrying back into the moonlight.[186]

In amongst the wealth of local knowledge displayed, one place name that might well have caught Terasawa's eye was *Luo Hou Ling* (羅喉嶺).[187] *Ling* is a common word for the ridge of a hill, and *Luo Hou* is the short form of *Luohouluo*, beginning and ending with the same character as Luohan, which is the Chinese phonetic approximation for Rahula, the only son of the Lord Buddha: thus "Rahula Ridge". The young Rahula became the

---

185 Ying Fashi, "Jietai Tanzhe Canyiji (Visiting Jietai and Tanzhe Temples)", in *Enjin*, Beijing, 3.10.1910, pp. 584-91, and 3.11.1910 pp. 640-48.

186 Li Zongfang's travel journal for 16th day of the 8th month, 1809, quoted in *Enjin*, Op. Cit. p.585.

187 The name was not new; Liu Tong and Yu Yizeng, Op. Cit. 1635, mentions 羅嶺喉 (Luohouling) both as a place to visit and in the title of a poem, "*Going from Jietai in the fog, crossing Luohou Ridge, and as it cleared, reaching Tanzhe.*" It also appears in a similar poem by Zhao Huailing (mid-Qing) and in Gu Zuyu's famous geographic compendium *Du shi fang yu ji yao yu tu yao lan*, juan 23, p. 15, published 1831, where it refers to a place in Wutaishan, Shanxi.

first person formally to be ordained as a novice, so it would have been perfectly appropriate to use his name for the ridge above the Jietai Temple, where so many novices were to receive instruction. A ridge of the same name can be found near Kunming and a *Luohousi*, Rahula Temple, dating from the Tang, stands to this day in the monastic complex of Shanxi's sacred Wutai Mountain. The name is not new; it appears in both scholars' essays and Ying Fa Shi recorded visiting two cave shrines there, one dedicated to Guan Di (關帝), the God of War and Righteousness, and the other Guanyin (觀音), the Goddess of Mercy. We will come back to these in a moment.

Apart from inadvertently revealing that the terracotta statues had been taken from a temple rather than retrieved from some caves, Ushikubo's letter provided four other pieces of information, First, Terasawa told Ushikubo that he had sought the assistance of "Chinese partners"; second, when the statues were removed from the temple, they were in bits and pieces; third, as noted earlier, "it was almost impossible to carry life-size figures in perfect condition such a long journey...."; and fourth, they had therefore had to leave at least some of the stands behind initially. As suggested earlier, the reference to distance clearly rules out the Daqingshou and Fa Yuan Temples, or any others inside Beijing, but not a temple in the Western Hills such as Jietaisi.

Perzynski's account provides us with one other clue. Before launching into the despicable diatribe against his Japanese colleague, he wrote that the latter "claims to have been the first to have discovered the commercial value of these demi-gods of the Buddhist pantheon..." If true, that statement would mean that Terasawa rather than C.T. Loo found the statues, which is intriguing. He was far too busy to have spent time foraging in the undergrowth of Perzynski's *Achtlohanberg*, but probably not so busy that he could not have spent a little time poking around

Fig.87 Entrance of the Cave Temple, or Guangong Cave on Rahula Ridge above Jietai Temple. Public Domain

Jietai Temple on his visit, or visits, there. We know that the temple had a Luohan hall that had collapsed in the 1880s. Even if a set of Liao dynasty terracotta statues had survived earthquakes and man-made disasters that long, the collapse would certainly have damaged them. We know from Jobst's booklet that the main hall had been rebuilt, but could it be that Terasawa stumbled on the remains of the Luohans gathering dust either in a shed, or one of the caves in the hillside behind the temple? Jobst mentions three of them, one dedicated to Guanyin, the Buddhist Goddess of Mercy, one to a "sacred Taoist Monk" and the third, two kilometres to the East, to the God of War and Righteousness. Despite its name, Jobst reported that the latter "Guan Gong Dong" (關公洞), housed a statue of the Buddha with another set of eighteen Luohans. And marked it as "Hohlen Tpl", or Cave Temple on his map (**Fig.87**)

Jobst said nothing of the dimensions of the caves he explored, and he was silent on the size of the Luohans he saw in one of them. Fortunately for us, a later, equally curious visitor, G.E. Hubbard, spotted the same shrines half-way up what he termed a *via sacra* leading along the ridge from Jietai Temple to the summit

Fig.88 The Abbot of Jietai Temple circa. 1920. Photograph by Messrs. Hartung, Peking

of Qianlingshan (千靈山), and took time to explore them and to chat with their guardian. **(Fig.88)** The latter told him that the largest of the caverns extended a couple of *li* (about one kilometre) into the hillside, and his own observation confirmed that platforms had been cut into the walls large enough to house eighteen life-size Luohans, with a pedestal in the centre to support a statue of the Buddha "[188] It is difficult to understand why the monks should have disguised the entrance to this Luohan cave with a Guan Di shrine. Perhaps they wished to hide or protect its injured occupants. Whatever the reason, at this remove, we cannot know whether that was the statues' original location, or whether their remnants were simply stored there. Imagine, however, Terasawa's initial disbelief when he first glimpsed the dust and bat-dung covered remains in the darkness of the cave, and then his delight on recognizing them for what they really were!

The length of the tunnel in the hillside suggests that the monks' choice of "Rahula Ridge" may have built on an earlier, earthier name, or it could be that the locals had a sense of humour. The middle character in the phonetic transliteration of Rahula's name *Hou* (喉) has several variants, one of which means "throat" or "larynx", which needs little imagination. The

---

188 Hubbard, GE, *The Temples of the Western Hills visited from Beijing*, 1923, p. 51. The "Arhats" he saw were probably replacements purchased with funds from the sale of their battered old predecessors.

first character being the same as that for *Luohan,* that allows "Luohan Larynx Ridge" as an alternative name. Be that as it may, Terasawa's first encounter with the Luohans could well have inspired the caves-in-Yixian ruse he subsequently used to distract Perzynski's attention. In any event, once he had found the statues and realized their potential commercial value, it would be only natural for him to seek advice and assistance from C.T. Loo, whose reputation was growing.

Here was the man who had somehow contrived to extract eight heavy 6th Century stone statues from the grottoes at Xiangtangshan, get them to Beijing and then spirit them abroad for sale. The path downhill to the plain was steep but manageable. Terasawa would doubtless have spotted the donkey trains taking coal down to the river and appreciated how they might assist in camouflaging the extraction, but donkeys can carry only about 100 lbs, or roughly the weight of one of the bases. The statues would need to be manhandled down the slope before they could be carted; so he would need help. Physical logistics aside, he would have welcomed C.T. Loo's silver tongue in helping persuade the monks to part with the statues. He would also have known of C.T. Loo's workshop and certainly needed the skills of his restorers for putting them back together again.

Taken as a whole, the circumstantial evidence linking the statues to Jietai Temple is reasonably strong. The temple was restored during the Liao dynasty and governed by an abbot of sufficient stature to attract the attention and sponsorship of the emperor. Its triple-tiered ordination altar marks it as the focal point of the Lu sect's late 11th Century drive to restore the discipline of the Buddhist canon. An imperial gift of the Eighteen Luohans would have been perfectly in keeping with that purpose, and proximity to the kilns at Longquanwu would have made transporting them relatively easy. Glazed as they were, it is conceivable that they originally graced the temple's broad Ordination Terrace. That would have been a truly dramatic sight, and portraits of the sect's most outstanding members, taken from life, some of them possibly recalling abbots who had kept the flame alive during the period of persecution, would have resonated with new recruits to its ranks.

Word of these wonderful sculptures would surely have spread among the monks of the Lu sect and the wider monastic community. Members of the court who attended on their installation would doubtless also have been impressed. Remember, however, that the temple was in lands newly lorded over by the Liao. For the rest of the Chinese empire this was enemy territory, off-limits to the scholar officials of the Northern Song. Beijing was not yet Beijing. For them, the focal point was the court at Bianjing (Kaifeng); the centre of their attention was the ongoing struggle between supporters of the radical reformer Wang An-shi (王安石; 1021-86) and the conservatives represented by Chancellor Sima Guang (司馬光; 1019-86) and that precocious genius Su Shi (蘇軾; 1037-1101). The latter had served briefly as a magistrate in Shandong, but he was recalled to the capital in 1068–69, probably before the Luohans were installed. He and other literati like him were aware of Guanxiu caricatures, but there was no reason why they should have heard of, or indeed paid any attention to artistic developments north of the border. A painting such as Zhang Zeduan's (張擇端; 1085-1145) sumptuous contemporary portrait of Kaifeng, *Along the River during the Qingming Festival*, would have attracted far more attention.

The area surrounding what we now count as China's capital would be fought over for the next two centuries. The Liao had captured it from the Northern Song. The Jin would shortly ally with the Song to take it from the Liao in 1125 and begin the construction of their splendid new capital, Zhongdu, in what is now Beijing. Less than one hundred years later, Genghis Khan would breach the Juyong Pass and destroy it. Another fifty years and Khublai Khan would declare himself Great Khan and Emperor of China and begin building Khanbaliq on the same site. Throughout this tumultuous period, however, there was no need for the monks to flee, nor reason for them to hide anything away. Khublai Khan's reverence is a matter of record and there is a possibility that he may have seen the Luohans with his own eyes. His daughter had become a nun at the nearby Tanzhe Monastery and he had established a summer residence there.

Quite when time or natural disaster took their toll on the terracotta figures may never be known The pointy non-original heads of the Luohans in the ROM and the Sezon are evidence of early damage and repair. The last serious earthquake had been in 1057, before the Abbot Fajun reached Beijing. The next, in 1337, jolted Huaitai to the northeast and may have been the culprit. The remnants of the Luohans might well have been shuffled off stage in the subsequent restoration to take refuge in the cave in the hillside above the temple, which had more than enough space to lodge them indefinitely. All we know with certainty is that the intriguing place name Rahula Ridge / Luohan's Larynx first appears in Liu Tong and Yu Yizheng's late Ming guide to the sights surrounding the capital. By this time the origins of the Luohans must have slipped from human memory, but the odd geographic feature where their dusty and dishevelled remains had been stored was still deemed a curiosity worth exploring, which suggests that they were retired well before that date.

We are lucky that Terasawa Shikanosuke shared that curiosity. His visit to Jietai Temple in connection with the sale of Prince Kung's collection provided the perfect opportunity for the re-discovery and acquisition of all that could be saved and fits neatly into the established chronology of events leading to the statues eventual sale. None of this may be proof positive, but taken together it provides the most plausible solution so far to the final elements of our five-part riddle. So, after a long and winding journey, let us re-cap our conclusions:

- the Luohans were commissioned by the Liao dynasty emperor Daozong (1055-1101), who was a devout Buddhist;
- they were produced at the Longquanwu kilns just to the west of Beijing by skilled sculptors and artisans whom the Liao had resettled from Longquan in Dingzhou, Hebei province;
- the emperor gifted the statues to the nearby Jietai Temple, when it was rebuilt by Abbot Fajun of the Lu sect in 1064 to spearhead the revival of Buddhism during the Liao restoration;
- they had gone unnoticed and unremarked by contemporary Chinese scholars because they originally lay beyond the Chinese pale, in land occupied by the Liao, and subsequently were no longer on prominent public display; and
- the set was incomplete because many of the statues had been damaged beyond repair, probably by the 1337 earthquake, such that when rediscovered in the early twentieth century, despite the best efforts of skilled restorers, only nine-and-a-half could be rescued from the rubble.

If future on-site archaeology eventually uncovers a stele confirming the imperial gift, there will be a certain irony in knowing that *Rahula Ridge* is recorded as a real place name at least three centuries before Friedrich Perzynski dreamed up his mythical *Achtlohanberg*, and that a young fellow countryman, blissfully unaware, saw but did not recognize the Liao Luohans in that cave above Jietai Temple just six years before Perzynski pursued but failed to find his "Gods" in the caves above Yizhou.

EPILOGUE

IN THE 1920s, there was still considerable uncertainty about how many of the Luohans had survived. In her 1923 note in the museum's Bulletin, Cornelia Harcum at the ROM, for example, listed the four already in the British Museum, the Met in New York and the Penn, mentioned another in the Matsukata Collection in Japan and then continued "a head in the Cleveland Museum and four others are said to be owned by private collectors and dealers."[189] That would have brought the tally to ten. In fact, the head in the Cleveland Museum had been acquired by Langdon Warner in November 1916 while in Beijing, and his correspondence with the museum "make it clear that, at the time, only shattered pieces of the other statues remained." His head was later determined, on the basis of stylistic comparison, not to be part of the set.[190] Likewise, the Luohans in the collection of General Munthe in Beijing were discounted by Otto Fischer, who inspected them in 1925. He found that they were made of coarser material and that one of them bore a 1339 date. Sickman's acquisition for the Nelson-Atkins Museum in 1933, brought the total to nine, including both the one in the Matsukata Collection and Fuld's torso. Perzynski's original estimate of eight had been close to the truth, only he reckoned without the ingenuity of C.T. Loo's gifted restorers somehow to bring even the basket cases back to life. Even so, stories continued to circulate about the

---

189   Harcum, Op. Cit., 1923.
190   The author is indebted to Paul R. Goldin of the Penn for the information in quotation
       marks.

existence of other Luohans.

As late as 1969 Marion Wolf felt obliged to record that "Several additional examples may be in private collections."[191] Prophetic? Or did she perhaps know something that others did not? For, thirty years later, number ten did indeed emerge from the shadows to take up residence in the Musée Guimet. This last survivor presents a mystery all of its own. Where had it been hiding all these years? Colin Sheaf of Christie's, who arranged its private sale in 1998, refers to it as coming out of a packing case. So it had been put in store, but for how long? As we saw in the last chapter, Richard Smithies reported a discreet reference to the statue having been in a private collection since the early part of the last century. Which begs the question: whose might that have been?

Any number of the French men and women who passed through Beijing on the heels of the Allied Forces at the turn of the century might have been in the market. Could it have been the polymath railway engineer Joseph Charignon whose daughter passed away in 1997, a year before the last Luohan appeared? Unlikely; Charignon was more philologist and philosopher than collector, and his home in Beijing was a much-visited *salon*, the centre of French intellectual life in the city at that time. What about other Francophones whom we have met along the way? Not Bishop Favier; he had gone to meet his maker in 1905. Not Paul Pelliot; he had returned to Paris with his discoveries from Dunhuang in 1909 to be met by a vicious smear campaign against both himself and Edouard Chavannes. The latter continued his mission surveying and recording the grottoes and other sacred sites until 1915, and died only three years later. Victor Segalen, who had accompanied him, died in mysterious circumstances

---

191   Wolf, Op. Cit., 1969, p. 53.

in a French forest at Huelgoat the following year. Possibly the adventurous, aristocratic friend, with whom Segalen had explored western China on horseback, in 1914, and visited the funeral mounds in Shaanxi? Comte Augustus Gilbert de Voisins was a prolific author, but was not known as a collector. Dr. G. Giesler, Chairman of France's Northern Railways Company, collected archaic jades rather than statuary. Or maybe Gillon Othon, Marquis de Trazegnies, who had invested in the railways and whose acquisitions of imperial furnishings have occasionally trickled onto the market? Except he was Belgian rather than French, as was the railway engineer, Jean Jadot, who collected bronzes. The Nobel prize-winning poet-diplomat St John Perse, perhaps? He was Secretary to the French Embassy in Beijing from 1916 to 21, but does not appear to have collected any antiquities either then or later. Little is known of Madame A. Saint, who purchased not one, but two of the Xiangtangshan Bodhisattvas from C.T. Loo and Paul Vignier, except that she allowed them to be published — only once in the 1930s, but at least they were published.[192] And that is precisely the point: the last Luohan was never either exhibited or published before it surfaced in Paris in 1998.

One has to ask, why would a private collector buy a sculpture of this size and beauty and then not display it? If it had been displayed, even if only briefly, it would have been noticed. Most collectors take pride in showing off their latest acquisitions. The collector would have to have been a peculiar sort of recluse to display it solely for his or her private gratification. Possibly it did not match the curtains and was consigned to storage? If that were the case, however, surely it would have made more sense

---

192 Steinhardt, Nancy S., "The Chinese Rotunda", in *Arts of Asia*, Sept-Oct, 2008, p.87. The author has since discovered that, in fact, they were later acquired by the National Gallery of Victoria, Melbourne, Australia in 1955.

to put it back on the market rather than have it clutter up the garage or the cellar. Somehow a *"private collection"*, in the normal meaning of those words, simply does not hold water.

The author has no wish to embarrass or impugn the integrity of any of those involved in this episode, whether living or gone before. However, in looking for closure for the Perzynski Myth, he feels compelled to try and tie up this last loose end. On a balance of probabilities, he has concluded that the statue was held by the dealer who first acquired it and, after his death, by the dealer's family. The main reason for the dealer not putting it on the market is, he believes, that this Luohan was the odd man out in that it was not of quite the same *sancai* glaze as the others. We have already discussed the problems that the dealers would have anticipated in disposing of such a large number of similar statues at the same time, and the care that they took in orchestrating exhibition and sale. Their foresight was borne out by the difficulty C.T. Loo experienced in trying to convince the Met in New York to buy the Older Monk. In the end he succeeded, but it took another twelve years and the opening of a new museum in Kansas City before he was able to find a home for number nine. The first difficulty that would be faced by whoever held number ten, would be explaining away the non-matching pattern and slightly bluer tint of its robes. Prospective buyers' immediate reaction was bound to be to question why it was not quite *sancai*, and possibly query its authenticity. The market was already saturated and so it was probably left to lie waiting for a buyer, while its owner got on with easier and more lucrative business, and eventually, maybe, forgotten. Forgotten, that is, until somebody had to clear out the cellar. What follows is, of course, entirely speculative reconstruction, but the sequence of actual events on which it hangs is intriguing and lends ample support to the hypothesis.

Since Luohan number ten surfaced in France, let us assume that the dealer managed to get it there before the outbreak of the First World War. Most of the Parisian dealers made careful arrangements ahead of the German invasion to move their stock to multiple safe storage locations. Given it was the odd man out, its owner would have been in no hurry to put it on the market and so it may well have stayed crated and gone straight into storage, staying there until the end of the war. By that time, as mentioned above, the market was saturated, so again there was no urgency about bringing it to market.

Also, the centre of gravity of the trade in Asian antiquities had shifted from Europe to the United States. Post-war Europe was enduring the Great Depression and there was no market for massive statuary. C.T. Loo discovered this at the 1935/36 International Exhibition of Chinese Art in London and, with consummate diplomacy, arranged for the enormous Sui (隋) dynasty Amitabha Buddha he had loaned for the exhibition to be gifted by the Chinese Government to the British Museum, rather than pay additional shipping or storage costs. Then came the Second World War and the need once again to shuffle stock into discreet stores ahead of the German occupation of Paris in June 1940.

Loo's youngest daughter, Janine, *"le garcon manqué de la famille"*, to use Geraldine Lenain's poignant phrase, was evacuated from China with her husband and three young children in 1946 after spending some eight years there, nearly half of them in an internment camp. On her return to Paris, her father took the opportunity to entrust the running of his gallery there to her so that he could concentrate on the American market. He had opened his New York gallery in 1915 and, although he had put an ostentatious architectural mark on the Parisian landscape with the opening of La Pagode in 1928, the same year that he was awarded the *Legion d'honneur*, he was by then already spending most of his time on the other side of the Atlantic. Then, three years after the Second World War ended, disaster struck. The defeat of the Nationalists in China's civil war left Loo with few friends in vital places. Confiscation by the Communist authorities of a major shipment of antiques in Shanghai forced him into retirement. He liquidated his stock in America, handed the business over to his long-time associate Frank Caro and returned to his adopted country, France, in ill-health. He died in a Swiss clinic in Nyon in 1957.

Few families of famous men deal well with the passing of the patriarch. Geraldine Lenain glosses over the petty disputes and deals humourously with what, at the time, must have been anything but amusing. It fell to Janine to deal with the French fiscal authorities, which took both time and tact. Indeed, she appears to have had a better head for business and bargaining with bureaucrats than her father foresaw. One of his earlier letters suggests that he did not think that she would run the gallery for long "*Je prends note que tu veux reprendre l'affaire a la fin de l'annee, mais supposons qu'il n'ait plus de l'ancien stock, espere-tu arriver a vivre avec les objects achetes en europe seulement?*"[193] She would run it for close on fifty years, not finally retiring until she was 82 years old. To judge from the catalogue of the final sale of stock at La Pagode, which was conducted by Daguerre on 4 July 2002, what they had been asked to put on the block was just leftovers. Janine had pretty clearly begun gradually running the business down from about a decade earlier, selling to other dealers as well as collectors, or through established auction houses as she judged fit. Parting with familiar pieces that had decorated the Pagoda for many years would have been an emotional affair, but

---

193   Lenain, Op. Cit., p. 255, letter from C.T. Loo to his daughter Janine dated 29 April, 1952..

that was as nothing compared with the clearing of the Augean stables below ground. Anybody with any experience as Executor of an estate, or inventorying businesses that have gone bust will be familiar with the surprises that come when sorting through the accumulated clutter of a lifetime.

It may simply be a coincidence that the private sale of the tenth Luohan to T.T. Tsui took place in 1998, but this author believes it was just a part of this Herculean and lengthy process of disposal. The fact that the family did not stumble on C.T. Loo's personal papers until fifty years after his demise speaks volumes, and a large, dusty old crate at the back of the *cave* might well have been left until last, behind a queue of numerous other more recent and more familiar acquisitions. However, once she opened the crate, Janine would have realized what she was looking at. She was nobody's fool; she had more experience than most in the trade and she had on hand friendly advisers such as her contemporary Michel Beurdeley. A private sale of the Luohan would have been a more prudent path than a public auction, and so it proved.

The Luohans had not been looted from an Imperial Palace, nor were they in any sense the trophies of war; rather they were damaged goods, discarded by the temple to which they had been donated a millennium before. Nevertheless, there would have been no point courting controversy given the size of the statue, the fame of its brethren and the stigma which by that time attached to C.T. Loo's name, as well as to the many iconic masterpieces that he had sourced over the years for museums in the West. Ironically, it was the French rather than the Chinese Government that was to prove sensitive to its sale and possible export from France, but better safe than sorry. Compare and contrast the media frenzy that accompanied China's anger at the attempted turn-of-the-century sale by Christie's in Hong Kong of a couple of bronze animal heads lopped from the famous Zodiac

Fountain in the Yuanmingyuan.

C.T. Loo had been left holding not one, but two babies. He had reserved the "Older Monk" for the Met and shipped it straight to New York. It seems likely that he had similarly sent the odd-monk-out to Paris with a view to selling it to the Guimet, for which we know he had a soft spot, only to be frustrated by the Great War and the Great Depression that followed.

So one of the babies was orphaned and, for a while abandoned, but it ultimately reached its intended adoptive parent, for which the Musée Guimet is doubtless thankful.

The artists and artisans who created these sculptural masterpieces a millennium ago have faded from memory, as have the remarkable, otherworldly men who sat for their portraits. All lovers of art must, however, be grateful that somebody should have spotted their incomplete remains, rescued what he could from the rubble and restored ten of them to their former glory.

REFLECTION ON MICHAEL ONDAATJE'S "COMPLETE CRIME."

Otto Kummel (1874-1952), whom we met in Chapter Four, was the German art historian who founded the Museum of East Asian Art in Berlin and went on to become Director General of the State Museums there. Unfortunately for him, his reputation was forever tarnished by a single report that bears his name. Commissioned in 1939 by Joseph Goebbels, Hitler's Minister of People's Enlightenment and Propaganda, it was Hitler's Christmas list. It catalogued all the plundered German art treasures that the Third Reich intended to retrieve from museums and private collections elsewhere in Europe, and a few other bits and pieces besides. Things did not go quite to plan, more than one nation got its hands dirty and several things disappeared. One, as we have seen, ended up in a storeroom in the Hermitage Museum in St. Petersburg. Others, such as the fabled Amber Room from Catherine the Great's palace at Tsarkoye Selo, whose panelling has had to be painstakingly recreated by modern master craftsmen, have still not resurfaced.

Not long ago, Hollywood reminded audiences of these events by paying homage to the work of the Monuments Men, the teams that hurried round Europe as the Second World War ground to an end, to locate and save from theft or destruction the countless works of art amassed by Hitler's Nazis. Hollywood's producers are not known for their sense of irony and nowhere in the film does any of its heroes raise a question about how many times some of these works of art had changed hands over Europe's war-torn centuries. The Nazis are still fair game, and useful as competing "baddies" in justifying plunder by American adventurers in films of the *Indiana Jones* variety. It is too much to hope that those who put the Monuments Men on their pedestal would ever turn the spotlight on America's museums, or others in the West whose collections have benefited from war or the temporary weakness of other nations.

The spoils-of-war argument is disingenuous. It assumes that all wars are just, that the victors are always in the right and deserve something for their pains. The arguments of those who claim that removal of artifacts to the West saved them from damage or destruction during a prolonged period of civil war and revolution are equally self-serving. What nation on earth has not at some time lost part of its heritage to internal strife or natural disaster? It is possible to distinguish between works of art that are manifestly a part of a nation's core cultural heritage and lesser items that were previously in private ownership and freely sold in the open market. However, in a digital world, the arguments for allowing retention of the former by public institutions, where they cannot be proven to have been a gift of the nation in which they were created, are wearing increasingly thin.

Much has been written on the subject of the return of cultural property to countries of origin and much good work done by UNESCO, which first took up the challenge in 1970. In practical terms, however, most of its achievements have been in the area of identifying the world's most important cultural sites and protecting them from future spoliation rather than righting past wrongs. On the latter, discussions continue and are regularly reported "regarding the delicate issue of the return of removed cultural property, on the requests formulated and reservations expressed, and on the claims and misunderstandings, in particular within the museum community."[194] As a former civil servant with some experience of the workings of multilateral organisations, I think I understand precisely what that means. Do not hold your breath!

The observant reader will have noticed references to this moral dimension scattered through the Luohan's tale. It is difficult to write about them without considering the broader historical context in which events occurred. I am not a Buddhist, but my heart is with Michael Ondaatje in his condemnation of the criminal pillage of the Tianlongshan grottoes (天龍山石窟). One such crime would have been bad enough, but the sacrilege was repeated, at Xiangtangshan (響堂山), at Longmen (龍門石窟), and numerous other sacred locations. Make no mistake this was desecration on an unprecedented scale.

The *sancai* Luohans were damaged goods that had been consigned to storage. Like the monks of Guangsheng Temple (廣胜寺) in Shanxi Province, those at Jietai Temple (戒台寺) were probably persuaded to part with the pieces for a sum that would assist in restoration of other damaged buildings. That might make it a little less objectionable, but it was still part of the same process of systematic pillage. The Luohans are great art and have a historic cultural significance that is not lessened, but rather heightened by their having been hidden from view for so long, and by the remarkable story of their rediscovery. If the hypothesis outlined in this book proves correct, and if further research can determine where they originally stood, reassembling the survivors there would recreate the collective magnetism that they must originally have exercised over the faithful.

Still more important, I believe, are the grottoes. UNESCO has pointed the way, but a process of formal request-and-response

---

194   UNESCO, *Return of cultural objects: The Athens Conference*, May 2009.

reverses the onus of responsibility. The country from which cultural objects were wrested or sold in time of weakness is forced into the position of *demandeur*. What is needed, in my humble opinion, is for one courageous curator to convince his or her governing board to take the lead in volunteering the return of a sacred object whose origins are known. Properly and sensitively handled such an approach could ultimately generate the momentum needed for real restoration. Any one of China's Buddhist grottoes would be a good place to start.

APPENDIX

JAGD AUF GOTTER
by Friedrich Perzynski
Translation by Richard Smithies

PERZYNSKI'S STORY[195]

This is the second time I have been in Yixian. Every tourist should see Yixian. For here, the graves (Qing Xiling–Western Tombs) of the Emperors of the last dynasty are laid out on a scale that would make one think that China existed only for its ruling families. The tomb of the Yongzheng Emperor, a name that makes the heart of a ceramics collector quicken its beat, shows to advantage the extremely broad-minded approach to the monumental building concepts of the Chinese who here created a mausoleum in the freest style in the midst of a perfect natural setting.

Art manuals maintain that Chinese architecture lacks monumental proportions. But these writers base their judgment on a limited perception. Only a few years after Poppelmann created the *Zwinger* in Dresden, northern China witnessed the erection of the Yuanmingyuan, the Chinese Versailles, the mausoleums of the Dongling and Xiling, the marble terraces of the Zhenjue Temple[196] and of the Biyun Temple near Beijing, whose monumental scale must be measured not by the scale of a Gothic cathedral but by that

---

195 Smithies' translation introduced sub-headings that do not appear in the original German text. I have removed these, but otherwise followed his formatting where the paragraphing differs from the original.

196 This is a mistake. The "*gelbes Tempels*" of the German original is normally taken to refer to the *Xihuangji*, the Western Yellow Temple, which was built in 1651 to provide a residence for the Dalai Lama. This is supported by the immediately preceding reference to marble terraces.

of a temple of antiquity, According to the well-known Japanese saying, Nikko–where the Tokugawa ruling family erected tombs at the time Rococo was all the vogue in Europe–is the only place where one can really appreciate the full meaning of the word *kekko* meaning splendid. Yet their blatant ostentation and gingerbread ornamental bombast present a striking contrast to the simplicity and composure of contemporary Chinese architecture of that kind.

Whoever comes to Yixian graciously shows his good manners by staying at the house of the Mandarin, who will arrange for an expert guide to visit the mausoleums. I draw up my fur collar, put on big black glasses to protect my eyes against the blowing dust and hurry away from the railway station to a nearby lamaist temple.[197] I have no rifle with me, although shooting for hare and pheasant is to be had for the asking. But I do have two loaded revolvers and ammunition, climbing ropes and an axe. I am hunting for Gods and not game!

In the absence of any government restrictions, China's Gods have become a lively article of trade. Some months ago, a statue of a disciple of the Buddha, larger than life-size, reached Beijing. Its owners feasted their eyes upon my profound amazement as they showed it to me. I had never seen anything like it. At the time, we called him the Priest, for despite the traditional long ears, he had the striking pictorial quality of a portrait. His eyes, with their dark shining pupils, looked as if into another world. He lived, spoke, dreamed. He was the realization of my hope that, here on the ancient soil of China, I would find sculptures that would completely revolutionize our conception of East Asian creativity, hitherto measured only by the standards of Japanese art.

Even without the weight and solemnity of its expression, the enchantingly honest silhouette, lifted above vulgar realism by a

---

197   This was the *Yongfu Monastery* (永福寺), where visiting members of the imperial family would stay.

slightly archaic trait, even without the mastery of form which revealed the hand of a master imbued with grace, and even if it were not a moving testimony of artistic and religious profundity, the material alone would have marked as a kind of wonder of the world (sic).[198] This larger-than-life ascetic was made of hard-fired clay and glazed in a great kiln in three colours–green, yellow and brown–the *sancai* of the Tang period. Tangara-like sculptures from this period are now being brought safely to light after a thousand years as the picks of Chinese railway workers tear up ancient Chinese graves.

A discovery in the history of art is a discovery like any other. It enraptures the finder, who hesitates for a long time before abandoning his find to the world. It produces a peculiar enchantment of the mind. A person who has never had a painting, a sculpture, that throws new light on the psyche of a whole period, alone in his possession, protected from covetous eyes, even the gaze of his friends, can hardly imagine the discoverer as he contemplates his find. Possession of a legion of slaves is a meager reward compared to the awareness of being master of the most radiantly transformed spiritual expression of that which inspired the elite of an entire age, and which was cast by the medium of the artist, out of elemental chaos into a precisely defined form.

The owners of the disciples of the Buddha were art dealers who naturally evaluated the treasure that had fallen into their hands in purely commercial terms. Did they suspect what torches of envy they had lit in me when they removed the wrappings from the sculptures? It was a nightly torment for me. This statue of the ascetic priest appeared in his world-renouncing serenity, his angular jaw resplendent, his eyes meeting mine and yet seeing past me.

---

198   An "it" appears to be missing between "marked" and "as".

THE MISSING BUDDHAS

Arrival in Yizhou

Now here I am in Yizhou for the second time. Back home, people are writing books about the history of Chinese art, and an authority such as Bushell leaps boldly over eight centuries in his treatise on Chinese sculpture, because he has nothing to recount from that period. Yet here in the mountains near the Qing Xiling, eight–or was it eighteen–larger-than-life statues were once produced and hidden in caves. All the while, English pheasant hunters have been climbing in the brush nearby without an inkling of their existence.

This is virgin territory, for no European, nor the art-dealers themselves, have any idea of where the luohan was actually found. This feeling makes me hot with joy and warms me in the cold temple guestroom, where I am told, Chinese princes are accommodated when they visit the imperial tombs. The Chinese standard of living is considerably lower than that of Europeans, and even more so of Americans and where an East Asian prince is content, a well-to-do middle class person from our part of the world would feel deeply sorry for himself without all the comforts. Paper window-panes, stone floors, hard *Kangs* to sleep on, a small fired-clay stove producing noxious fumes, all these are obstacles not easily overcome in winter-time and we must adapt our spoiled European habits to them. However, camping and life under canvas are good bridges.

I cannot expect to find the luohan still in their caves. It may never be established who first took it into his head to fetch them out of their hiding places. It was certainly not the inhabitants of Yizhou. They number about 85,000–a few thousand Chinese and Chinese Moslems and the rest Manchus. The Manchus are brave, well-mannered and chivalrous, but they are, as their most eloquent Chinese defender, Gu Hungming, even admits, ignorant and helpless blockheads. Now that the handsome allowance which used to be distributed to them regularly before the revolution has been abolished and they have abandoned the building of the mausoleum for the Guangxu Emperor, the cruelest poverty reigns among them, a poverty that does not beg, but is borne dully and as proudly as a Kismet behind crumbling mud walls.

A Japanese claims to have been the first to have discovered the commercial value of these demi-gods of the Buddhist pantheon—one of those jackals who scout the continent of Asia, under every conceivable pretext, to tailor a comfortable and durable jacket for themselves out of the skin of the poorest. No American is more cunning, no German more brutal, no Englishman more unscrupulous than this human pestilence, which the island kingdom, gripping the Asian continent as with a dragon's claw, discharges like pus from its teeming populace. And no physiognomy is more base, more deeply etched by all the evils of covetousness and perfidy than that of the Japanese emigrant who seems to have the slogan 'survival of the fittest' written in monumental letters on his belly.

No, the luohan were torn from Samadhi, from the deepest and clearest peace, long ago, by night, when the north-western mountains lay in silence. Moslems, followed by ruffians of every description, loaded these clay colossi on long bamboo poles and carried them down into the valley where they were buried. Many statues were thereby destroyed. The commandant of Xiling used his soldiers to rescue what was left and threw those he caught in jail for many years. One after the other, the many Beijing curio-dealers who had come trooping along when they heard of the discovery were taken into custody until a cloud of fear spread among the inhabitants and out into the remotest parts of the region.

I myself am not entirely without concern as my laissez-passer has still not arrived. I have had my informants here for a long time. One of them, whom I have been paying handsomely, has been feeding me anecdotes and stories for months. He was a Moslem and he did honor to the reputation of his fellow-believers, whose dishonesty is proverbial among the Chinese. Another succeeded in locating two statues, supposedly buried beneath the flagstones of a Manchu house. I commissioned him to inspect one of these statues for me, but the gendarmes arrived on the scene just as they were about to carry the *disiecta membraii* out of the house to a safer place. Everyone fled. One took the head, another the arms and torso and each considered whatever he had saved was now his own property. One owner had now become six, who, in typical Chinese fashion, distrusted one another. In ten years' time, no doubt, they might probably agree on their shares of the booty. But they took the money from the man in whom I had placed my trust. They dragged him off to the *yamen* (local government offices) for questioning, where he was successful in pleading for his freedom but not for my money.

Nothing daunted, I sent another Chinese, this time an academic, to Yixian. We agreed upon a secret number code which he wrote upon his chest. So that this emissary could 'save his face' in an emergency, the code referred only to 'paintings' of a 'goddess'. I received the first telegram early one morning in Beijing, while I was still in bed. I hurried barefoot to my desk, where with pounding heart, I decoded:

0006–I have ferreted out the torn painting and know where the face is.

Hurrah! Thought I.

3054–The goddess's face and other parts of the torn painting still exist, but they are in a dangerous place and I have not seen them.

'The Chinese are all blockheads', the Japanese bandit who

claims to have tracked down these controversial statues, said to me one day.

Another figure in code:

1165-The complete painting is still in its old place and has been carried away.[199]

So this unbroken sculpture still rests beneath the flagstones of the Manchu house and nothing has happened in all this time.

In the meantime, my new emissary has made a few valuable acquaintances–a lamaist priest expelled from his monastery for theft, who spends the night behind a teahouse and cannot write, and another no less disreputable character whose head also sits uneasily on his shoulders. Both have offered to serve me as spies. In the manner of a scholar, my informant brings me nobler information: an old lamaist priest claims to know that the luohan were made on the orders of the great Chinese traveler Xuanzang. Xuanzang travelled to India at the beginning of the seventh century and came home laden with works of art and manuscripts. The landscape around Yixian aroused his enthusiasm and he is reputed to have founded a temple with his disciples and made them produce such images as these. In my excitement, I pound the table with my fist. Xuanzang, whose invaluable manuscripts Marc Aurel Stein discovered in a temple on the borders of Gansu and which are even now being translated by all the great Sinologists of Europe, traces of Xuanzang in the mountains of Yixian! If only it were true! If only we could prove that! I stagger around my room, as if intoxicated. This discovery would be finer than Marc Aurel Stein's findings, more valuable for our understanding of East Asian art than all the scientific expeditions so far.

---

199 The formatting of the text in Hsu's book has gone awry here, with the whole of this section printed in a smaller font. For ease of reading, I have restored the larger font for Perzynski's commentary.

No the old priest had no book, no document of any kind. It is all oral tradition, handed down to him by his teacher, an old monk. A few days pass in idleness.

Now I am in the middle of the battlefield. Full of expectation, I look over the walls of the temple courtyard which rises in terraces, down onto the silent village. The cold seems less painful here than in dusty Beijing. The air is pure, transparent; beautiful undulating hills sweeps (sic) down blue from the west, the smoke of mountain fires descends like incense into the valley. Mighty old conifers stretch out their boughs and twigs with expressive gestures to the sky. The Qianlong Emperor, who enjoyed a noble tree as an aesthetically perfect living thing no less than the Bostoner Oliver Holmes did a century later, gave some of them names by which they are still called today: 'Dwarf,' 'Crooked Neck,' and 'Dragon's Claw'. Beneath the temple, a few other giant trees extend their branches into the gossamer air, a bird's nest sticks like a woolly ball of cotton to the tangle of the treetops. The beauty of a tree bereft of leaves in the winter was felt by Chinese painters as a deep experience of the mind.

We hold a council of war. I decide not to show myself for the time being. My Chinese friend draws a hideous bright blue smock over his aristocratic silken robe and sets forth on a tour of inspection. Just as he returns and I am bursting with curiosity, we are joined by a senior lamaist priest. The art of the Chinese, who are able to draw insignificant things out at length by detailed discussion, ornamenting them with onomatopoeic garnishings, until they are as loaded as a Levantine woman's bosom, never fails to arouse my astonishment. And even more, the immense courtesy with which they respond to their interlocutor's every utterance, even the most banal. My friend excels a master of ceremonies at the Austrian Court in politeness. He sits on his chair, his legs together, leaning forward in an obliging manner, showing his white teeth in an amiable smile, his porcelain eyes directed at his interviewer as if in thankful expectation. My Chinese friend tells him that I am a foreigner recovering from an illness and who is seeking inner refreshment by climbing in the mountains. He then asks, 'Have you climbed the Eight lohan Mountain?' The Lama says he has not.

A soon as he has left, I impatiently ask my Chinese friend what he has found out in his talk, He tells me that a mighty sculpture, that of Guanyin on the Guanyin Mountain, has been broken into pieces by the inhabitants of Yixian and carried off to places of hiding. What madness! Apparently it was made of mud and rags, simply painted over and gilded. It was shown to me some months ago and I turned it down–it could not be carried and was splendid where it was, providing a delightful surprise for whoever might come across it climbing in the hills. What vandals! Vandals!

Now they say that the statue was not made of mud and rags. That is only the outer covering. Beneath that lies Goddess's ceramic body, decorated in three-colour glazes like those of the luohan. The thief proposes to bring us some pheasants and hare this evening and to smuggle into the house one of the feet of the Guanyin which he has cleaned of its covering . I am to be convinced that it is made of the same material as the luohan.

The hunter makes his appearance just after eight that evening. He drags a heavy sack into my room and then disappears. We open it. I gaze in awe at the Goddess's foot. It is the same material–chalky-white burnt clay, fairly hard, with a coating of white-greenish glaze, which shows finely meshed cracks of age. A few toes are missing from the powerfully beautiful shape of the foot. Did he have the whole statue in his possession? I asked. Yes, but in about 60 pieces. The audacious young fellow draws back the curtain of the room and the candlelight falls on his face, it is brown and wrinkled by sun and mountain wind, the eyes blazing with irrepressible fire. A fur hat with earflaps gives him an almost Prussian appearance. His head will certainly fall if the Commandant learns the temple has been pillaged.

We fail in our attempt the next morning to get a guide to visit the Eight Luohan Mountain. Nobody in the temple will admit to having climbed it. Finally, we go looking for a man who 'knows mountains.' The night crackles with the cold. I mix myself a stiff grog, wrap myself up in my blankets and, as I dream of the statues, hear the sweet plaintive sound of a Manchu flute, which pierces the night and reaches me in the darkness of the temple.

Guanyin Mountain Caves

The morning air is as cold and clear as mountain water, the donkey bells tinkle and the locals out gathering brushwood stand still as our long procession of baggage carts jolts by. The soldiers standing outside the barracks cast embarrassingly interested glances at us as we pass. We follow the path over half-frozen streams. 'Korr, korr,' shout the donkey drivers, warning their beasts not to make a false step. They are all Moslems with quite un-Chinese facial features.

A small grove of elm trees marks the entrance to the wild nature park, which now opens before our rested eyes like a multi-coloured fan. The soft curves of the chain of hills become more and more angular and the donkeys' hooves carefully seek a hold in the rubble, while the dew-laden brush that reaches to the farmer's chest or the donkey's belly in summer now wets our boots.

In the north-west, the mountains tower up in mighty naked blocks, embracing all Yixian in a wide half-circle. A large cave, that looks like a cliff-temple draws me like a magnet. How can we get up there? My guide, trotting on ahead on an old nag, lent to him at the temple, shakes his head. Nobody, he says, has ever been up there and along the ridge of the mountain, where only the wolf and ibex live. My Chinese friend smiles and comments that the wolves flee from men by day.

The path becomes more difficult and finally ceases altogether, as we approach our goal, the Bafowa, the Eight-luohan Mountain. Oh for the Taishan in Shandong Province, where one can climb to the summit up elegant stone steps, and where I groaned that Buddhism dispenses its blessings with so much discomfort. We unload the donkeys, pack our cameras, provisions and cooking equipment on our people's backs and begin the climb. The ground is slippery, thorn bushes catch our clothes, tangled branches set snares for our feet and one after the other we get stuck. Often we are forced to scramble up on all fours and I can see from the look on our guide's face that he cannot make up his mind.

There is the first cave (*Cave 1*). He points, high above us. It is too small for the great sculptures! Perhaps we are climbing the wrong mountain! Only chamois can make their way up here!

Our guide announces that he does not want to continue. Angrily, I bite my lower lip. All the inhabitants of Yizhou only seem to think of misleading me. A thought flashes through my mind–the shrine off the Guanyin is nearby. I visited it when came up here during the summer. Her foot lies in my trunk. But is it really hers? Months ago, when I visited her ensconced in the cave, she was still intact. Hers was a strange, almost raw beauty, a mixture of styles, standing on a mighty tri-coloured faience stand, whose material and colouring contrasted curiously with the perishable clay-like substance of her body. My guide at the time, a young Moslem with thieving eyes, had climbed onto the stand, barely reaching the shoulders of the goddess. Coarse and lacking any reverence, he had broken off a finger from one of the hands.

The Guanyin Mountain lies on the western wing of the long mountain range and can be climbed, on all fours, in a good half-hour. We pull ourselves up the steep rocks. The path becomes even narrower and I run ahead breathlessly. Half way up the knoll, standing on a cliff-ledge, is the little temple hewn into the rock face (*Cave 2*). Our guide, whom we had left below so that he could not spread the news in Yixian about the destruction of the Goddess and jeopardize all my plans, makes a move to follow us. Like a trumpet call, my *tang-i-tang* echoes of the face of the mountain.

And now I am up. Rubble blocks the entrance. I climb over it only to find a scene of heart-rending desolation. The Goddess still rests on what is left of the stand. But the vandal has broken her legs from her body, all that remains of her right arm is a stump and there is a gaping deep hole in her breast. Sadly, her nose is gone and her countenance is not even a pale reflection of its once brittle but expressive beauty. My Chinese friend arrives panting. Gazing on the sorry remains of the statue, he hurls vain imprecations against the robber.

After a while, we both break into laughter for the Goddess has cruelly made a fool of the violator of her temple. A narrow path runs along the edge of the cliff. There two commemorative stone tablets relate that a pious man from the district had found the goddess broken, and with the help of other charitable inhabitants of the region, had repaired and gilded the statue in 1624. The robber was obviously illiterate.

Footprints, cigarette ends and other evidence that is difficult to describe, show that the shrine had been desecrated in the past 36 hours. The iconoclast must have climbed the mountain during the night, knocked off the clay covering by the dim light of a lantern and finally reached the ceramic core. His had been a noble work to strip the statue, worthy of the best museum restorer! He amputated the legs. The pheasant's plaintive piping had long ceased and there was not a soul on the mountain when his axe blows had echoed through the night. Then he struck the hole in the breast of Guanyin. The idol remains unmoved, still wearing her impenetrable smile. No writing on the wall appears in flames of phosphorous. The robber puts his hand into the open breast–the head is made of wood! He pulls the arm off the shoulder–wood again! Nothing now remains but a headless, armless goddess with a covering which had been added much later of a mixture of clay and mud, with new head and arms, a piously patched up remnant, against which the hand of a fool had sinned. In a rage, he had destroyed the base with blows from his axe–this deceptive base, which had brought dozens of Beijing curio dealers to Yixian, because they had rightly suspected that behind this patched up image of Guanyin lay something much more valuable.

So now we sit amid the ruins of the cave, lamenting a China that in gnawing poverty thus destroys its noblest art treasures. How inconceivably beautiful this Guanyin must once have been! I clean some of the folds in her robes and cut free a piece of the hair-bow that falls in long ribbons down the Goddess's back. The robe had been fashioned with tender love, ornamented with clouds and flowers engraved beneath the glazing. A cinquefoil patterned frieze in high relief, yellow on a green base, seems to have formed the front border of the robe which flowed down in wide folds. The statue had once been two metres tall and stood on a base which itself measured one metre high and two metres wide. In what gigantic kiln did they fire this colossus and how did they manage to get it up here?

On the stone commemorative tablet, erected at he (sic) beginning of the seventeenth century, the restorer had chiseled a poem celebrating the difficulty of the climb:

Longmensi is an old temple.
Like some mighty screen; the mountain enfolds it.
Shanzidong lies not far from here, to the west,[200]
While in the west, the mountain descends steeply
to the plain.[201]
It is silent here.
Of all the mountains, this one is deemed to be the
most holy and renowned place.
Yet the passer-by is gripped with fear on venturing
here, and his skull shatters should he climb in fear.
From the distant valley, clouds and whisps (sic) of
mist ascend and human voices are seldom heard.
Trees spread their limbs and crows caw in their
midst.
Woodcutters come and then they go.
Wild monkeys scavenge through the trees.

The story of these sculptures becomes stranger still. On the commemorative tablet is inscribed this curious phrase–*All these Buddhas came from afar.* Were they from Henan, the most artistic of China's ancient provinces, brought here by pious pilgrims? Did they want to save them from the Mongol incursion in the thirteenth century and hide them in these almost totally inaccessible caves?

I wonder if there might be some piece of writing concealed in the Goddess's body or in the base and for quarter of an hour I rummage through the rubble. Suddenly, I come upon a piece of paper. I hand it to my Chinese friend, but he shakes his head with a smile. It is a prayer for a sick mother, undated and barely legible.

---

200 "West" is either a typo, or an error in translation; the German original reads "*Ost*".
201 Here Perzynski's memory is at fault; the mountains descend steeply to the East, not the West.

Driven by curiosity, that cardinal feature of the East Asian, our guide now magically appears on the mountain ledge. He sees our axe lying on the ground, but says not a word. The axe, the long time we have spent in the cave and the foot of the Guanyin in my bag are damning evidence enough.

Finally, we make our way down at snail's pace. Arriving at the foot of the mountan, we trot back in silence through fields empty of humanity. We pass by the grave of the Guangxu Emperor, the moonlight shining through the roofs of the halls where building has barely begun. Hewn stones lie around, tiles and logs neatly stacked in piles. Once it begins to get colder and all the Gods have been sold, they will come and steal the wood from the Emperor's mausoleum for their hearths. Frost and hunger destroy all reverence. Cixi, the old Empress, made better provision for mortal remains–her corpse lies in a splendid palace in the Eastern Graves, the Dongling, which was completed before she died. She had incense vessels made, of gold, silver and jade, to be placed in her mortuary chamber like an ancient ruler and her coffin raised on a jewel encrusted catafalque. As for her nephew's mausoleum, only the deficit of the Higher Accounting Office remains. He reigned for a hundred days in an independent and not unmanly fashion, staring for what remained of his life into the eyes of a medievally violent death. His brittle bones could well have rested comfortably enough beneath some beautiful tree, far from the people, but that was not grand enough; it was not the way of the Manchu. So they measured out the area of half a city for his tomb. It lies there now, piteously illumined by the moon, like some heap of ruins with a mangy dog sitting on a pile of cement for its only guardian, growing into a giant silhouette in the chalk-white light.

Are those clouds on the horizon?

There was disturbing news the next morning. I learn that the authorities have been continuously collecting information on the purpose of my journey and that soldiers have searched the temple by night. The Commandant of Qing Xiling has forbidden the inhabitants of Yixian to sell me any of the luohan. I do not feel at all at ease without my laissez-passer. The foot of the Guanyin was returned to its owner last night with a new offer of pheasants and hares. We eat pheasant every evening. It reminds me of the fate of the consular official in the extreme north of China, who wrote to Berlin complaining that surely he could not be expected to eat snipe every day. A Privy Counsellor wrote back offering to exchange places with him!

The Commandant's authority certainly has an effect–there is not a guide 'for the mountains' to be had in the entire district. Knowing that his head sits loosely on his shoulders, the destroyer of the Guanyin makes it plain that he does not want to be seen anywhere in the vicinity. The sun rises in the sky and I wander dejected up and down the temple terrace. Everywhere I turn, I meet with passive resistance or a smile that betokens refusal, and promises that go unkept.

We walk over to the tomb of the Yongzheng Emperor to give the impression that I am simply on a world tour. We stop at the elm grove and I to set up my tripod so that the unfrocked lama from the village can join us without raising suspicion. He now sports a splendid braid on his once shaven head, his nose and mouth almost meet and his forehead even mirrors his delightful spiritual depravity. I tell him not to look down at the ground whenever he speaks to us. He understands readily enough. He overwhelms me with a veritable cornucopia of promises: tomorrow he will accompany us to the Eight Luohan Mountain, this evening he will show me the head of the sculpture rescued from the Manchu house a few weeks ago and he even promises to introduce me to the owners of an undamaged luohan. I place two shining dollars on the grass.

A churchyard peace reigns in the grand park surrounding the mausoleum of the Yongzheng Emperor. A charming moat of clean masonry surrounds it, designing graceful curves. Ch'ienlong, who had this tomb built for his father, was a consummate master at playing with nature. The building itself is laid out according to the plan of Ming tombs and offers no surprises; all the gates, bridges and paths bordered by old conifers simply echo the prospect of the Temple of Heaven in Beijing or that of the mausoleum of the Yongle Emperor. As with the Ming tombs, stone figures of mandarins and animals line the ceremonial way and the patina of age will only increase their charm.

Our footsteps echo, but no deer starts for the cover of trees, not a breath of wind ruffles the stillness of this clear, sun-warmed November day and, like a wall blanking out any worldly sound, the mountains frame this park dedicated to a departed soul. Chinese architecture is composed to blend into the landscape, becoming only a small part of it. An arched bridge, which suddenly appears to the west, half-covered by conifers, is set, with a painter's eye, against a background of green fronds and undulating blue hills where, once again, the north-south axis is emphasized by the five arches of an open stone gate, flanked by two side-porticos to the east and west. There is no artificial wall to obstruct the view. Through the middle opening of the gate, one can see beyond across a balustraded bridge, whose graceful curvature is lyrically calculated. And the eye is led towards a gentle rising mountain peak, behind which one's fantasy can imagine anything, and over which a dreaming soul can reach out over mountains, over chasms, over a distant sea, ever onwards.

Of course, we did not get to see anything that evening. My heart yearns for a luohan and my banknotes burn in my pocket. After a meal of pheasant, we wander over to the wretched tea-house where the worthy lama brother spends his nights. My friend went in, looking up at the night sky as if to seek the Plough, Cassiopeia or the Pleiades. There were soldiers there, but no lama in sight.

This morning we breakfast at that magical early hour when the sky is spun over with a transparent gauze that threatens to tear apart at any moment and shortly after seven, our donkeys arrive at the door. The cook and the boy merrily gallop on ahead beneath the ever-cheerful sky of China now filled with blue. I sing loudly and quite out of tune. The mountain scenery gradually becomes clearer, caves appear once more, lit with promising points of light and a stream snakes its way across the meadow. According to my friend, the lama said he would wait for us here. Our eyes scan the furthest reaches of the valley but only a few people gathering brushwood are to be seen.

After waiting for an hour, I sit down in a tea-house and dispatch one of my retinue on the fastest donkey in Yixian to look for the lama and finally stride on alone. There is a shout behind me–we have found a guide! A peasant makes his obeisance. Where is the way to the Eight Luohan Mountain? From the east. Has he been there before? Yes, twice. We shoulder our knapsacks and climb up the steep pathless mountain slope. Thorns pierce our gloves, one of my coolies falls, the ball of his foot bleeding profusely. I rip my handkerchief in two for a bandage. Forward! Forward! We slide and stagger, clutching at rocks white with bird droppings. We throw ropes to each other and wipe the sweat pouring form our foreheads with our sleeves.

When we reach the crest, high up, we lie down exhausted. The stillness is even more palpable through the soft twittering of the pheasants. Waves of hills spread out below like a brown surging sea. To the north-east, laid out in straight lines and as

small as a village built of children's blocks, we spot a farmstead–
that is the village of Xiagaosi. Its inhabitants had tried to get a
luohan down into the valley, but it was smashed to pieces in the
process.

We start walking again, fairly comfortably, along a footpath
that runs just beneath the ridge, quickening our pace as the sun
is high. Shall we be able to cover the deep indentations that lie
ahead of us in the few hours before dusk and reach the Eight
Luohan Mountain? A cry of joy rings out! Here is the first cave!
We climb up. I almost race forward but when I get up there,
disappointment falls as heavy as lead upon my heart yet again.
A cave it is, with a fresh-water spring, but with a sorry-looking
altar upon which squat three roughly painted idols, as in any
simple village shrine (*Cave 3*).I sit down on the rock ledge, let
my legs and head hang down and exercise my self-control. My
Chinese friend, pale from the climb, argues bravely with the
guide. We march on, slowly in my case, the two Chinese at a
faster pace. Suddenly, they disappear in the scrub. I call out and
a voice reaches me, 'This way!' I see a great hole, slide forward
on all fours and find myself standing in a deep cavern (*Cave 4*).
It is called Shanzidong and is mentioned in the poem composed
by the restorer of the Guanyin. A few shards lie at my feet. I look
down at them and begin laughing like a child–there (sic) are
from a luohan!

Inside, a series of platforms are cut into the cave.[202] In the
antechamber, a commemorative stone tablet dating from the
reign of the Kangxi proclaims the provenance and renovation
of the Buddhas and the shrine, but without giving any details.
There is an unglazed clay statue of 'Milefo', who laughs amicably,

---

202 This is incorrect. The original German does not include the word "cut", "hewn", or
similar. It simply notes that there are platforms going up inside the grotto. Perzynski's
photograph of the cave confirms this and suggests that the platforms have been
assembled.

with twinkling little eyes and two accompanying figures. But the shrine itself, with a roughly hewn wall at the back and the cave vaulting for a ceiling, is nothing more than a heap of ruins. On the steps of the altar there are some incense vessels. I lift one up only to have it break apart in my hands. I let out a joyous shout–the fragments are covered with the most splendid light blue glazing! It is a Yuan dynasty ceramic from the thirteenth century. One fragment after another finds its way into my bag.

I hurl questions at our simple guide. How many luohan stood here? He tells me he had seen three here six months ago. No, no European has ever been up here before me. I ask myself question after question. Why and how were these colossal statues brought up to these heights so far from the world? Certainly Buddhism knows how to artificially heighten the yearning of its adherents by bringing its idols up to the heights where the spirit spontaneously leaves behind all human pettiness. And the mountain itself is identical to the divine. But Chinese piety is loth to rise to such uncomfortable meditation exercises. No, these caves were used as hiding places. Time and again I think of the iconoclastic eras such as the time of the Mongol invasions or during the ninth century, when imperial persecution decrees resulted in the destruction of tens of thousands of Buddhist temples and the annihilation of so many splendid art treassures.

We discover a new monument made of stone, which recounts the renovation of the altars at the time of the sixteenth century. What had been restored then must have existed for centuries before. I literally run along the narrow path, believing that I can see new caves on the cliff wall opposite, but our guide shakes his head–no one has ever been able to get there. There is no path.

As twilight falls, we make our way down by another better track and it becomes clear to me that our guide, innocent as he seems, has done all in his power to slow down my day's work.

Once below again, a lama priest awaits us with his accomplice. In the tea-house, which smells of rotting straw, he introduces me to the owner of one of the luohan heads. He has all the appearance of a manure carter or a butcher dealing in donkey meat. The owners of the tea-house bring tea, but politely stay outside. Of course, they are in league with local robber bands, just like everybody else about here in the mountains, including the police–of course not those in uniform, but the local mountain wardens who go about clad in rags. It is agreed that tomorrow, at the latest, I am going to see the head of the luohan, but first it has to be dug up.

The little bridge leading to our temple lodgings is occupied by some soldiers. Only the *laissez-passer* protects me from the commandant's bullying. I send a wire to the German consulate in Tientsin and then we sit down to our meal of pheasant.

No luohan head makes its appearance and we are kept waiting in the most disgraceful and incomprehensible manner. But the next morning, the sun rises in all its radiance and another blue sky greets us. Two guides accompany us this time. One is the lama priest, who charmed by my promise of a double-crown, will show us a cave with three intact statues today. The other is a pheasant hunter, who opens his mouth to show a gap in his teeth that he has a climbing party on the Eight Luohan Mountain to thank for. It sounds like a good recommendation. Before we start the climb, I catechize the lama brother: has he really seen the three sculptures himself? No, it was the pheasant hunter who told him about them. So the hunter gets the ten dollars not the lama!

I leave the lama behind and the hunter with the missing tooth takes over as our guide. He appears to know what he is doing and strides forward as if on springs. He leaves the Guanyin

Mountain on our left. He points to two caves on the so-called Eight Luohan Mountain (*Caves 5 and 6*). They are larger than they look and two statues are supposed to have stood in each cave. Not far from there, further north and higher up, another luohan once sat in meditation (*Cave 7*). The soldiers arrived just as it was about to be stolen. Seized with panic, the thieves tipped it over the precipice and it was smashed.

The guide, flattered by our attention, talks incessantly. He stops and points to a peak which is not particularly high. There is the cave he wants to show us. He shows me where to place my feet. Sand and stones come loose as we pull ourselves up an 80 degree incline. I become giddy and curse my mission. The guide pulls me into the cave. I close my eyes for a while, but we can see nothing but great rocks, tipped one on top of the other. A mighty temple-like cave with something shining inside, is suspended under the crest just opposite. From where we stand, the sky is only a narrow patch of pale blue.

The cave is big enough for five people to stand in. A luohan was here, fragments of him lie all around–a piece of chin, a few fingers reflectively touching the temple, an eye, sunken and without its pupil. How were these statues carried up here? I ask myself this question again and again.

We are ravenous. Stumbling hesitantly like old men, we find our way down. Only the guide manages to swing down with the agility of a lizard. He proudly announces that his brother can carry a weight of 2oo catties down the mountain.

Arriving at the tea-house of the Guanyin Mountain, which is maintained by the half-starved local police, we eat our mid-day meal in silence. We hardly chew and greedily devour the tinned meat in great lumps. A black spitz dares to creep between my legs; he is covered in dust and sand and even eats some little fish-bones which the policemen eye enviously. When I lift him up by his forelegs, a fountain stream is sprayed upon my Chinese photographer's pastry. The donkey driver brays with laughter, but the photographer picks the wet part out with equanimity and stuffs the rest into his mouth.

After the meal, all sorts of unshaven individuals arrive. My Chinese friend gets up and I follow him. A fine party has now gathered in the little temple behind the tea-house. Their spokesman is an eighteen-year old boy with filthy nails. These hirsute 'knights of plunder' possess a seated luohan with a beard. He is not in Yixian, but is buried somewhere else. Whenever a warning signal has been received, he has been spirited away, from one place to another, even as far as Baoding. Do I want to see him?

My answer is no, thank you very much–a few days travelling in a Chinese cart with this rabble in tow does not appeal to me. But my photographer can stay behind and take some pictures and then I will decide.

We ride back to our lodgings at the temple. Tomorrow at noon our train leaves for Beijing. My mission is accomplished. It is impossible to buy everything here now. I even ask myself if the commandant is afraid of competition. I have sat in the cave where one of the luohan once reposed–the most amazing and alive statues that a Chinese sculptor has ever produced. I have wound my way through a jungle of lies and I am on the track of just half of the truth. Nobody gets to know the whole truth in China.

My passport arrives the following morning and my Chinese friend breathes an audible sigh of relief. Now we can tackle our arch-adversary, the commandant, who jails anyone showing any interest in the luohan. I am told that his rank is no more than that of a major. I know his kind of Chinese general, who exerts his influence mainly by his great boots and has begun to play providence in China.

Before we go. Manchu inhabitants offer us all kinds of mythical monsters and the pheasant hunter from yesterday offers us another luohan that is buried somewhere. He knows the place. My friend smiles, hands out addresses and hastens our departure.

The inhabitants literally line the street in my honour. 'That is the European who wants to buy a luohan.' I can read it on their lips. A hotel landlord bows and invites us into lowly hostel, where important and confidential announcements are said to await us.

We make an impressive sight as we stride into the *yamen*, to 'beard the lion' in his den. Twenty years ago, they would have brought us here under escort on the very first day. Today, they have too great a need of Europeans in China. I present my card and passport and we wait in a little house, where my friend makes conversation in a wonderfully light manner. Eight porcelain eyes shine upon each other. An announcement is made: the Commandant is pleased to receive us. We go through courtyards, courtyards and yet more courtyards–an uninformed person would lose heart in the process. We are led into a sparkling clean room. I sit in the place of honour, to the left of the *kang*, while my friend sits politely on a stool with his legs together. Through the gauze window in the curtain, eighteen eyes observe us with curiosity–everything is public in China! A door opens and the major appears. 'Oh! He is old!' cries my friend in surprise.

[A gentleman, with drooping white whiskers and a magnificently aristocratic head, appeared, dressed completely in dark blue silk. He greeted us with a dignity whose freedom immediately disarmed me. We instantly changed our tactic.][203]

What a wonderful art, East Asian conversation! I hang upon my friend's lips in admiration. He speaks of common acquaintances in the lightest of tones as if dancing a waltz. There is a calligraphic scroll hanging on the wall. Is it not, he asks, by the former Deputy Minister of Agriculture–who naturally knows more about the classics than pig breeding. Beijing gossip is exchanged with darting glances from four eyes. The old gentleman, delighted to receive a breath of air from the great city, calls for tea, drinks himself and primes his water-pipe. I receive a 'pirate' cigarette.

Little by little, my friend turns the conversation along a more sensitive path. He tells the major that I have come to China to study ancient monuments and have already written many thick books–in short, that I am a European celebrity, How old am I? asks the Commandant. Forty-nine. Oh, he is over 70. I make an interjection, for I feel my self-esteem has been insulted in the most ridiculous way. My friend says, half aloud, 'When you have written so many books, you are at least fifty years of age in China. Only wise old people write books here.'

I have, continues my gracious Baron Munchausen in epic style, seen a great luohan in a Paris museum at which the great multitude of men, women and children gaze every day full of wonderment. Beside this sculpture, the museum curator had hung a plaque, which announced, 'This is the only sculpture of its kind in the world and it comes from China.'

The Commandant rises from his seat on the *kang,* as if something had stung him and sits down on a little. He now gazes directly at my friend. Outside, eighteen eyes follow his lips, eyes that burn through the gauze window in the curtain with curiosity.

Now I, the great learned gentleman, says my friend, have

---

203 The paragraph in square brackets is omitted without explanation from Richard Smithies' translation in Hsu's *Monks in Glaze.*

heard from a very knowledgeable German source in Beijing, that several luohan have been found in the neighbourhood of the Qing Xiling. The local people have told me that two of the luohans were now in the *yamen*.

The Commandant puffs mightily on his water-pipe. A slight sarcastic smile plays upon my lips throughout this exchange. I am enjoying the artistry with which my friend slowly roasts the destroyer of my carefully laid plans.

He continues, telling the Commandant that I live in the temple of the lamas. Lama priests are supposed to be blockheads, but I have been told that an old monk knows something about the history of the statues. But he is not in Yizhou and so I have been referred to the Commandant, who must naturally be the best informed about the luohan's past. So now I have come, first to pay my respects–three people bow at this point–and second, because I cherish the hope of seeing the two luohan and to learn about their history from someone of authority.

The Commandant nods, puffs on his pipe, then runs his fingers through his white triangular beard, His hand seems to tremble slightly. He apologizes for not being able to respond properly to my attentions because of his rheumatism. Yes, the luohan have given him some serious problems. Thieves have taken them from their places of concealment, smashing most of them in the process. But he has had all the fragments collected together and the last bits have been brought down from the mountains. A few of the thieves have been caught and clapped in jail for ten years. All the commemorative tablets had been copied and sent to Beijing, where they are now displayed. He would be glad to have copies made for me and also to show me the luohan in his possession.

We get up, cross a few courtyards with a tiring exchange of civilities. Finally, we stand before the trunk of the luohan. His head has been knocked off at the neck, as has part of the shoulder blade and the feet. In his hand he holds a scroll. The head is leaning against the wall next to the torso. With its yellowing ivory tone, it looks like the head of a man who has been executed. Once again, the powerful sense of life in his face runs through me like an electric shock. He is fairly old-looking, thin with lips that are tightly compressed. I think of the Japanese Noh masks of the Yase-Otoko, emaciated by involuntary asceticism.

No, he only has the one luohan, the Commandant corrects me. The other has been destroyed, the pieces filling several baskets. Other baskets contain smaller fragments and sculptures, probably dating from the Ming Dynasty. He himself was not able to keep the luohan in the *yamen* and he was thinking of sending it to a temple, where, as my friend remarks, one could buy it.

Back at our lodgings, the Commandant's calling card is already lying on the table. We have a last meal of pheasant and make our way to the station, where I hand out some cakes, which are greedily snatched from my fingers. A gentleman of some forty years of age, with cunning eyes and shining cheeks, makes a deep bow to my friend, who responds just as respectfully. He is one of the thieves, capable of changing his expression to suit the occasion. He wants to bring two new luohan down from the heights, of course. We promise mountains of gold and wave to our servants to climb aboard.

Then, amidst this operatic scene, we take one last look at the mountains shimmering in violet haze, in whose caverns the luohan had, for perhaps a thousand years stared straight ahead, ignoring mankind, looking into the far distance, through basalt rocks, seeing yet not seeing, literally worn down by so much concentration, creating so much ecstatic tension of the mind that it threatens to issue forth from this heavy skull, this powerfully bulging forehead, like a glowing stream of lava.

THE MISSING BUDDHAS

APPENDIX
The Steles at Yixian

A TOTAL OF five commemorative tablets, or steles, are referenced, four of them by Friedrich Perzynski in *Hunt for the Gods*. Two of the latter are also referred to by Zhang Hongyin and Dr. Eileen Hsiang-ling Hsu in their respective researches on Yixian, together with a fifth, which Perzynski apparently did not see. Although Perzynzki subsequently claimed that he alone had transcriptions of all of the steles, he never published them, nor were any found in his papers after his death. In his account, *Hunt for the Gods*, he provided neither transcriptions nor photographs of the steles he saw, but simply recorded what he regarded as significant. Since neither Zhang nor Hsu found the first two claimed by Perzynski, such information as he provided or quoted from them is given below in lieu of transcription. This is followed by full transcriptions of the other three in chronological order.

The inscriptions on the latter three steles found by Zhang Hongyin and Dr. Eileen Hsiang-ling Hsu on their explorations of the area around the caves at Yixian are reproduced in translation as far as their weathering will permit. The translation, punctuation and suggested filling of lacunae are all by Dr. Hsu, who very helpfully, in her words, *"placed square brackets around characters that are illegible but which can be adduced on the basis of context, and used empty pairs of square brackets to designate characters that are completely undecipherable"*. Similarly, relevant explicatory notes have been borrowed from hers.

THE FIRST STELE, DATED 1624
- FOUND BY PERZYNSKI NEAR THE GUANYIN
PAVILION

Perzynski noted only that the first commemorative tablet recorded *"that a pious man from the district had found the goddess broken, and with the help of other charitable inhabitants of the region, had repaired and gilded the statue in 1624."*

THE SECOND STELE, DATED "BEGINNING
OF THE 17TH CENTURY"
- FOUND BY PERZYNSKI NEAR THE
GUANYIN PAVILION

Perzynski noted that on the second tablet, *"erected at the beginning of the seventeenth century, the restorer had chiseled a poem celebrating the difficulty of the climb."* He reproduced this as:

> *"Longmensi is an old temple; the mountain encloses it like*
> *a mighty screen.*
> *Shanzidong lies not far from here, to the east, while to the*
> *west,*
> *The mountain descends steeply to the plain; it is silent*
> *here.*
> *Of all the mountains, this is deemed to be the most holy*
> *and renowned place.*
> *Death grips him who enters here, and his skull will shatter,*
> *if he climbs in fear.*
> *Clouds and mist from the valley rise and human voices are*
> *seldom heard.*
> *Trees spread their branches, crows caw in their midst.*

*Woodcutters come and go, and wild monkeys hunt in the
trees."*

The same commemorative tablet also had the
following words engraved on it:
*"Alle diese Buddhas kommen von weither.
All these Buddhas came from far away"*,

(Both quotations translated from Perzynski's German
rendering in *Jagd auf Gotter*.)

THE THIRD STELE DATED 1519
– FOUND BY PERZYNSKI IN THE SHANZIDONG
GROTTO

Record of the Successful Completion of the Images,

The *Book of Changes* says: 'The family that accumulates goodness
is sure to have a surplus of happiness; the family that is not good
is sure to have a surplus of misfortune.' Laozi says: 'Esteeming
goodness is like [making good use of] water because it can
benefit all things.' Confucius says: 'What is not good must be
corrected; choose the good and accord with it.' The Buddha
says: '[If one] cultivates all [sorts of] goodness, then one attains
complete Sambodhi.'

Clear are the words of the three great sages: none [of them] but
encourages the good and warns against evil. How could there be
divergence in their shared goal, which is to teach and encourage
everyone to do good? There was a certain Song Jun, posthumously
[Song] An, who served in the Rear Unit of the Maoshan Guard of
the Daning Regional Military Command. From his grandfather's
and father's generations onward, his family esteemed the good.

They accumulated much merit by practicing anonymous good works, giving vegetarian meals to monks and alms to temples. They cared for the elderly and commiserated with the poor, and aided those who had lost a spouse. They set free the animals caught alive, and were honest with strong moral rectitude. They were not attached to material things, and did not treat others unfairly. Once [Song] Jun returned some money he found to the person who had lost it. Indeed this kind of honesty and integrity were truly rare! Born with fine quality and a benevolent nature, he carried on the family tradition of giving to charity after his father passed away. Realizing that nothing in the world is permanent and the corporeal body is just an illusion, he generously donated his family's wealth to sponsoring the making of images.

Beginning in the sixth year of the Zhengde reign-period [1511], his efforts [in this regard] continued uninterruptedly, nor were they limited to a single one place. [In that year, he sponsored the] making [of] a Buddhist image for the Guanyin Hall of the Emo temple[1] on the West Mountain; in the seventh year [1512], [he sponsored the] making [of] an image for the Three Officials (Sanguan)[2] Daoist Temple in this prefecture, a luohan figure for the Xingguo Buddhist temple in this prefecture, and an image of Maitreya for his own family. The following year [1513], he commissioned three large Buddha images for Chuiyun temple in Xiahuanghao village, one image of a Daoist deity Zhenwu [for a temple] in Dongguan (Eastern Gate), in the eastern part of the prefecture, and a large Buddha image for the Wulihe temple. Moreover, [he donated] thirteen [wooden] sculptures consisting of twelve Complete Enlightenment Bodhisattvas and one Buddha, all magnificently gilded with bright and dazzling

---

1   The Emo Temple was later renamed Longmensi, which is recorded in the fifth (1741) stele q.v.

2   The "Three Officials" refer to the Daoist deities, the Officials of Heaven, Earth and Water.

appearances. [For their installation], workers were ordered to prepare niches, one for each of [the thirteen sculptures]. [The thirteen figures were then] sent to the mountains.

On the Hundred Flowers Mountain about 40 li (20 km) northwest of the Yizhou seat, there is a grotto named Shanzidong. A body of water inside it never dries out; it is cool and tastes fresh all year round. The mountain is high and precipitous and the tall trees grow unevenly. The cliffs are steep and jagged as if they were cut by a sword and chipped with an axe. This wonderfully strange and stunningly beautiful landscape is difficult to draw by even the most skilful artisans. This is a place where visitors become oblivious of the outside world and forget to return home. Indeed this is the site for ancient recluses and modern pursuers of immortality. The grotto is large enough to accommodate a hundred people.

[I], Monk Daojinshan of the Bajian village, whose lay surname was Wen, practiced in this mountain site for many years, living a frugal and simple life. [I] have endured hardship and loneliness, and given up family life, love and material desires. Together with [my] friend Qi Yuan, we built a three-bay [worship] hall in the grotto, its beams and columns beautifully painted. [In this hall, we] practiced Daoist and Chan meditation and burned incense to pray for the blessing of the people, thus [undertaking] an enterprise for public well-being.

The making of the images [under the sponsorship of] Song Jun, began in the sixth year of the Zhengde reign-period (1511). and was completed in the fourth month of the fourteenth year of the Zhengde reign-period (1519) with the dispatch of the images to the grotto (i.e. the Shanzidong) and their safe installation [therein], thus successfully completing this exalted task. Rejoicing [at this successful installation], I proposed to all: 'The good deed has been done, and my wish has been fulfilled. But if we do not erect a stone tablet for posterity, after a long period of time, who will know when and by whom these images were created?' We calculated the money needed, ordered the craftsmen to prepare the stone, solicited the text [for the inscription], and had it carved in commemoration

Encomium:
Song Jun had many [sacred] images made, as he followed in his father's footsteps sowing seeds for the good cause. Neglecting his familial obligations he carried out this sacred service; he was pure of heart and faithful to the task.

When the enterprise was complete and the stone grotto filled with the safely installed images, the blessing spread to all people. [We] erected this stone tablet so that his name and virtue could be known to posterity. The lofty mark he has inscribed in history will last for eternity.

Hymn:
Mr. Wen took Daojinshan as his practice soubriquet, and cultivated asceticism in the forests and [mountain[springs for many years. Enduring physical and mental solitude in seeking the way of the sages, he built a three-bay [worship] hall inside the grotto. Abandoning worldly obligations, cutting off worldly attachments, and forgetting fame and profit [he] craved neither jade nor gold. He swore brotherhood with Qi Yuan, so that when he passed the hundred-year boundary (i.e. death) he would board the Dharma boat (i.e. achieve enlightenment).

Brushed by [Mi] dao[3], a wild old man from the Baofeng temple, on a mountain north of the Yi River, at the end of the

---

3   Hsu surmises that the first character of the name is probably an obsolete variant of *mi* meaning 'to seek' Thus the recluse calligraphist's name might be rendered 'Seeker of the Way'.

summer in the *yintao* cyclical year (year 14) of the **Zhengde** reign period [**1519**] of the Great Ming dynasty. Jointly engraved by Li Gang, a craftsman from this town, and Li Da, a stone carver from Quyang.

THE FOURTH STELE DATED 1667
– FOUND BY PERZYNSKI NEAR THE SHANZIDONG GROTTO

Record Of Renovation

Stele-Record of the Renovation of Shanzidong on the Hundred Flowers Mountain, Thirty-five li Northwest of Yizhou in Baoding Prefecture of Zhili Metropolitan Area.

For we have heard that sages rose in the West, and all the heavenly [spirits] transcended obstacles to ascend the path of enlightenment. The Dharma flowed to the land of the east, and for ten thousand kalpas has helped those lost in delusion to cross over. Because the teaching of the Dharma responds without fail to all prayers and ensures that no road in extinction (i.e. *nirvana*) is impassable, the moon [one character illegible] ten thousand things initially lack [one character illegible] people do not cease to place their good faith in it.[4] This is because the fragrant traces of the ancient sages never disappear, and the Buddha's divine teaching began long ago.

The Baihua Mountain northeast of this [prefectural seat] [one character illegible] is embraced by the Yi River on the southeast and vies for beauty with Mount Ning on the northwest. The scenery is truly unsurpassed among the wonders of nature within the seas, with ranges of hills and layered peaks, winding

---

4   Two indecipherable characters obscure the meaning of this phrase.

paths and [two characters illegible].

[Moreover] there is a famous site, named Shanzidong, a grotto created by heaven and [designed] by earth. [In it] there are two side-by-side caverns. For ascending the mountain and treading the peak, using just two feet is insufficient. Judging by the finely executed paintings and sculptures of the Buddhist deities and Daoist immortals made by those who came before us, this place must have once been filled with rich incense fires (i.e. was a popular place of worship). The vicissitudes of time have caused its decline, however, as prosperity is usually followed by decline, and anything completed must perish.

Thereupon the Buddhist abbot, Jia Shouzai, having seen [the ruined condition of the images], came up with the idea of [restoring them]. He raised funds from a lay patron, a Mr. Liu [two characters illegible] and other pious devotees from the neighbouring villages. [The many divine images thus repaired] included those of the 'multiple Buddhas' from the east and west caverns. The bodhisattvas, the Dizang (Ksirigharba), the Ten Kings [of Hell], the Dharma protecting guardians on the left and the right, and the Prominent Physicians from Ten Periods[5] and their sacred plinths. The gold and polychrome [one character illegible] colours on these images appeared almost as if new [three characters illegible]. The restoration project was completed in a short period of time, and the original appearances of the Buddhist and Daoist images were once again revealed [one character illegible], as they had been of yore.

By divination an auspicious day was sought to erect [this] stone with an inscription [carved on it], so that it could be immortalized. We often say that the divine grace of the Buddhist deities brings salvation to all, and the myriad gods bestow [one

---

5   The Ten Prominent Physicians became part of the Daoist pantheon in the Yuan dynasty.

character illegible] favour [two characters illegible] pervasive fragrance, the power of the Dharma is broadly manifested and the myriad deities send down the joy of restful peace. That this phenomenon is inevitable is [one character illegible]. As for the fulfillment of wishes and the realization of thanksgiving, this is the masses' greatest fortune [three characters illegible] to have their prayers answered, [be that] from the Buddha, the immortals, or any other deities.

Composed by Dong Mu, Added Student at Yi Prefectural School, with good reputation and in accordance with sincerity. Calligraphy by Dong Mu, Supplementary Student at Yi Prefectural School, with good reputation and in accordance with sincerity.

Stonemasons Cui [ ] and Cui Wenxiang. Respectfully [assisting in the] engraving by Dong Mu.

Erected on the fifteenth day of the last month [ ] of spring, in the sixth year of the Kangxi reign period (1667) of the Great Qing.

THE FIFTH STELE DATED 1741
- FOUND BY ZHANG HONGYIN AT THE LONGMEN TEMPLE

STELE RECORD OF LONGMEN TEMPLE ON WHITE JADE MOUNTAIN

As seen in historical records and gazetteers, each of the Nine Prefectures[6] has its own spectacular landscapes and sceneries. The greatest among these are mountains and rivers. The Emo Mountain, located fifty *li* (about seventeen miles) northwest of the Yizhou prefectural seat, and now known as the Baiyu (White

---

6 Jiuzhou, the Nine Prefectures, is an ancient name referring to the entire pre-Han Chinese empire.

Jade) Mountain, are indeed the most wonderful scenery in Yizhou.

The mountains and rivers echo one another as if expressing their mutual affection, and this site certainly has not lacked for visits by famous people. But without the accompaniment of Buddhist temples, there is no medium through which this natural beauty could be transmitted. Moreover, by what [other] means could the comments of those gentlemen have reached [their audiences]?

An old Buddhist temple, Emosi, used to be nestled in the middle of the mountains, its name has now been changed to Longmensi. About 5 *li* (two-and -a-half kilometers) further up [from the temple compound] there is a Guanyin Pavilion. An investigation of its origin [indicates that] the temple was probably established between the Song and the Yuan dynasties (i.e. thirteenth- fourteenth centuries), but no reliable records are available for its history further back. It was repaired during the Jiajing reign-period (1522-1566) of the Ming dynasty, more than two hundred years ago. Although the tall beams [of its halls] soared high into the sky and penetrated into the clouds, dust had accumulated on the flying eaves [of the pavilion] and the stone beams had also begun to crumble. While the sounds of wood-cutters were occasionally heard amidst the green forest and huge trees, the sounds of Buddhist chanting under the moonlit pine trees were no longer heard.

In the eighth year of the Yongzheng reign-period (1730), it was divined that the Auspicious Site of Ten Thousand Years[7] was to be located in front of these mountains. [An area] of about thirty *li* (sixteen kilometers) in circumference was then marked by red posts, and [two characters illegible] by imperial order the

---

7   The Auspicioius Site of Ten Thousand Years is a euphemism for the imperial mausoleum.

Buddhist and Taoist temples located in the area within the posts were to be repaired without exception. [After the repair], the main gate of the temple compound stood so high that it could even catch the light through mountain mists. The Maitreya Buddha sits cross-legged [there] and with a perpetually smiling face. The front hall has three [main] columns, and one can enter its main door to gaze up at the image of Tathagata (i.e the Buddha Sakyamuni), the rear shrine has five roof beams, and one can ascend the terrace to worship images of the Buddha.

[Two characters illegible] the Guanyin Pavilion is located half way to the sky, the water from the willow branch vase[8] ferries over those trapped in delusion. As for the auxiliary halls, the bell tower, monks' quarters, refectory, walls, stone by-ways, and brick terraces, these have without exception been repaired and restored anew. We shall soon be able to see [one character illegible] images regaining their brilliance of yesteryear, and happily gaze into the gem-like chapels glistening with bright colours. Moreover, because wood-cutting has been forbidden, the forest is becoming more luxuriant; since herdsmen and cattle have been sent away, the mountain peaks are turning greener every day. The spirit of the mountains [two characters illegible] the surroundings of the temple are always tranquil. Pure streams flow past long mountain paths, and seekers of wonder can have their dusty hearts cleansed. Layered rocks occasionally emerge as steps [on which] those who climbed them make their temporary rest. Hearing the birds singing in the breezes of spring always provides opportunities for *cham* insights, the autumn moon [two characters illegible], appearing like nothing less than the Jetavana garden.[9]

Thenceforth verdant mountain cliffs surround the imperial

---

8   The vase held by statues of Guanyin typically holds a willow branch.
9   Jervana is a famous park which the Buddha Sakyamuni often visited.

tomb site, providing everlasting solid protection, and the brilliance of the monastery [i.e. the Longmen Temple] is as bright as that of the sun and moon. Ten years have passed since the completion of that repair project, stone tablets were left blank as no one composed texts to be inscribed on them. In the spring of the fourth year of the Qianlong reign-period (1739), I came to Yi under imperial order in my capacity as Vice Chancellor of the Imperial Academy, to inspect the construction of public works and oversee financial affairs and the food distribution service. I twice visited [the Longmen temple] site on my days off, leisurely enjoying its vistas and scenery; the memories of those visits are still vivid in my mind. In the sixth year [1741], a monk from the Chang [one character illegible] temple known as Tianyun came to my door and asked me to compose a record [of the renovation of the Longmen temple] [one character illegible] to be inscribed. Hence I carried out a careful investigation and conducted interviews, obtaining the information successfully recorded here.

Written by Sai'erdeng, Vice Chancellor of the Imperial Academy, with two additional ranks ad three honorary records, chief manager of finance for the construction project at the Taiping Ravine.

Carved on stone on the fifteenth day of the [three characters illegible] month in [1741].[10]

---

10   Hsu comments that though the date of the stele inscription is not formally noted in the traditional manner, it can be inferred from the text.

THE STELE OF 1519
Record of the Successful Completion of the Images

造像圖滿之記
易云：積善之家，必有餘慶；不善之家，必有餘殃。
老子日：尚善若水，能利萬物。孔子：不善則改之，
擇善而從之。釋氏日：修一切善則成正覺。

詳乎三大聖人之言，莫不勸蕭(善)懲惡，欲令人人咸歸于善，豈
有異也？茲有大寧都司茂山衛後所宋均，諱安。自祖考已(以)
來，其家崇蕭(善)，積惪(德)修陰，齋僧布施；愛老憐貧，賙濟
鰥寡；活物放生，處心正直；不愛物，不虧于人。亦曾有人遺金
若干，均得不昧而還，吁哉勘有也。昔有X(靈)根，天性純善；
父沒非倦，愈加其善；継父之道不改也，行善之志不忘也。悟世
非常，知身是幻；不吝家貲，發心造像。

自正德六年已來，節次不休，非止一處。西山莪磨寺觀音殿
造佛一尊；七年，本州三官廟造相一尊，本州興國寺造羅漢一
尊，本家造彌勒相一尊。又次年，下黃蒿村垂雲寺造大佛三尊，
州東關造真武一尊，五里河寺造大佛壹一尊，全金又雕十二圓
覺佛菩薩十三尊，金光晃耀，燦爛輝煌。命匠做龕已成，每尊一
龕，送山。

去易城西北四十里百花山睬子洞，洞中有水一灣非涸，清涼
甘美，冬夏恆如。其山嵯峨，陡峻杪槎，壁立萬仞，似刀砍之
樣，如斧劈之形。山奇水秀，巧匠難圖。翫(玩)景之人非思于
世，游觀之士忘歸于家；古人遁世之場，修僊(仙)學道之地。洞
寬司容百人。

僧道金山，俗姓溫，百尖村人也。于此居山學道已有年矣。
苦形煉性，受寂寞，甘澹薄，棄家緣，絕愛慾。同友祁原，洞中

蓋殿三間，彩梁繪棟，辦道參禪焚香祝祐民，是公之事業也。

造相，宋均始自正德六年，落於正德十四年四月內為終，送像安洞，聖業事圓矣。子心樂矣，謂眾議曰：善事已圓，我願既滿，若不樹石于后，歲月悠久，莫知何人之所造欤？輪(論)金若干，命工X石，征文勒琨為記。

頌曰：
宋均造相許多尊，踵父增修種善因。
弗顧家緣營聖事，貞心篤志辦功勛。
行圓果滿安石洞，福被 群氓一切人。
豎石留名彰后世，高標萬古與千春。

偈曰：
溫公立號道金山，苦行林泉已有年。
寂寞身心求聖道，洞中修蓋殿三間。
棄恩割愛忘名利，白玉黃金捴(總)不貪。
誓與祁原為志友，百年限盡上法船。

大明正德十四歲次已卯孟夏末旬，易水山北寶寺埜(野)叟[覓?]道書。

本邑匠人李剛曲陽石匠李達同刊。

The Stele of 1667 – Record of Renovation
直隸保定府易州西三十五里百花山睒子洞重修碑記

蓋聞聖作西方，諸天超登覺路. 法流東土，萬劫永渡迷津。有求必應，無滅不通，月[]萬相初無[]人之善信不絕. 斯前聖之芳踪不泯，佛神之其祇祇所由久也。

茲本[州][]治之西北有百花山者，易水環抱於東南，寧山競秀於西北，一方方勝X，海內奇觀。層巒疊嶂，路轉[][]。[又]有所名睒子洞者，其洞也，天造地[設]，兩洞并峙. 登峰躋頂，二足莫容。前人穷繪塑畫之工。建佛聖神仙之像，彼時香火極勝可知。但年深歲久，物換時移，由勝而衰，有成必壞。

爰有住持道人賈守齋，觸目興思，募化檀越刘[][]，并左[右]各村善信人等，將東西兩洞諸佛，1菩薩，地藏，十王，左右護法善神，十代明醫等神塌，洞聖像丰有餘尊[]，金妝彩畫[]色見新…神[][][].不日告成。佛仙之妙像依[]，神聖之儀容如故。

卜吉立石[]文於[]，以垂不朽。子惟日慈航普渡，諸佛3佈[]優[][]馨。法力洪施，眾神降休寧之福，此理之必[]也。至於求則必應，感而遂通，此是[]眾至福[][][]不[]以自得之耳。佛也，仙也，神也，何得而移易之哉。

易庠首增生員榮捷秉誠董沐撰
易庠副學生員流芳秉誠董沐書

石匠崔[]崔文相董沐敬刊。
大清康熙陸年歲次丁未季春望月[]旦立。

The Stele of 1741
Stele Record of the Longmen Temple
on White Jade Mountain

白玉山龍門寺碑記

歷觀志書所載，九州風土各具形勝。山水者，其形勝之大者也。易州西北五十公里有峨磨山焉，今改為白玉山。茲山也，實易州之形勝也。

然山圍水繞，回互有情，名流勝跡，固所不棄，使無招提梵宇以為佐之，則山水之靈秀無因而傳。而士大夫之記誦何由而致？

茲山之半舊有峨磨寺，今改為龍門寺焉。更上五里許有觀音閣焉。考厥始基，大約創自宋元間，遠不可考。至前朋嘉靖年間，為之重修，至今二百餘年。雖危甍插漢，聳入雲衢，而飛閣凝塵，漸摧柱石。青林巨木時聞樵采之聲，松月禪燈不聽梵音之誦。

至雍[1]正八年，卜萬年吉地於此山之前，計程三十公里，此寺亦圈入紅椿之內，[][]椿內所有寺觀無不奉旨官修，是以重為修葺。山門高峙，時挹嵐光，彌勒盤居，常開笑臉. 前殿三楹，入門瞻如來之像；後宮五棟，登台拜古佛之尊。

[][]觀音閣高居天半，楊枝水普渡迷津。至於配殿，鐘樓，僧房，香積，牆垣，泊岸，石徑，磚台無不一一經營，恍如新構。將見[]像重輝，已復當年之璀璨. 琳宮3煥彩，快睹往日之宏規. 且嚴禁採樵，叢林日漸以蓊郁；遠驅牧犢，峰巒益顯其青蔥。山靈[][]梵境常寧，清泉甲道以長流，探奇者一洗塵心. 盤右成臺而時出，登臨者暫為駐足. 春風鳥語，聽來總是禪機；秋月[][]，看去無非祇樹。

自茲以往，翠嶂拱山陵永固，精藍同日月增輝矣。奈工程即峻，十易春秋；碑碣空存，無人撰述。至乾隆四年春，余以國子監司業奉命來易，總理工程錢糧事務，暇日曾兩至其地，曠覽遐矚，其景象無一不在胸臆間。六年，長[]寺僧，號天雲者，踵門求記，[]勒貞琨，因細加詢訪，歷述其原委焉。

總理太平峪工程錢糧事務，國子監司業加二級紀餘錄三次賽爾登撰。[][][]月中元日勒右。

---

1   This appears to be a printer's error for "雍" in Hsu's transcription in *Monks in Glaze*.

244

BIBLIOGRAPHY

Abe, Stanley, *Rockefeller Home Decorating and Objects from China*, in Rujivacharakul, Vimalin edit., *Collecting China: The World, China and a Short History of Collecting*, pp.107-123, University of Delaware Press, 2011.

Aldrich, Robert, *Vestiges of Colonial Empire in France*, Palgrave Macmillan, 2005.

Allison, Graham T., *The Essence of Decision–Explaining the Cuban Missile Crisis*, Little Brown, Boston, 1971,

Anon, *International Exhibition of Chinese Art, Catalogue*, Royal Academy of Arts, London, 1935.

Anon, *Record of Restoring the Buddha Relic at Minzhong temple*, c. 713-756, displayed in *A Promise to the Buddha–Devotion and Praxis in Buddhist Stele Inscriptions*, Academica Sinica 2014-15.

Archaeological Report of the Longquanwu kilns in Beijing, *Beijing Longquanwu yao fajue baogao*, in *Beijing shi wenwu yenjiaosuo*, 2002, ed., Beijing.

Bishop, C.W., *A Pottery Statue of a Lohan*, in The Museum Journal, vol. 5, no. 4 (September 1914).

Bishop, C.W., *Notes on Chinese Statuary*, in The Museum Journal, vol. 7, no. 3 (September 1916).

Bosch Reitz, Sigfried Chretien., '*A Large Pottery Lohan of the T'ang Period*', Metropolitan Museum of Art Bulletin, XVI, (January 1921).

Bosch Reitz, Sigfried.Chretien, *A Second Pottery Lohan in the Metropolitan Museum of Art*, Metropolitan Museum of Art Bulletin, XVI, (January 1921).

Bredon. Juliet, *Beijing, A historical and intimate description of its chief places of interest,* Second edition, revised and enlarged, Shanghai, 1922.

Brysac, Shareen Blair and Meyer, Karl. E, *The China Collectors: Americas Century-long Hunt for Asian Art Treasures,* St. Martin's Press, 2015.

Burton, William, *Porcelain, a sketch of its nature, art and manufacture,* B.T. Batsford, London, 1906.

Bushell, Stephen W., *Chinese Art,* New York, 1904.

Bushell, Stephen W., *Oriental Ceramic Art: Illustrated by Examples from the Collection of W.T. Walters,* 1896.

Bushell Stephen W., *Chinese Pottery and Porcelain,* OUP, Oxford, 1910.

Chen Shen, *Objectives and Challenges: Past, Present and Future of Collecting Chinese Antiquities in the ROM,* in Jason Steuber and Guolong Lai ed. *Collectors, Collections & Collecting the Arts of China: Histories & Challenges,* University Press of Florida, 2014.

Cox, Warren E., *The Book of Pottery and Porcelain,* New York, 1944 and revised edition New York,1979.

Currelly, Charles T., *I Brought the Ages Home,* Toronto, Royal Ontario Museum, 1976.

Davids, Roy and Jellinek, Dominic, *Provenance: Collectors, Dealers and Scholars of Chinese Ceramics in Britain and America,* Great Britain, 2011.

Dohrenwend, Dorie, *Far Eastern Department: Arts of Buddhist Asia,* Arts of Asia 9, no. 2 (1979).

Feugere, Laure, Anne Bouquillon, Beatrice Beillard, and Martin Bailly, *Le Lohan en terre vernissee du muse Guimet,* Techni 16 (2002) 20-25.

Fischer, Otto, *Wanderfahrten eines Kunst-freundes in China und Japon,* Stuttgart, 1939, Deutsche Verlags Anstalt.

Fischer, Otto, *Die Kunst Indiens, Chinas Und Japans,* Berlin, Propylaen Verlag, 1928.

Fischer, Otto, *Chinesische Plastik*, Munchen, R. Piper & Co., 1948, pp. 132 ff.

Fong, Chow, *Chinese Buddhist Sculpture*, Metropolitan Museum of Art Bulletin, XXIII, May 1965.

Fu Zhenlun, *Zhongguo yishu gunji zhanlan canguan ji* / Record of Viewing the International Exhibition of Chinese Art, in *Beiping gugong bowuyuan nian kan*, 1936.

Gies, Jacques, *Revue du Louvre*, February 1998,

Gillman, Derek, *General Munthe's Chinese Buddhist Sculpture: An Embarrassment of Riches?"* in The Buddhist Forum, London, 1992.

Gillman, Derek, *The Penn's Glazed Luohan in Context–Chinese Buddhist Art during the 10th-13th Centuries*, a lecture delivered at the Penn Museum, 8 August 2011.

Gillman, Derek, *The Imperial Luohans of Zhongdu and the Reassertion of Chan (Zen) Buddhist Influence in North China*, a lecture given on 3 November 2013, Bulletin of the Oriental Ceramic Society, London, pp. 41-42.

Glaser, Curt, *Ostasiatische Plastik*, Berlin, B. Cassirer, 1925.

Gray, Basil *Chinese Sculpture Examples at Burlington House*, in The Connoisseur: An Illustrated Magazine for Collectors, 1936, Volume 97 (February).

Gray, Basil, *Early Chinese Pottery and Porcelain*, London, Faber & Faber Ltd., 1953.

Gridley, Marilyn, *Chinese Buddhist Sculpture Under the Liao; Free Standing Works in Situ and Selected examples from Public Collections*, International Academy of Indian Culture and Aditya Prakashan, New Delhi, 1993.

Gridley, Marilyn, *Three Buddhist Sculptures from Longquancun and the Luohans from Yi Xian*, Oriental Art, vol. 46, no. 4, (1995).

Gridley Marilyn & Gadden Paul: *China: where were these monks made and how did they get there?* Asian Ceramic Research Organization, June 1996.

Griswold, Alexander B., *Monastic Dress in Chinese Sculpture*, Artibus Asias, XVII, No. 4, ad XXVI, No. 2, 1962 and 1965.

Harada Yoshito, *Chokureishoekiken kyuzai to rakan ni tsuite* in *Toa kobunka kenkyu*, November 1940.

Harcum, Cornelia G., *Chinese Pottery Statue of a Lohan*, Bulletin of the Royal Ontario Museum of Archaeology (Dec. 1923).

He Li, *Ceramics of the Song, Liao, Western Xia and Jin Dynasties*, in Li Zhiyan ed, *Chinese Ceramics from the Paleolithic Period through the Qing Dynasty*, 2010;

Heinrich, Theodore Allen, *Art Treasures in the Royal Ontario Museum*, McClelland and Stewart, Toronto, 1963.

Hobson, R.L., "A New Chinese Masterpiece in the British Museum", in *The Burlington Magazine*, XXV, May 1914.

Hobson, R.L., *Chinese Pottery and Porcelain: an Account of the Potter's Art in China from Primitive Times to the Present Day*, 1915.

Hobson, R.L., *Chinese Pottery Statue of a Luohan*, British Museum, London 1925,

Hsu Hsiang-ling Eileen, *Monks in Glaze: Patronage, Kiln Origin, and Iconography of the Yixian Luohans*, Brill, 2016.

Hubbard G.E., *Temples of the Western Hills visited from Peking*, La Librarie Francaise, Peking and Tientsin, 1923.

Jacquemart, Albert, *Historie artistique, industrielle et commerciale de la porcelaine*, 1862, co-authored by Edmond Le Blant.

Jarrige, Jean-Francois & Robert, Jean-Noel, *Nara, Tresors Bouddhiques du Japon Ancien: le Temple du Kofukuji*, Paris 1996, Maertz.

Jarrige, Jean-Francois, *Activites du Musée national des Arts asiatiques–Guimet*, Arts Asiatiques, tome–53-1998.

Jayne, Horace F., *Loan to Burlington House*, University Museum Bulletin, Philadelphia 6, No. 1, (Oct. 1935).

Jayne, Horace F., *Chinese Art in the University Museum*, Parnassus 11, No. 1, (Jan. 1939).

Jayne, Horace F., *The Chinese Collection of the University Museum*, Handbook of the Principal Objects, Philadelphia, 1941.

Jin Shen, *Yixian Bafowa sancai tao Luohan de shidia*, 1998

Jin Shen, *"Tan Hebei Yixin Bafowa Liaodai Sancaitao luohan"*, Wenwu chunqiu, 2003, no. 2, China Academic Journal Electronic Publishing House.

Jirka-Schmitz, Patrizia, *The Trade in Far Eastern Art in Berlin during the Weimar Republic (1918-1933)*, Journal for Art Market Studies, vol. 2, no. 3, 2018.

Jobst, Fritz, *Geschichte des Tempels Tja Tai Tze*, Tianjin, 1905.

Johansson Perry, *Saluting the Yellow Emperor: A Case of Swedish Sinography*, Brill, 2011.

Karlbeck, Orvar, *Selected Objects from Ancient Shou-Chou*, Ostasiatische Museet (Bulletin of the Museum of Far Eastern Antiquities), Vol. 27, Stockholm, 1955.

Kerr, Rose, *Countess Wilhelmina's Chinese Treasures: the Hallwyl Museum, Stockholm*, a lecture delivered on 23 October, 2014, Bulletin of the Oriental Ceramic Society of Hong Kong, No. 16, 2013-15.

Kogel, Eduard, *The Grand Documentation: Ernst Boerschman and Chinese Religious Architecture (1906-1931)*, Berlin, 2015.

Kummel, Otto, *Die Austellung Der Sammlung Perzynski Im Berliner Kunstgewerbemuseum*, Ostasiatische Zeitschrift. Jahrg. 2, Heft 4 January- March 1914.

Laufer, Berthold, *Chinese Pottery of the Han Dynasty*, 1909.

Lally James J., *J.P. Morgan (1837-1913): An Early American Collector of Chinese Porcelain*, a lecture given on 26 November 2007, the Oriental Society of Hong Kong, Bulletin No. 15, 2015.

Lawton, Thomas., *A Time of Transition: Two Collectors of Chinese Art*, Spencer Museum of Art, University of Kansas,1991.

Lenain, Geraldine, *Monsieur Loo: Le Roman d'un Marchand d'Art Asiatique / Mr. Loo: The Novel of an Asian Art Dealer*, Philippe Picquier, 2015.

Levi, Sylvain and Chavannes, Edouard, 'Les Seize Arhats Protecteurs de la Loi', in *Journal Asiatique*, 1916, XIe serie, Tome. 8.

Liang Sicheng, *History of Chinese Sculpture* (中国雕塑史), 1985, China Architecture and Building Press; published posthumously.

Lippe, Aschwin von, *Fortieth Annual report for the Year 1915*, Museum of Fine Arts, Boston, 1915.

Lippe, Aschwin von, Catalogue Card No. 20.114, Metropolitan Museum of Art, New York.

Liu Tong and Yu Yizheng, *Di jing jing wu lue* (Notes on the Sights of the Imperial Capital), 1635, reprint ed. Peking, Guji, 1980.

Liu Qi , *Beijing Mengtougou qu Longquanwu faxian Liaodai ciya*, 1978

Loo, C.T., *An Exhibition of Chinese Sculptures: C.T. Loo & Co. New York City*, New York: Loo, 1940.

Medley, Margaret, *Yuan Porcelain and Stoneware*, London, 1974.

Menshikova, Maria L. *The Arhat from I-chou*, Transactions of the State Hermitage 39 (2008), pp.: 114-118.

Menshikova, Maria L., *Date, History and Restoration of a Ceramic Lohan Sculpture from Yizhou*, a lecture delivered at the School of Oriental and African Studies, University of London, March 2014.

Meyer, Karl E., and Blair Brysac, Shereen, *The China Collectors: America's Century Long Hunt for Asian Art Treasures*, St. Martin's Press, 2015.

Murowchick, Robert E., editor (1994), *China: Ancient Culture, Modern Land*, Cradles of Civilization series, Weldon Russell, North Sydney, Australia.

Naquin, Susan, "Sites, Saints and Sights at the Tanzhe Monastery", in *Cahiers d'Extrême-Asie*, 1998, 10, pp. 183-211.

Naquin, Susan, *Peking Temples and City Life 1400-1900*, Berkeley, University of California Press, 2014.

Newman, Robert, *The I-Chou Lohans and the Stages of Realization*, Loka, New York, Anchor Books, 1975.

Newman, Robert, *Disciples of the Buddha: Living Images of Meditation*, Cool Grove Press, 2001.

Ondaatje, Michael, *Anil's Ghost*, McClelland and Stewart, 2000.

Peirce, Nick, *A Group of Chinese Stoneware Buddhist Sculptures Reunited*, Transactions of the Oriental Ceramic Society 58, 1993-94 (1995), pp. 37-50.

Perzynski, Friedrich, *Jagd auf Gotter* in *Die Neue Rundschau*, October, 1913; republished in *Von Chinas Gottern*, Munich, 1920.

Priest, Alan, *Chinese Sculpture in the Metropolitan Museum of Art*, Catalogue Card No. 74, New York, 1943.

Rackman, Bernard, *Ceramics*, in *Catalogue of the International Exhibition of Chinese Art 1935-36*, Royal Academy of Arts, London, Faber & Faber Ltd., 1935.

Reischauer, Edwin O. and Fairbank, John K., *East Asia the Great Tradition*, Boston, 1958.

Reidemeister, Leopold, *Keramische Funde aus Jehol und die Lohan von I-Chou*, Ostasiatische Zeitschrift Neue Folge XIII, Heft 5, 1937.

Rosch, Petra, *Chinese Wood Sculptures of the 11th to 13th centuries: Images of Water-moon Guanyin in Northern Chinese Temples and Western Collections*, ibidem Verlag, Stutgart, 2014.

Royal Ontario Museum, *Chinese Art in the Royal Ontario Museum*, Toronto, 1972, No. 111.

Royal Ontario Museum, *Homage to Heaven, Homage to Earth: Chinese Treasures of the Royal Ontario Museum*, Far Eastern Department, ROM, 1992, University of Toronto Press, Toronto.

Rujivacharakul, Vimalin edit., *Collecting China: The World, China and a Short History of Collecting*, University of Delaware Press, 2011.

Saint-Raymond, Lea and Howald, Christine, *Tracing Dispersal: Auction Sales from the Yuanmingyuan loot in Paris in the 1860s*, Academia on-line.

Segalen, Victor. *Mission Archeologique en Chine*, 1914.

Sharf, Robert H. and Sharf, Elizabeth Horton Ed., *Living Images: Japanese Buddhist Icons in Context*, Stanford University Press, 2002.

Sheaf, Colin, *A Gift for the Guimet*, in Christie's Magazine, Jan/Feb 1998.

Shen Hsueh-man, *Gilded Splendor: Treasures of China's Liao Empire (907-1125)*; New York, Asia Society, 2006.

Shou Pengfei, *Yixian Zhigou* / Draft Gazetteer of Yixian, 1944.

Sickman, Laurence and Soper, Alexander, *Art and Architecture of China*, Pelican History of Art, 1956.

Silcock, Arnold, *Introduction to Chinese Art and History*, New York, Oxford University Press, 1948.

Siren, Osvald, *The Chinese Marble Bust in the Rietburg Museum*, Artibus Asiae, 1962, pp.9-2.2

Smithies, Richard, "*The Search for the Lohans of I-Chou (Yixian)*", Oriental Art 30. 1984, pp. 260-74.

Smithies, Richard, "*A Luohan from I-chou (Yixian) in the University of Pennsylvania Museum*", Orientations 32. 2001, pp. 51-6.

Smithies, Richard, *Friedrich Perzynski and the Hunt for the Gods of Yixian*, published as an Addendum to Hsu Hsiang-ling Eileen, *Monks in Glaze: Patronage, Kiln Origin, and Iconography of the Yixian Luohans*, Brill, 2016.

Springer, Anton, *Die ostasiatische Kunst, in 1929*, Handbuch der Kunst- geschicte, 1929, Volume 6, 43, 50.

St. Clair, Michael, *The Great Chinese Art Transfer: How So Much of China's Art came to America*, Farleigh Dickinson University Press, Maryland, 2016.

Steinhardt, Nancy S., *Liao Architecture*, Honolulu, University of Hawaii Press, 1997.

Steinhardt, Nancy S., "The Chinese Rotunda", *Arts of Asia*, 38 (5), September-October 2008.

Steinhardt, Nancy S., *The Luohan that Came from Afar*, in The Magazine of the University of Pennsylvania Museum of Archaeology and Anthropology, 2010, 52 (3), 7-8.

Steinhardt, Nancy S., *Chinese Architecture in an Age of Turmoil, 200–600*, Honolulu, HI: University of Hawaii Press; Hong Kong: Hong Kong, University Press, 2014.

Stibbs, Anami Virginia, *Encounters with Ancient Beijing: Its legacy in trees, stone and water*, 2004.

Strahan, Donna; Leidy, Denise Patry; et al., *Wisdom Embodied: Chinese Buddhism and Daoist Sculpture in the Metropolitan Museum*, 2010.

Sullivan, Michael, *The Arts of China*, University of California Press, 1967.

Swann, Peter. *The Art of China, Korea and Japan*, Frederick A. Praeger, New York, 1963.

Swarzenski, Georg, *Die Sammlung Henry Fuld in Frankfurt*, Das Kunstblatt, II, 3, Weimar, 1918.

Takeda Kazuya, *Summary Report on the Investigation of Khitan Relics found in the area of Chifeng City in the Inner Mongolia Autonomous Region 2004-05.*

Trevor-Roper, Hugh, *A Hidden Life: The Enigma of Sir Edmund Backhouse*, London,1976. (Note: the title of the American edition of the same book is *Hermit of Peking: The Hidden Life of Sir Edmund Backhouse*.)

Trubner, Henry, *Royal Ontario Museum: The Far Eastern Collection*, Royal Ontario Museum, Toronto, 1968.

Walravens, Hartmut, *Friedrich Perzynski (1887-1965) Kunsthistoriker, Ostasienreisender, Schriftsteller: Leben–Werk– Briefe (Art Historian, East Asia Traveler, Writer. Life–Works– Letters)*, Wagner Edition, Melle, 2005.

Wang Shuyan and Huang Weihan, 法源寺志稿, / *Fayuansi Zhigao*, Jiangsu Guangling Guji Keyanse, Yangzhou,,1996.

Wang Yiyou, Daisy, *The Loouvre from China: A Critical Study of C.T. Loo and the Framing of Chinese Art in the United States, 1915-1950*, a dissertation presented to the faculty of the College of Fine Arts of Ohio University in partial fulfilment of the requirements for the degree Doctor of Philosophy, 2007.

Watters, T., *The Eighteen Lohans of Chinese Buddhist Temples*, in Journal of the Royal Asiatic Society, vol. 30, 1898, pp. 329-47.

Wen Fong, *The Lohans and a Bridge to Heaven*, in *Occasional Papers*, Smithsonian Institution, Freer Gallery of Art, vol. 3, no. 1, (1956).

Whitehall, Walter M., *Museum of Fine Arts, Boston*, 2 vols., Cambridge, Mass., Belknap Press of Harvard University Press, 1970, Vol. I.

Walters, William and Henry, *The Oriental Collection of W.T. Walters*, Baltimore, 1884.

Wolf, Marion, *The Lohans from I-chou*, Oriental Art 15, no. 1, 1969, pp. 51-7.

Wood, Nigel, Doherty, Chris., Menshikova, Maria, Eng, Clarence. and Smithies, Richard., *A Luohan from Yixian in the Hermitage Museum: Some Parallels in Material Usage with the Longquanwu and Liuliqu Kilns near Beijing*, Bulletin of Chinese Ceramic Art and Archaeology, No. 6, Beijing, December 2015.

Ying Fashi/影法師, *Jietai Tanzhe Canyiji*, in *Enjin*/燕塵, Beijing, 3.10.1910, pp. 584-91, and 3.11.1910 pp. 640-48.

Young, William J., *Some Notes on Shoso-in, T'ang and Ming Pottery*, Far Eastern Ceramic Bulletin I, No.1 (July 1948).

Zhang Hongyin, *Yixian Louting Longmensi Shanzidong Diaochaji/* Report of the Investigation of Shanzidong and Longmen Temple in Louting Village, Yixian County, Wenwu chunqiu, 2003.2, pp. 56-60

Zhao Guanglin, *Longquanwu yaozhi diaochaji /* Account of the Investigations of the Longquanwu Kiln Site, Yandu, 1987, No.5, p. 32.

ACKNOWLEDGEMENTS

MY THANKS go first to my wife, Nga-ching, my blindman's stick in everything Chinese, for encouraging my research and putting up with me when obsession takes hold.

Professor Peter Lam, retired Director of the Art Museum at the Chinese University of Hong Kong, deserves a special mention for generosity with his vast learning. He has been my mentor since I first became interested in carved Chinese porcelain of the late Qing dynasty, and has never failed to respond to my queries, or to point me in the direction of reference material that I would otherwise not have found. I am indebted to both him and Rose Kerr for scrutinising the book in draft.

Curatorial staff of the museums that house the surviving Luohans have kindly responded to e-mails from out-of-the-blue, seeking clarification on the history of their acquisitions. Many have gone out of their way to search their records in order to check a detail. Particular thanks are due Ms. Miwako Shinkai at the Sezon Museum of Modern Art, Professor Maria Menshikova at the State Hermitage Museum in St. Petersburg and Archivist Evan Peugh at the Penn. I am likewise grateful to the staff of numerous libraries both in Hong Kong and abroad, none more so than Jeannette Lindner at the Universitaedts-Bibliothek, Heidelberg and her counterparts in the Universitaets-und-Stadtbibliothek in Koln for tracking down Lieutenant Fritz Jobst's 1905 pamphlet and scanning a copy for me.

The debt to others who have ploughed this stony field before me should be obvious, chief among them Richard Smithies and Professors Nancy Shatzman Steinhardt, Paul Goldin, Marion

Wolf and Marilyn Gridley, as well as Messrs. Jin Shen, Derek Gillman and Eileen Hsu Hsiang-ling. That I have reached conclusions different from theirs means no disrespect. Dr. Daisy Wong's thesis provided a vital clue, and a paper by Professor Susan Naquin at Princeton put me on the trail of a rare Japanese travel article on two of the temples in the Beijing's Western Hills. However, I would never have found the latter without the help of our Hong Kong friends Gerard and Taeko Millet, and their friends, Ryujiro Yagasaki and his wife Yoko. The latter trekked from Karuizawa to Tokyo, to knock on the doors of the Kokuritsu Kokkai Toshokan, the National Diet Library, unearth the original and persuade staff there to part with a copy.

Dr. Helmut Sohmen kindly came to my aid when my Langenscheidt Dictionary failed me. Friends and colleagues at Hong Kong's Oriental Ceramic Society listened politely to an early and highly speculative version of my debunking of the Perzynski Myth. Their encouragement persuaded me to pursue the subject further. Special thanks for this go to Dr. Roz Hammers for her honest critiquing of my occasional notes and to Edith Terry for introducing me to Graham Earnshaw. No amateur could wish for a friendlier or more helpful and constructive editor.

To all of the above, and to many more unmentioned, my sincere thanks for your assistance on my journey.

CHRONOLOGY

618-907	Tang Dynasty
907-1125	Liao Dynasty
960-1126	Northern Song
1062	Abbot Fajun arrives in Beijing
1115-1234	Jin Dynasty
1126-1279	Southern Song
1213	Genghis Khan breaches the Juyong Pass
1260-1368	Yuan Dynasty
1264	Khublai Khan chooses Khanbaliq (Beijing) as his capital
1290	Major earthquake strikes Yixian in Liaoning Province
1337	Huaitai earthquake northeast of Beijing
1368-1644	Ming Dynasty
1644-1911	Qing Dynasty
1731	November 30, devastating earthquake strikes Beijing, killing an estimated 100,000 inhabitants.
1839-42	First Opium War
1851-64	Taiping Rebellion leaves 20 million dead, three times the toll in America's Civil War.
1860	British and French troops sack the Yuanmingyuan, the Old Summer Palace, at the end of the Second Opium War.
1868	Japan opens to the West sparking interest in Oriental arts.
1870	Metropolitan Museum established in New York.

1876	Boston Museum of Fine Arts opens its doors.
1879	Art Institute of Chicago established.
1879	Musée Guimet opens in Lyon, moving to Paris ten years later.
1886	Norwegian Johan Wilhelm Normann Munthe joins Chinese Customs Service, later becoming a General in the Chinese army and friend of would-be-emperor Yuan Shi-kai.
1888	Prince Gong retires to the Jietai Temple in Beijing's Western Hills
1889	Pennsylvania Museum of Archaeology and Anthropology opens in Philadelphia.
1895	Sadajiro Yamanaka opens his antique store in New York.
1895	Brooklyn Museum founded.
1897-1904	China's railway projects uncover many ancient sites.
1898	Musée Cernuschi opens in Paris.
1899	George Crofts, fur trader, arrives in Tientsin, later developing a profitable business sourcing antiques for foreign museums.
1900	Boxer Rebellion, 55-day siege of Beijing's Legation Quarter relieved by foreign forces; Imperial family flees to Xi'an.
1902	Empress Dowager and Guangxu Emperor return to Beijing.
1902	C.T. Loo accompanies Zhang Renzhie, attaché to the Qing Minister in France, to Paris and helps him run a curio store.
1904	June 21, Trans-Siberian Railway opens.
1905	Summer, Lieutenant Fritz Jobst surveys the Jietai Temple and publishes his researches in an

	illustrated booklet.
1905-06	Duanfang, statesman and connoisseur, tours Japan, Europe and the United States with four other Commissioners to research possible constitutional reforms.
1906-07	Charles Freer visits China and Japan.
1906-09	Ernst Boerschman conducts architectural survey of Chinese temples.
1908	Puyi becomes Emperor on death of Guangxu Emperor and Empress Dowager.
1909	Marc Aurel Stein discovers Diamond Sutra at Dunhuang.
1909	French Sinologist Eduoard Chavannes publishes photographic survey of China's ancient monuments and inscriptions.
1909	C.T. Loo establishes Laiyuan & Co. in Paris, with branches in Beijing and Shanghai; and later New York.
1909 & 1910	Charles Freer makes two trips to China.
1910	C.T. Loo acquires eight 6th Century Bodhisattvas from Xiangtangshan.
1910	Guide to Jietai and Tanzhe Temples appears in October and November editions of *Enjin*, a Japanese journal published in Beijing.
1911	Duanfang, statesman and connoisseur, killed in Wuchang by mutinying troops.
1912	January 1, Republic of China declared.
1912	12 February, Puyi abdicates; end of Qing Dynasty.
1912	Sadajiro Yamanaka appointed exclusive agent by Puwei, grandson of Prince Kung, for disposal of family's collection.
1912	Pre-summer, Friedrich Perzynski arrives in Beijing

	and is shown bust of a luohan by dealers he does not identify.
1912	Summer, C.T. Loo takes Trans-Siberian Railway to Beijing.
1912	Summer, Friedrich Perzynski makes first visit to Yixian, tipped off by Terasawa Shikanosuke.
1912	November, Friedrich Perzynski makes second visit to Yixian.
1913	Summer, C.T. Loo takes Trans-Siberian Railway to Beijing.
1913	June, two luohans exhibited by German art dealer Edgar Worch at Musée Cernuschi, Paris, without bases, are purchased by Boston's MFA and the Penn.
1913	Terasawa Shikanosuke sells a luohan to Japanese ship-builder and collector Kojiro Matsukata.
1913	Mid-year, British Museum purchases a luohan from S. M. Franck & Son, who had obtained it from George Crofts.
1913	Langdon Warner takes up residence in Beijing working for the Smithsonian.
1913	October, Friedrich Perzynski publishes *Jagd auf Gotter* / Hunt for the Gods in the Munich Review, *Neue Rundschau*.
1913	November, Friedrich Perzynski exhibits two luohans at Berlin's *Kunstgewerbemuseum*, selling one, a bust, to German collector Harry Fuld, and the other to the Met, New York.
1913-14	China passes law banning export of antiquities.
1914	Royal Ontario Museum (the "ROM") opens in Toronto.
1914	Summer, on visit to London, Mrs. Sarah Warren

	buys a luohan for the ROM from S. M. Franck & Son, who had obtained it from George Crofts.
1914-18	First World War
1914	August 1, C.T. Loo arrives in Beijng from Paris but, following outbreak of WW I, is unable to return.
1914	December, C.T. Loo meets Charles Freer on train from Toronto and moves to New York, opening gallery there the following year.
1916	Langdon Warner gives Cleveland Museum a luohan head he claims he found in Yixian, reporting that only fragments are left of the others there. Head later judged not part of set.
1916	April 27, C.T. Loo writes to John D. Rockefeller, Jr. urging hm to view another luohan (the "Older Monk") and buy it for the Met
1916	June 6, Yuan Shi-kai dies and Warlord Era begins, lasting until 1928.
1916	March 27, John Ellerton Lodge at Boston's MFA tells Director he doubts their luohan's head is original one; later makes enquiries about provenance with Yamanaka & Co. in New York.
1916	September 6, Yamanaka & Co.'s Mr. Ushikubo reports to Boston's MFA what he has learned from Terasawa in Beijing, and Lodge makes further enquiries with C.T. Loo.
1916	C.T. Loo gifts original stands to Boston's MFA and the Penn.
1917	January 18, Francis Stewart Kershaw of Boston's MFA thanks Loo for his clarifications confirming Perzynski's account.
1918	George Crofts spots "his" luohan on a ROM postcard and calls on the curator.

1920	Met, New York takes delivery of "Younger Monk" bought from Friedrich Perzyinski in November 1914.
1920	Perzynski reprints his account in a collection of essays, *Von Chinas Gottern* / on the Gods of China.
1920	December, learning Langdon Warner claimed he had discovered the luohans, Perzynski writes him seeking clarification and photographs, but gets no reply.
1921	Met, New York buys second luohan, "Older Monk" from C.T. Loo.
1923	Freer Gallery opens in Washington.
1924-28	Liang Sicheng studies at University of Pennsylvania, where he sees one of the luohan.
1925	German art historian Otto Fischer meets Perzynski in Beijing, visits Yixian and inspects Munthe's two Luohan statues, finding one dated 1339 and both coarser than others in the West.
1925	April 5, George Crofts dies in England.
1928	C.T. Loo awarded *Legion d'Honneur* builds *La Pagode* in Paris.
1928	June 12, Warlord Sun Dianying systematically loots Eastern Tombs, including Empress Dowager's.
1928	October 10, General Chiang Kai-shek appointed Chairman of Nationalist (KMT) Government of the Republic of China.
1930s	Kojiro Matsukata sells his luohan to former chairman of Seibu Railway Corporation Yasujiro Tsutsumi.
1933	Nelson Atkins Museum opens in Kansas City.
1933	Harry Fuld's collection confiscated by Nazi party and sold, his luohan bust going to Berlin's *Museum*

	fur Ostasiatische Kunst.
1933	Lawrence Sickman buys ninth Luohan for Nelson-Atkins Museum from C.T. Loo in Beijing.
1935	General Munthe dies in Beijing, his collection going first to Los Angeles County Museum and then the West Norwegian Museum in his native Bergen.
1935-36	International Exhibition of Chinese Art held at Royal Academy, London; among the exhibits the Penn's luohan.
1936	Chinese scholar Fu Zhenlun laments dispersal of Chinese antiquities to museums and private collections around the world in his report on London exhibition.
1936	October 30, Yasujiro Yamanaka dies.
1939-45	Second World War.
1942	March 27, Friedrich Perzynski sets sail from Lisbon for Buenos Aires, where he would spend the rest of his life.
1944	The luohan bust in Berlin's *Museum fur Ostasiatische Kunst* is believed lost in war-time bombing.
1946	C.T. Loo's daughter Janine takes over running of gallery in Paris.
1948	July, William Young, pioneer of scientific analysis at Boston's MFA, publishes results of his tests on its luohan.
1949	October 1, founding of the People's Republic of China.
1949	C.T. Loo retires following confiscation of his stock in Shanghai by authorities at end of China's Civil War.
1957	C.T. Loo dies in Nyon, Switzerland.

1965	August 11, Friedrich Perzynski dies in Buenos Aires aged 88.
1972	Edgar Worch dies in New York.
1982	China introduces Cultural Relics Law designating all antiquities found in tombs and grottoes as national property.
1983	Liao dynasty kilns discovered at Longquanwu near Mengtougou in western suburbs of Beijing.
1987	Thermo-luminescence tests conducted on Boston MFA's luohan.
1996	Thermo-luminescence tests conducted on Penn's luohan.
1997	Zhang Hongyin, Director of Yixian Bureau of Cultural Relics conducts field studies in hills above Yixian.
1998	Tenth Luohan appears in Paris and is donated by Hong Kong collector T.T. Tsui to the Musée Guimet.
2001	Luohan bust believed lost in bombing of Berlin found in storeroom of State Hermitage Museum, St. Petersburg.
2002	July 4, final sale of Janine Loo's stock at *La Pagode*, Paris.
2005	China launches Cultural Relics Recovery Programme covering museum-quality antiquities removed between 1860-1949.
2008 & 2011	Dr. Eileen Hsu Huang-ling conducts field studies at Yixian.
2015	Nigel Wood et al. confirm that clay used to make both luohan bust in State Hermitage and luohan in Musée Guimet came from small and distinctive deposit to West of Beijing.

Index

THE MISSING BUDDHAS

About The Author

Tony Miller (苗學禮) is a long-time resident of Hong Kong with a keen interest in Chinese painting, porcelain, jade and the conversations across borders that have influenced art and style through the ages. He is a former President of Hong Kong's Oriental Ceramic Society and a member of the Min Chiu Society, and has published a variety of papers on previously unresearched aspects of Chinese antiquities. Since 1979, he and his wife Nga-ching (雅貞) have wandered all over China, happily exploring its historic sites and natural wonders.